The series „Neue Studien zur Politischen Ökonomie"
is edited by

Volume 16

David Christoph Ehmke

Institutional Congruence

The Riddle of Leviathan and Hydra

Nomos

The Deutsche Nationalbibliothek lists this publication in the Deutsche Nationalbibliografie; detailed bibliographic data are available on the Internet at http://dnb.d-nb.de

a.t.: Berlin, Humboldt-Universität zu Berlin, Wirtschaftswissenschaftliche Fakultät, Diss., 2018

ISBN 978-3-8487-5599-8 (Print)
978-3-8452-9775-0 (ePDF)

British Library Cataloguing-in-Publication Data
A catalogue record for this book is available from the British Library.

ISBN 978-3-8487-5599-8 (Print)
978-3-8452-9775-0 (ePDF)

Library of Congress Cataloging-in-Publication Data
Ehmke, David Christoph
Institutional Congruence
The Riddle of Leviathan and Hydra
David Christoph Ehmke
224 p.
Includes bibliographic references.
ISBN 978-3-8487-5599-8 (Print)
978-3-8452-9775-0 (ePDF)

1st Edition 2019

To Magda, Hans, and Phil

Table of Contents

Acknowledgments

My PhD in economics would not have been possible without the outstanding support and guidance of my supervisor and mentor Prof. Dr. Charles Beat Blankart. For several years, I have had the great privilege to work together with Charles Blankart. Our collaboration has resulted in several co-authored papers and presentations on sovereign/public debt, insolvency, and federalism, which have provided me with the fundament for my PhD and my understanding of economics. In regular meetings, Charles Blankart and I reviewed and discussed my PhD, which made my PhD research an incredibly exciting and inspiring time. I will remain forever highly indebted and grateful to my teacher Charles Blankart for his role model and his fabulous support.

For my PhD research, I could always rely on the invaluable feedback of Prof. Dr. Christoph Paulus, Prof. Dr. Katharina Pistor, and Prof. David Skeel. Many thanks to Steven Kargman for his insights on municipal bankruptcy. An inspiration for the interdisciplinary approach in my education and research has been the late Prof. Dr. Dr. Dr. h.c. Christian Kirchner, for whom I had the honour to work as a research assistant and with whom I co-authored my first article on sovereign insolvency. Prof. Dr. Dirk Engelmann provided a very helpful and accurate feedback in the report of my PhD. I am grateful to Prof. Dr. Ulrich Kamecke and Dr. Sebastian Schweighöfer-Kodtrisch for their participation in the doctoral committee. My uncle Prof. Dr. Dr. Helmuth Rolfes has been an academic role model for me throughout my life and a great support in the preparation of my oral exam. Moreover, I should like to express my gratitude to so many for their support and feedback through conversations and lectures. Amongst those I have not already mentioned, I like to name especially: Prof. John Armour, Prof. Dr. Dan Awrey, Prof. Dr. Barry Eichengreen, Dr. Sven Höppner, Prof. Dr. Howard Jones, Prof. Dr. Oren Sussman, and Prof. Dr. Kristin van Zwieten. The comments and questions of participants at different seminars and conferences at in particular Humboldt-University of Berlin, Columbia University, the Annual Conference of the Hayek-Society, the Annual Meeting of the European Public Choice Society, and the Christian Kirchner Memorial Symposium have been of great help for my PhD project.

My PhD research was generously funded by the Hayek Foundation.

I am extremely grateful to my family for their amazing support. Thank you so much!

I. Introduction

1. Two Ways Towards Financial Sustainability

In a perfect world, citizens decide about expenditures for a public goods. Public goods and their prices are flawless reflections of the citizens' preferences. Public goods are funded by revenues from tax and debt. Since all debts are repaid when they are due, debt acquisition is nothing than delayed or future taxation. The citizens who enjoy the public good pay for it. The unity between the circles of decision-makers, beneficiaries, and payers is complete.

In reality, the world is not perfect. Citizens vote for politicians whom they believe to realise their preferences for spending, taxation, and debt acquisition. Politicians, however, may follow their own agenda. Concerns for current popularity and re-election overshadow the long-term plan for a solid financial architecture. The citizens themselves play false and favour deficit-spending over tax-funded spending for the presently consumed public good in the hope and expectation that the bill will be paid by future generations or by taxpayers of other sovereign or public entities in a bailout. Absent a bailout, several sovereign and subnational public debtors fall short of their promise to repay debts when they are due. They become factually insolvent. While debt is the chance to realise an investment with future taxation and while it may be the fountain of growth, it is also the vehicle of burden-shifting. Quite often, it can be the cause of chaos in public finances.

The goal of this book is to answer the question about what constitutes a solid financial architecture for sovereign and subnational public entities. The key research hypothesis which will be developed and tested throughout this book is that the pre-requisite of a solid financial architecture is *institutional congruence*, i.e., the highest possible overlap of the circles of decision-makers, beneficiaries, and payers and that there are two ways to achieve institutional congruence and thus financial sustainability: *autonomy* and *integration*. Various mixed models, with the core elements of autonomy and integration mixed up, exist. The financial architecture of mixed models is unsustainable and requires reform towards the autonomy or the integration model.

(Fig. 1) Autonomy and Integration in a Nutshell

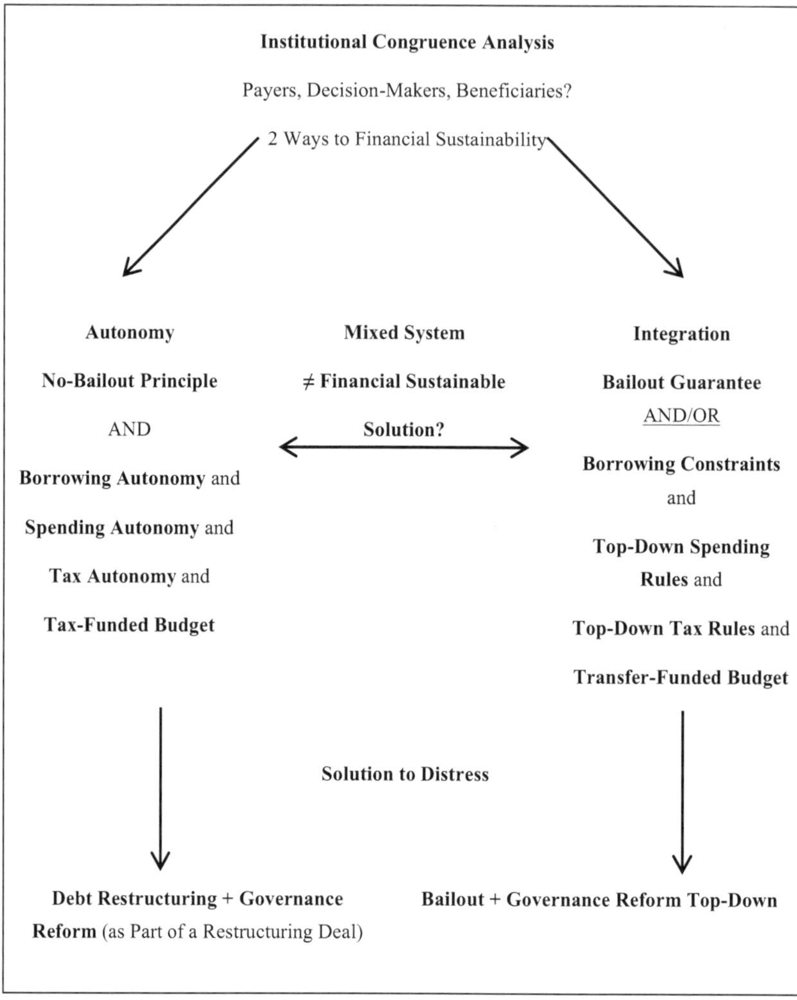

In the decentralised *autonomy* model, the sovereign or subnational public entity is independent when making decisions about spending, debt acquisition/service, and taxation. No bailout is to be expected. The sovereign or subnational public entity has to face its creditors, to signal a diligent budgetary policy for low capital costs, and to bargain about debt restructuring and governance reform in case of financial distress. Financial sustainability requires effective creditor control.

In the centralised *integration* model, several sovereign and subnational public entities cling and swing together in a multi-tier fiscal union. A central/collective body has the final say about spending, debt acquisition/service, and taxation. Spending is common pool financed by (shared) taxes, transfers, and debts; i.e., it exists a mutual commitment to carry the burden of funding together. As long as the subnational units are relatively free to borrow within the limits set by the centre, the centre and the subnational parts commit to be responsible for the debts of subnational units in financial trouble. Strictly enforced borrowing and deficit constraints form an alternative to a bailout commitment. Financial sustainability requires an effective chain of commands top-down. The integration model functions like a private business with multiple regional branches. The board holds the reigns in its hands–how tight or loose may vary from firm to firm. Nonetheless, the board has the final responsibility.

A *mixed* system is in essence an incomplete autonomy or integration model. A mixed system is not financially sustainable. Misallocation of resources, overspending, and/or underinvestment are its natural consequences. The only way to escape the quandary of financial unsustainability is a reform towards either the autonomy or the integration model.[1]

---

1 For the theory of institutional congruence, the autonomy model, the integration model, and the faulty design of hybrid/incongruent systems see: CHARLES BLANKART and DAVID EHMKE, 'Collective Decisions on Public Debts' (2016) 14 (3) CESifo DICE Report 43; CHARLES BLANKART, *Öffentliche Finanzen in der Demokratie* (9th edn, Vahlen 2017), especially 419–499; CHARLES BLANKART, *Föderalismus in Deutschland und Europa* (Nomos 2007); CHARLES BLANKART, 'The Process of Government Centralisation: A Constitutional View' (2000) 11 (1) Constitutional Political Economy 27; CHARLES BLANKART, 'Wie finanzieren sich Völkergemeinschaften? Vom Kaiserreich zur Eurokrise–Drei Modelle im Vergleich' (2012) 61 (3) Zeitschrift für Wirtschaftspolitik 241; CHARLES BLANKART and DAVID EHMKE, 'Kommunaler Bail-Out oder beschränkter Insolvenzfähigkeit–Zum Umgang mit überschuldeten Kommunen' (2014) 63 (2) Zeitschrift für Wirtschaftspolitik 173; CHARLES BLANKART and ACHIM KLAIBER, 'Subnational Government Organisation and Public Debt Crisis' (2006) Economic Affairs 48. The idea of the institutionally congruent autonomy and integration model is also present in the groundbreaking work of Jonathan Rodden on fiscal federalism. See: JONATHAN RODDEN, 'Reviving Leviathan: Fiscal Federalism and the Growth of Government' (2003) 57 International Organization 695; JONATHAN RODDEN, 'Soft Budget Constraints and German Federalism' in Jonathan Rodden, Gunnar Eskeland, and Jennie Litvack (eds) *Fiscal Decentralisation and the Challenge of Hard Budget Constraints* (Massachusetts Institute of Technology 2013) 161; JONATHAN RODDEN, 'The Dilemma of Fiscal Federalism: Grants and Fiscal Performance Around the World' (2002) 46 (3) American Journal of Political Science 670; JONATHAN RODDEN and ERIK WIBBELS, 'Beyond the Fiction of Federal-

2. Structure

This book is divided in five parts:

Political Decisions on Sovereign and Public Debt: The methodological fundament is established in Chapter II. The homo economicus enters the stage of politics. The perfect world assumptions for political decision-making in matters of sovereign and subnational public debts in relation to spending and taxation are adjusted to the imperfections in reality and reviewed in light of public choice theory.

Public Finances in a Multi-Tier Playing Field: Chapter III forms the theoretical mainstay of this project and is concerned with taxation, debt, and spending in a multi-tier playing field. The analysis will start with a discussion of decentralisation versus centralisation in fiscal federalism before the theory of institutional congruence, i.e., of the institutional superiority of the autonomy and integration model over mixed systems, will be presented. The institutions which define the autonomy and the integration model will be discussed in detail.

Lessons from Subnational Fiscal Experiments: The theory of institutional congruence will be road-tested first in Chapter IV. The theory of institutional congruence will be applied to several national fiscal concepts, i.e., to the fiscal relations of the federal/central government with the subnational public entities.

The Challenge of Integration: The European Monetary Union: The challenge of integration in a bailout union of multiple sovereign nations will be analysed in Chapter V. The European Monetary Union forms the single example for such an integration project of integration in our times. The institutional framework for decisions about spending, debt acquisition/service, taxation, and transfers, the European 'rescue mission' for troubled sovereign debtors, and the possible way forward will be discussed in this chapter.

The Challenge of Autonomy: Autonomous Sovereign Debtors: Chapter VI. eventually will deal with the vast majority of countries across the world which cannot expect a comprehensive bailout. For these countries and

---

ism: Macroeconomic Management in Multitiered Systems' (2002) 54 World Politics 494. For the concept of fiscal equivalence linked to the idea of institutional congruence see also MANCUR OLSEN, 'The principle of "fiscal equivalence": The Devision of Responsibilities among Different Levels of Government' (1969) 59 (2) The American Economic Review 479. Olsen's idea of fiscal equivalence best relates to the autonomy model.

their creditors, the absence of an orderly insolvency framework creates an awkward and chaotic situation in distress. The challenges faced by sovereign debtors and their creditors in a game with presently weak rules will be analysed before a proposal for the design of a sovereign insolvency regime will be presented.

II. Political Decisions on Sovereign and Public Debts

1. Preliminary Considerations

The analysis of sovereign and public debt starts in a (quite) perfect world. Politicians make decisions with the intention to maximise the welfare of their citizens. An all-wise and benevolent government is in charge. Taxpayers and voters calculate the net present value of debt acquisition, spending, and taxation. Externalities, i.e., costs which would be paid for by taxpayers in future generations or by taxpayers of other sovereign or public entities, are not discounted from the net present value calculation. Sovereign and public debtors regularly repay their debt. If they default, e.g. because of an external shock out of their control, they will play fair and repay as much as it is possible. Similarly, the political agents of sovereign or public 'rescuers' bailout other debtors because they believe that this would create a shared surplus for the taxpayers of rescued and of rescuing entities. Ulterior short-term political interests do not exist.[2]

If the forenamed assumptions were true, institutions would not matter. The distinction between fiscal systems following the autonomy, integration, or a mixed model would be pointless.[3] Institutions, however, matter because the world is not perfect, as public choice theory highlights. In this

2 Especially political decision-makers seem to have avoided a discussion about how the behaviour of investors, voters, and politicians is influenced by the calculation for different possible scenarios in financial distress. Even though it is troubling if policy decisions are made based on an incomplete calculation of their factual consequences, it is quite understandable why political decision-makers prefer to focus on the acute ex post problems. A debate about the ex-ante consequences of different ex post scenarios of distress is first and foremost concerned with questions of public choice and distorted incentives of political decision-makers. The debate about ex post problems instead, i.e., the debate mostly about the problems of opportunistic creditors, is certainly a more comfortable debate for politicians in office, but quite often a scapegoat strategy.

3 Also the often cited argument that a model of decentralisation (such as the *autonomy* model) would have an information advantage does not hold in a perfect world. Political agents at different levels of government would simply have to establish smooth communication channels for information to travel bottom-up. Distortions in the communication of information first arise when the homo economicus in politics acts in asymmetric information relations (see II. 3.2.).

chapter, political decision-making in matters of debt acquisition, taxation, and spending in the shadow of distress will be discussed, primarily from a public choice perspective. Perfect world assumptions will be questioned in the respective sub-chapters in which they are presented.

In an imperfect world, questions arise of how the expectations of a default, a bailout, a transfer commitment, or, alternatively, of an (orderly) private or public ordering insolvency procedure influence the actions of political agents, voters, taxpayers, and creditors. Questions have to be answered of why governments grow beyond reasonable size, why public spending explodes, or why political decision-makers delay necessary but unpopular governance reforms when deficit financing on the costs of 'rescuers' and future generations is possible. An understanding of the interests and positions of all players precedes the design of institutions which are established in order to overcome the problems identified. In this sense, chapter II. will lay the fundament for the institutional analysis.

2. *Debt Relations in a Quite Perfect World*

2.1 Ricardo-Barro Equivalence Theorem

A government in a capitalist society has primarily two ways of raising capital in order to finance its budget: The government can collect taxes from its residents/citizens or borrow capital from other countries/public entities, from banks, or on the capital markets. [4] If the government decides to borrow capital, 'capital now' will have to be repaid in the future in principal plus accrued interests. In a quite perfect world, sovereign and public debtors always repay their debt and debt is considered to be risk-free. It is, however, not cost-free. Capital is scarce and if investors choose to entrust their capital to a debtor, they cannot invest it elsewhere, i.e., they expect a compensation for the lost opportunities of an alternative risk-free investment. The price for goods in different time periods, similarly the price for capital, is found on the markets as a result of the individuals' subjective val-

4 Certainly, the state itself can engage in entrepreneurial activities. For the sake of this project, the assumption is that individual and corporate players can do business more effectively than the state, so that state ventures will not be discussed as a third stream of income. On this discussion about capitalist v socialist enterprises see: JANOS KORNAI, 'Resource-Constrained versus Demand-Constraint Systems' (1979) 47 (7) Econometrica 801.

uation in supply and demand, as Kenneth Arrow and Gérard Debreu[5] discovered when taking the idea of the marginal revolution one step further.[6]

Because all debts will have to be repaid by sovereign and public debtors one day, debt acquisition cannot ease the burden of taxation. Similar to the Modigliani-Miller Theorem, according to which corporate debtors should be indifferent between debt and equity capital acquisition,[7] the Ricardo-Barro Theorem postulates that sovereign and public debtors should be indifferent between taxation and borrowing. Taxpayers will perceive borrowing as delayed taxation, since all debt outstanding will have to be repaid. The present taxes collected plus the present value of the principal borrowed plus accrued interests in future periods is accounted for as the burden of present taxation.

From the Ricardo-Barro Theorem follows:

$$\mathbf{TB1} = \mathbf{TR1} + [\mathbf{D1} \times (\mathbf{1} + \mathbf{i})^{tx}] \div (\mathbf{1} + \mathbf{i})^{tx} = \mathbf{TR1} + \mathbf{D1}$$

Explanation: TB1 = tax burden experienced by taxpayers in period 1; TR1 = tax revenue collected in period 1; D1 = debt-financed deficit in period 1, i.e. spending minus tax revenue in period 1; tx= time period x when debt has to be repaid; i=risk-free interest rate.

Inference: Taxpayers are indifferent between taxation and borrowing.[8]

The Ricardo-Barro theorem works under some perfect world assumptions, of which two are in particular problematic: (i.) sovereign and public debtors always repay their own debts, (ii.) taxpayers account for the debt

5 KENNETH ARROW and GERARD DEBREU, 'Existence of an Equilibrium for a Competitive Economy' (1954) 22 (3) Econometrica 265.

6 The marginal revolution was brought by William Stanley Jevons, Carl Menger, and Léon Walras. See therefore: WILLIAM STANLEY JEVONS, Theory of Political Economy (Macmillan and Co. 1871); CARL MENGER, *Principles of Economics* (original: Grundsätze der Volkswirtschaftslehre 1871, tr James Dingwall and Bert Hoselitz, Ludwig von Mises Institute 2007); LÉON WALRAS, *Elements of Pure Economics* (original: *Éléments d'économie politique pure* 1874, tr William Jaffe Routledge 2010).

7 FRANCO MODIGLIANI and MERTON MILLER, 'The Cost of Capital, Corporation Finance and th Theory of Finance' (1958) 48 (3) The American Economic Review 261; MERTON MILLER and FRANCO MODIGLIANI, 'Dividend Policy, Growth, and the Valuation of Shares' (1961) 34 (4) The Journal of Business 411.

8 ROBERT BARRO, 'Are government bonds net wealth?' (1974) 82 (6) Journal of Political Economy 1095; ROBERT BARRO, 'On the Determination of the Public Debt' (1979) 87 (5) Journal of Political Economy 940; DAVID RICARDO, 'Essay on the Funding System' (1820) in John Ramsay McCulloch (ed.) *The Works of David Ricardo* (Morrison and Gibb 1888) 516. See the discussion by BLANKART (2017) at 272–274.

obligations of future generations at present value. In respect of the first assumption (i.), chapter VI. will deal with the problems of autonomous sovereign or public debtors unable or unwilling to repay their debt while the case that a sovereign or public debtor is (partly) financed by vertical/ horizontal transfers/bailouts will be discussed in chapters III., IV., and V. In each of the aforementioned scenarios, the sovereign or public debtor does not (always) repay its own debt. The debtor defaults or the debt is repaid by a third party. The assumption that taxpayers would account for the debt burden of future generations at present value is quite idealistic. The second assumption becomes even more disconcerting when the challenges to the first assumption, that sovereign and public debtors would always repay their own debt, is refuted.

2.2 The Sustainability of Sovereign and Public Debt

When Anne Krueger addressed the public with a proposal for a Sovereign Debt Restructuring Mechanism in 2001, the ultimate question of how to re-establish a sustainable debt level was the hot topic of the session.[9] A widely used framework to test the sustainability of the sovereign/public debt level is the intertemporal budget constraint, designed to picture the dynamic relation of interest and growth in gross national product. A factor which is, however, not included in the calculation below, is the risk of political opportunism.

The intertemporal budget constraint is defined by the public spending excl. interest payments (S), the sovereign/public debt (D), the real interest rate on D (i), the real GDP growth rate (g), and the tax income (T). Assuming that a budget is currently sustainable, the budget will remain to be sustainable as long as

$$\mathbf{0 \geq (S'-T) \div GDP + (i-g) \times D \div GDP}$$

is true. If $i > g$, the debtor has to yield a budget surplus large enough to compensate for the increase in the debt-to-GDP-ratio due to accrued interests. Vice versa, only in times where $g > i$, the debtor can acquire additional debts without that the debt-to-GDP-ratio increases. Thus, depending on real growth and interest rates, the debtor may have to adjust spending or tax-

9 ANNE KRUEGER, A New Approach to Sovereign Debt Restructuring (2001) Address by Anne O Krueger, First Deputy Managing Director, IMF, Given at the National Economists' Club Annual Members' Dinner, November 26.

ation to balance its budget or to re-approach a sustainable debt-to-GDP-ratio. The more the debt-to-GDP-ratio increases, the higher have to be the debtor's budget surplus in future periods as a result of higher taxes or lower spending in order to make good for the sins of the past.[10]

The debt sustainability calculation, however, becomes more complicated if one accounts for the following:

- All variable factors S, iD, g, D, and T are mutally dependent on each other. The correlation is flexible. To illustrate this: Spending cuts can affect growth, especially when a scale back in infrastructure investments (i.e. spending cuts) inhibits business activity.[11] Similarly, an increase in taxation can affect growth negatively, and while it may currently fill the treasury, excessive taxation can erode the future tax potential in a recession. The risk-free interest base is dependent on factors which the debtor cannot influence, i.e., the capital supply and demand, while the risk-premium is determined by the debt level in relation to the potential for growth, taxation, and spending cuts.
- The debt structure has a significant influence on the actual debt burden in distress. It has to be taken into account as to whether the body of creditors is concentrated or dispersed, as to whether the indebtness is external or internal, i.e., national or foreign, in which currency the debt is denominated and which law governs the debt contract. The distinct interests of creditors have to be identified as well as hidden and potential debts have to be taken into consideration, e.g., debts which would arise as the consequence of a national bank bailout programme. An analysis of the debt structure is a cornerstone for a successful debt restructuring.[12]

---

10 For the intertemporal budget constraint equation and the inferences as they are presented in this sub-chapter see BLANKART (2017) 268–269 (equation 17.4) in reference to OLIVER BLANCHARD, JEAN-CLAUDE CHOURAQUI, ROBERT HAGEMANN, and NICOLA SARTOR, 'The Sustainability of Fiscal Policy: New Answers to an Old Question' (1990) 15 OECD Economic Studies 8.

11 This is in particular true when the bureaucratic, judicial, law enforcement, energy, or transportation infrastructure is insufficient as a result of spending cuts. Some activities which have previously been performed by public entities, e.g., energy supply and transportation, can be assumed by private investors. A prerequisite therefore is that the debtor sends out a credible signal to protect private investments from its own hold-up strategies in the future. To put it differently, the 'rule of law' has a hard market value.

12 For a discussion of the forenamed factors see especially the debt sustainability analysis framework of the IMF for market-access countries and of the IMF and the World Bank for low-income countries: MARK ALLEN and DANNY

- "... an emerging market may be defined as a state in which politics matters at least as much as economics" (Ian Bremmer).[13] A debt sustainability calculation would be incomplete if it only accounted for the economic sustainability of the debtor's debt burden. In case of a corporate debtor, the case is comparatively easy. If the debtor wants to continue trading, its creditors will have to be convinced that the going-concern value and a debt reduction will yield a higher return for them than a liquidation of the debtor's assets. In case of a sovereign or public debtor, liquidation is no option and no threat. Enforcement options are limited. The debtor finds itself in quite a strong bargaining position. It is not only its economic capacity. It is the often the debtor's political choice as to whether and to which percentage debts will be repaid. The less stable the debtor's political regime is, the less weight the rule of law has as a principle of political action. The higher the risk of political opportunism is, the higher is also the risk that debts will not be repaid (in full).[14]

2.3 The Sirens' Song: Low Interest Rates

In recent years, interest rates have dropped significantly. For some borrowers, considered to be risk-free, interest rates are close to zero; even a long-time period of negative interests rates is said to be a possible scenario for future lending practice. The low-interest rate phenomenon can be explained differently. Following the theory of boom and bust by Ludwig von Mises, the central banks flood the market with capital and banks lend capital in an amount which by far exceeds their assets. Investments go up and

LEIPZIGER, 'Operational Framework for Debt Sustainability Assessment in Low-Income Countries–Further Considerations' (International Monetary Fund and International Development Association 2005); MARK ALLEN and DANNY LEIPZIGER, 'Applying the Debt Sustainability Framework for Low-Income Countries Post Debt Relief (International Monetary Fund and International Development Association 2006); TIMOTHY GEITHNER, 'Assessing Sustainability' (International Monetary Fund 2002); TIMOTHY GEITHNER, 'Assessing Sustainability–Review of Application and Methodological Refinements' (International Monetary Fund 2003); CARLO COTTARELLI and REZA MOGHADAM, 'Modernizing the Framework for Fiscal Policy and Public Debt Sustainability Analysis' (International Monetary Fund 2011). See also the discussion in Chapter VI. 2.

13 IAN BREMMER, 'Managing Risk in an Unstable World' (2005) June Issue, Harvard Business Review 2, 2–3.

14 Sub-chapter VI. 2. is concerned with these questions.

the prices for 'real values' rise. The oversupply of capital, however, leads to less selective investment decisions, more risk-taking, and, eventually, to an oversupply with production goods, real estates, etc. In von Mises' theory, low interest rates are only a temporary problem. The boom period has to come to an end when the false game of central banks and commercial banks is unmasked. Prices drop and the bubble busts.[15]

Another prominent explanation put forward sees low interest rates as a permanent result of changing economic conditions and demographics worldwide. In 2005, Ben Bernanke, then President of the Federal Reserve Bank of the United States of America, warned the public of the danger of a so-called 'savings glut'.[16] Carl Christian von Weizsäcker presented an academic explanation of the savings glut: In a nutshell, the saving glut arises in consequence of changing demographics worldwide. Thanks to rising living standards, especially nutrition and healthcare in developing countries, the life expectancy across the world increases steadily. At the same time, changing living conditions such as a focus on less labour intensive businesses and the overall availability of birth control measures have contributed to a falling birth rate. The idea of an intergenerational contract by which the working population commits to care for the elder is not sustainable. Because everyone is ultimately responsible for themselves, those able to save for their retirement look for opportunities to invest their capital. The supply of capital rises. If the demand for capital does not positively correlate with this development, i.e., if there are not enough additional and worthwhile investment opportunities, the oversupply of capital and low (even zero/negative) interest rates are the natural consequence of the savings glut.[17]

Following the 'saving glut'-theory that oversupply of capital and low interest rates are a permanent phenomenon (and not just the reflection of

---

15 LUDWIG VON MISES, *The Theory of Money and Credit* (first published 1912, English version, Yale University Press 1953) discussed by BLANKART (2017) 274-276. On the risk of malinvestments as a consequence of low interest rates see further PAUL MASSON, 'The Dangers of an Extended Period of Low Interest Rates: Why the Bank of Canada Should Start Raising Them Now' (2013) C.D. Howe Institute Commentary 381.

16 BEN BERNANKE, 'The Global Saving Glut and the U.S. Current Account Deficit' (March 10, 2005) Remarks by Governor Ben S. Bernanke, At the Sandridge Lecture, Virginia Association of Economists, Richmond, Virginia.

17 CARL CHRISTIAN VON WEIZSÄCKER, 'Kapitalismus in der Krise?' (2015) 16 (2) Perspektiven der Wirtschaftspolitik 189 discussed by BLANKART (2017) 276–282.

an artificially blown up bubble), the question arises how this affects the case of sovereign and public debt. At first glance, one might assume that the debt problem would be washed away with low, zero, or in particular negative interest rates. Public and sovereign debtors could refinance their debt at low costs and pay off a previously pressing/unsustainable debt burden. This assumption is misleading though.

The problem of sovereign and public debt persists. While debtors with a strong financial and economic performance and a high degree of accountability in politics might benefit from low interest rates, low interest rates are likely to exacerbate the indebtness problem for debtors with an already weak financial/economic performance and with low levels of accountability in politics. As the economists Tim Besley and Peter Hennessy pointed out in their letter to Her Majesty The Queen, an oversupply of capital, as a consequence of the saving glut, could have been an accelerator for the recent financial crisis.[18] If capital is cheap and easily available, the competition for capital is less intense. The incentive for sovereign and public debtors to develop their investment offer, i.e., to present themselves financially and economically sound, vanishes. Governance reforms can be delayed.[19] Sovereign and public debtors are more likely to become economically distressed before they are eventually financially distressed. Under the assumption that financial markets are rational and accurate risk-monitors (in a quite perfect world), this becomes in particular an issue for sovereign and public debtors in a bailout/transfer union.

Greece is an excellent example for the danger of low interest rates in a bailout/transfer union. After Greece had joined the eurozone, interest rates for Greece fell sharply, and Greece benefitted from interest rates in a pooling equilibrium. Greece could have, theoretically, restructured its outstanding debt positions, could have used the cheaply available debt capital for the development of its economy, could have reformed its economy and its bureaucratic system, and could have eventually closed the gap between present spending and present tax income. The story went different. While interest rates fell, the Greek government missed the chance for overdue reforms. The Greek government had chosen the easy and popular path. Greece's debt problem became worse.[20]

---

18 TIM BESLEY and PETER HENNESSY, Letter to Her Majesty the Queen (British Academy, 22 July 2009).

19 The case of debt finance and political opportunism will be further explored in section II. 3.

20 The case of Greece will be discussed in more detail in Chapter V.

While an oversupply of debt capital will bring the risk-free component of any debtor's interest rate down, (potential) creditors will require an adequate risk premium for their investment once the risk of a future default rises. For weak debtors at a high risk of default, the risk-free interest rate will then constitute an almost insignificant portion of their interest rates. Low interest rates might be a blessing for debtors which are able to resist the temptation to fund spending with easily accessible debt capital and to delay necessary but unpopular governance reforms. For other debtors unable to resist the Sirens' song, low interest rates may turn out to be a fatal temptation once they are trapped in the vicious circle of economic slowdown and financial distress.

3. *Debt Relations in an Imperfect World*

3.1 The Homo Economicus in Politics

The homo economicus is based on a sheer positive assumption of human nature and interaction. Humans are not wild and evil, in need of the guidance of a benevolent and all-wise ruler, may it be a King/Queen, a President, or the Church.[21] Not a central authority which prescribes the narrow path of virtue to pleasure and salvation but the individuals themselves are capable of increasing first their individual utility and by means of trade their mutual utility. Individuals make self-interested and rational decisions. Trade facilitates an optimal allocation and use of scarce resources. Actions by self-interested and rational individuals, therefore, have a positive outcome for society as a whole.[22]

A problem arises once the homo economics enters politics. The world becomes quite imperfect at once. When citizens compete for public goods, when politicians act as their citizens' agents, the assumption of self-inter-

21 The rather pessimistic illustration of the human being is most famously associated with the philosophy of Thomas Hobbes, often referred to by the widely known Latin proverb "homo homini lupus est". See therefore: THOMAS HOBBES, *Leviathan or the Matter, Forme, and Power of a Common Wealth Ecclesiasticall and Civil* (1651) PART I On Man, and PART II On Commonwealth.

22 ADAM SMITH, *An Inquiry into the Nature and Causes of the Wealth of Nations* (original 1776, MetaLibri 2007). Christian Kirchner has, therefore, described the optimistic and positive concept of human nature in the homo oeconomicus model as the Anti-Leviathan position. See CHRISTIAN KIRCHNER, 'Ökonomik: Eigennutz, Fairness und Empathie' (manuscript) Chapter 2.3.1.

ested and rational decision-makers often leads to suboptimal rather than efficient outcomes. This is in particular true when information is asymmetrically distributed.[23] Different from the creation of private goods and the performance of private services and their respective exchange on the markets, public/political actions are not meant to produce original wealth in a capitalist society. The supply with public goods is often a question of re-distribution, which relates to the question of institutional congruence, i.e., to the (in-)congruence of the circles of those who order, enjoy, and pay for a good.[24] The re-distribution of wealth as a matter of public policy (e.g., for health, education, and arts, or to the benefit of the poor and weak) shall not be questioned in this book at all. Certain public goods, indeed, are a prerequisite for a society to thrive. If some goods were not provided, this would cause gross injustice. The question in this book, however, is how the framework for decisions about the creation, funding, and 'access key' to goods provided by the government can be designed to achieve a Pareto-improvement in public finances.

When decisions are to be made about the re-distribution of resources, each citizen acting in accordance with the homo economics model will strive for the highest possible benefit, i.e., order as much and enjoy as much of the public good as possible. If tax-funded, families will order to enjoy the best possible child care and education for their children, older people will ask for an increase in pension plans, and anyone will demand a highly developed infrastructure especially for their home region. While every individual has to balance the benefits and costs of a private good, this link does not exist when individuals make up a calculation for public goods. The costs are shared amongst all taxpayers in proportion to their individual tax contribution. The public good is relatively 'cheap' for those who enjoy it if compared to a private substitute. Since public projects are financed by a pool of taxes and debts, but since the benefits are often only enjoyed by specific interest or regional groups, an excessive amount of orders is placed. The use of tax money and debts for the funding of an unrestricted amount of public projects suffers from the 'common pool dilemma.' Similar to the 'tragedy of the commons,' there exists an incentive to overuse the resources or to demand an extension of the resources which are

23 See therefore section II. 3.2.

24 In many cases, this is inevitable, since the provision of public goods almost always entails some element of re-distribution. The degree of institutional congruence, nonetheless, differs dramatically depending on the respective institutional design.

available to the community.[25] It depends on the process of decision-making about the creation, funding, and access to goods provided by the government how well the allocation and supply is managed. The process can be hostile and competitive (winner-takes-it-all), leading to an exploitation of some to the benefit of others, or cooperative, with the risk of oversupply.

Decisions about the (re-)distribution of resources in politics often involve some element of delegation and representation. At this stage, politicians enter the stage to decide about public goods as agents of their principal citizens. Even though they might be formally expected to maximise the welfare of all citizens, i.e., to form a benevolent legislative and executive government, the more realistic assumption is that of self-interested and rational political agents. Politicians, for example, often tend to advance the interests of their regional or special interest support group. They are inclined to advocate projects on the cost of all citizens and to the benefit of those parties whom they expect to support their claim to power; in elections in a democracy or as a matter of factual support in an authoritarian regime. [26] One major concern of politicians, in this light, is the desire to gain and to maintain power. If support is crucial therefore, they can be expected to overvalue the opinion of their support base and too discount negative effects of their actions as long as they do not affect their supporters. The better a political system works to proportionally reflect the different interest groups in a society, the less of a problem is an understanding of politicians as special interest representatives. If some groups are overrepresented or if the legislative is hostile/competitive in relation to the opposition, it will come to cost-shifting to the disadvantage of under-represented and minority groups.

It would, however, be too simplistic to assume that all politicians seek office for the sake of power itself, i.e., that they would adjust their agenda to whatever direction momentarily secures them the highest support. While this is true for some politicians, most politicians can be expected to follow an own agenda, i.e., a personal belief about how the society 'ought

25 For the 'tragedy of the commons' see: GARRET HARDIN, 'The Tragedy of the Commons' (1968) 162 (3859) Science 1243. Hardin re-discovers the idea first developed by WILLIAM LLOYD, *Two Lectures on the Checks To Population* (Oxford University Press 1833).

26 See therefore STEPHEN COATE and STEPHEN MORRIS, 'On the Form of Transfers to Special Interests' (1995) 103 (6) The Journal of Political Economy 1210; GENE GROSSMAN and ELHANAN HELPMAN, 'Electoral Competition and Special Interest Politics' (1996) 63 (2) The Review of Economic Studies 265.

to be' designed. The value of projects which would be associated with their person presently and in the future will then be multiplied with a political factor. The politicians' projects, thereby, do not necessarily have to be in the best interest of their principals. This might be because the politicians are subject to a bias in evaluating the actual impact of their project, or because they expect that their supporters will see the benefits though they will not be able to identify the real costs of the projects.[27]

It is not the purpose of this book to answer fundamental questions of redistribution, the supply of public goods, and the political process of representation and delegation in general. The question to be answered is the one of the optimal fiscal regime to enhance fiscal and economic performance. The assumption of voters, taxpayers, and political agents as self-interested and rational beings with distinct interests is crucial in order to understand the real impact of institutions when it comes to spending, taxation, and debt acquisition decisions.

3.2 Political Agents in Asymmetric Relations

The fundamental reason of why politicians can realise their interests in conflict to their citizens' interests is an information problem, i.e., the asymmetric distribution of information between principals and agents. Principal-agent relations have been first and foremost analysed in context of the firm. In a firm, the interests of the principals as residual claimants and of the agents (i.e., directors, employees) can differ substantially. While, in theory, the principals can order their agents to follow a strategy in the principals' best interest, the principals' ability to influence the course of action is heavily limited. Though the delegation of work and leadership, i.e., the separation of ownership and management, is a pillar of capitalism, it creates the problem that the agents, who are specialised to work with the principal's resources, possess superior information.[28]

The principal agent (or team production) theory of the firm has been transferred to the case of political relations. The citizens (in a democracy, as

27 See therefore section II. 3.2.

28 For principal agent relations in context of the firm see: ARMEN ALCHIAN and HAROLD DEMSETZ, 'Production, Information Costs, and Economic Organization' (1972) 62 (5) The American Economic Review 777; MICHAEL JENSEN and WILLIAM MECKLING, 'Theory of the Firm: Managerial Behaviour, Agency Costs and Ownership Structure' (1976) 3 Journal of Financial Economics 305.

voters and taxpayers) are the principals as 'owners' of the country. The (elected) politicians are their agents with, as pointed out in the previous section, possibly distinct interests. The same as for principal-agent relations in context of the firm, politicians are 'full-time experts' with specialised knowledge and access to superior information. The more complex it is to process information, the easier it is for political agents to exploit the asymmetry of information. [29]

In case of a fiscal regime, an opaque system of taxation, spending, and budget responsibility can increase the cost for citizens to evaluate their political agents' budget decisions. Different from a perfect world scenario, citizens and taxpayers can be misled by a 'fiscal illusion'. They may underestimate the costs of a spending decision, especially when the costs are not realised immediately but with delay or with uncertainty, e.g., when such costs will only arise conditional upon a future event. A good example for this case are the loans and guarantees granted to Greece as part of the Eurozone bailout mission. The rescuing countries do not keep their accounts adjusted to the default risk of their sovereign debtors, i.e., they do not depreciate the value of their claims against a sovereign debtor with questionable prospect. Moreover, taxpayers are often not properly informed about the present value reductions already granted to the bailout recipients.[30] The short-term benefits for the rescuer – the avoidance of spillover effects and of an economic turmoil – are not properly balanced with the costs of a future default on the rescue loans. Such costs regularly remain in disguise for many taxpayers in the rescuing countries.[31]

Taxpayers may also have an illusion about the revenues/resources received by their political agents and about the real costs of a project. In particular when grants are transferred from one to another institution or level of government, it becomes increasingly complicated for citizens to associate revenues and spending. The 'flypaper effect' relates to such a problem of asymmetric information. Local politicians increase public spending dis-

---

29 For a discussion of the principal-agent model in politics see: RICHARD WATERMAN and KENNETH MEIER, 'Principal-Agent Models: An Expansion?' (1998) 8 (2) Journal of Public Administration Research and Theory 173. For the political agent's opinion to enforce their own political agenda, i.e., to realise their own beliefs, as they may be contrary to the citizens' interests, see: JOSEPH KALT and MARK ZUPAN, 'The Apparent Ideological Behaviour of Legislators: Testing For Principal-Agent Slack in Political Institutions' (1990) 33 Journal of Law and Economics 103. Especially see the discussion in II. 3.3.

30 See section V. 3.5.3.

31 BLANKART (2017) 267. Blankart calls this 'cameralistic accounting'.

proportionally, the higher their revenue stream from intergovernmental transfers is, as compared to the situation where the local citizens' income (available for taxation) increases. Put differently, politicians are less likely to cut local taxes when they receive (unconditional) transfers, which they could theoretically use to unburden their taxpayers, than to raise local taxes in order to achieve a similar spending level absent transfers. An explanation therefore is that it is more complicated for local taxpayers to evaluate public expenditures when they do not perceive the costs of a project as an increase in taxes (as opposed to possible but not exercised tax cutes).[32]

Eventually, the distinction between present taxes and future debt repayments is not only a problem of inter-generation burden-shifting but also of a lack of transparency. While the tax burden is presently and transparently perceived as a cost, the future repayment obligation – as a consequence of information asymmetries – is possibly calculated with an inflated discount factor so that present expenditures at the cost of future debts are overestimated to increase the citizens' net benefit.[33] Especially in a multi-tier transfer and bailout union with different levels of government and multiple units with individual accounts, the situation becomes more and more cloudy.

There has been much discussion about how one can mitigate the principal-agent problem in a firm by the implementation of control mechanisms, e.g., by the appointment of a monitor, by the design of incentive schemes to align the interests of principal and agent, or by a combination

32 For the 'flypaper effect' see BRUCE HAMILTON, 'The Flypaper Effect and Other Anomalies' (1983) 22 Journal of Public Economics 347; JAMES HINES and RICHARD THALER, 'Anomalies: The Flypaper Effect' (1995) 9 (4) Journal of Economic Perspectives 217; GEOFFREY TURNBULL, 'Fiscal Illusion, uncertainty, and the flypaper effect' (1992) 48 (2) Journal of Public Economics 207.

33 William Niskanen prominently criticised the US Republican fiscal strategy to cut down taxes in order to contain public spending, commonly referred to as 'Starve the Beast'. Niskanen argues that lowering taxes while allowing for deficit spending/indebtness would actually increase the demand for present public spending. See: WILLIAM NISKANEN, 'Limiting Government: The Failure of "Starve the Beast"' (2006) 26 (3) Cato Journal 553; WILLIAM NISKANEN, 'Comment on Tax Policy from 1990 to 2001' in Jeffrey Frankel and Peter Orszag (eds) *American Economic Policy in the 1990s* (MIT Press 2002) 184. The idea of 'fiscal illusion' is elaborated in relation to the tax system and deficit financing by JAMES BUCHANAN and RICHARD WAGNER, *Democracy in deficit: The political legacy of Lord Keynes* (Academic Press 1977).

of both.[34] Similar questions about accountability and incentive structures have to be answered in case of politics. The question is how can politicians be incentivised to act in the best interest of their citizens and how can citizens generate information to monitor and control their political agents' behaviour. The question of centralisation or decentralisation of budget authority and funding responsibility plays a crucial part in this game and will be further discussed in Chapter III, where it will be shown that centralisation and decentralisation both carry a risk to increase information asymmetries for different reasons.

3.3 Building Bureaucratic and Public Empires

In a perfect world, the government would try to generate as much revenues from tax and debt as required to satisfy their citizens' demand for public goods. In our world, governments have often been described as being 'revenue-hungry', so that they would increase their income stream from tax and debt acquisition for the construction of bureaucratic and public empires. Geoffrey Brennan and James Buchanan prominently discussed the idea of the government as 'revenue-hungry Leviathan' in their seminal work *The Power to Tax*.[35] The reasons for why the homo economics in politics often does not perfectly represent the citizens' interests has been subject to quite extensive research. Fundamentally, the question relates to the politician's desire to gain and maintain power and to their desire to build a legacy.[36]

The politicians' desire to gain and especially to maintain power is often reflected in the way that political decisions are influenced by the election cycle. The proposition made by William Nordhaus and other scholars is that politicians adjust their fiscal policy in a 'political business cycle' so that they increase spending, make election gifts, enter into long-term commitments, and artificially blow up the economy in the pre-election period in order to buy votes. The short-term gains which are visible to voters will have to be paid for in mid-term/long-term costs which are less visible and

---

34 The theoretical foundation of the principal-agent theory of the firm was laid with the seminal work of MICHAEL JENSEN and WILLIAM MECKLING, 'Theory of the firm: Managerial behaviour, agency costs, and ownership structure' (1976) 3 (4) Journal of Financial Economics 305.

35 GEOFFREY BRENNAN and JAMES BUCHANAN, *The Power to Tax: Analytical Foundations of a Fiscal Constitution* (Liberty Fund 1980).

36 See section II. 3.1.

more complicated to evaluate.[37] While the 'political business cycle' theory has a rather global approach, since it focuses on the overall economic performance in the pre-election period, another line of research inspired by Douglas Hibbs, known as 'partisan theory,' concentrates on the political ideology of those in power. While left-wing governments are supposed to foster employment on the cost of high inflation, right-wing governments would follow a low inflation path on the costs of higher unemployment figures. The 'partisan theory' suggests that politicians pursue an agenda not necessarily suited to increase welfare in the interest of all citizens, but that politicians would promote special interests,[38] and that they might even increase debt-funded special interest expenditures in order to limit their successors' scope of action to alter the political agenda, i.e., that they would force their legacy into stone.[39]

The concept of the revenue-hungry government 'Leviathan,' as presented by Buchanan and Brennan, finds its equivalent in the Niskanen model of the budget-maximising bureaucrat. According to the Niskanen model, civil servants, i.e., the executive agents in charge to perform the politicians' agenda, aim to increase the budget of their respective office so as to increase their own utility (e.g., for the sake of power and reputation). Since bureaucrats are regularly life-time experts in one profession, they possess superior information about the efficient input-output ratio for their office, so that they can deceive their political superiors when they communicate

37 See the formalised model presented by WILLIAM NORDHAUS, 'The Political Business Cycle' (1975) Review of Economic Studies 169 and further: WILLIAM NORDHAUS, ALBERTO ALESINA and CHARLES SCHULTZE, 'Alternative Approaches to the Political Business Cycle' (1989) 2 Brookings Papers on Economic Activity 1; LUDGER SCHUKNECHT, 'Political Business Cycles and Fiscal Policies in Developing Countries' (1996) 49 Kyklos 155.

38 See the seminal work of DOUGLAS HIBBS, 'Political Parties and Macroeconomic Policy' (1977) 71 (4) The American Political Science Review 1467 and further: FREDERICK CARLSEN, 'Rational Partisan Theory: Empirical Evidence for the United States' (1998) 65 (1) Southern Economic Journal 64; CHARLES FINOCCHIARO and DAVID ROHDE, 'War for the Floor: Partisan Theory and Agenda Control In the U.S. House of Representatives' (2008) 33 Legislative Studies Quarterly 35; DOUGLAS HIBBS, 'Partisan theory after fifteen years' (1992) 8 European Journal of Political Economy 361; DOUGLAS HIBBS, 'The Partisan Model of Macroeconomic Cycles: More Theory and Evidence for the United States' (1994) 6 (1) Economic and Politics 1.

39 ALBERTO ALESINA and GUIDO TABELLINI, 'A Positive Theory of Fiscal Deficits and Government Debts' (1990) 57 Review of Economic Studies 403.

about the optimal budget allocation.[40] While the Leviathan hypothesis has been widely studied theoretically and empirically, the Niskanen model of the budget-maximising bureaucrat remains primarily a theoretical argument awaiting further empirical discussion.[41]

A corollary from the propositions of the revenue-maximising politicians' pursuit for power and legacy, of the politicians' information advantage if compared to their citizens' information level, and of the politicians' own dependency on information communicated to them by budget-maximising bureaucrats is that the public budget should grow continuously; the same as the debt level to fund the budget should increase. The reason for why some fiscal regimes follow this prediction, i.e., the reason for why the Leviathan-hypothesis seems to be confirmed by some governments, while other fiscal regimes are capable to contain expenditures, taxes, and debts within reasonable limits has to be found in an institutional analysis.

3.4 Interest Group Lobbying

Lobbying is a reciprocal process influencing political decision-making. The focus is often on lobby groups representing the commercial interests of specific industries. This, however, does not at all cover the multifarious world of lobbying. Not only do commercial industries invest into lobbying, but also trade unions, stakeholders of a religion, or representatives of a region. The motivation of the lobby groups' representatives is to achieve an improvement for their constituency/principals. Such improvements are typically realised by the implementation of or the relief from regulation or by the supply of subsidies. While some regulations and subsidies may result in a pareto-improvement for the entire population, other regulations and subsidies are cross-funded with externalities to other citizens.

---

40 WILLIAM NISKANEN, *Bureaucracy and Representative Government* (Aldine Transaction 1971).

41 For a discussion of the Niskanen model and its critics see: ANDRÉ BLAIS and STÉPHANE DION, 'Are Bureaucrats Budget Maximizers? The Niskanen Model & Its Critics' (1990) 22 (4) Polity 655. A related subject is investigated by SIMON LUECHINGER, STEPHAN MEIER, and ALOIS STUTZER, 'Bureaucratic Rents and Life Satisfaction' (2008) 24 (2) Journal of Law, Economics & Organization 476. The authors present an empirical analysis of the question in how far bureaucrats are able to extract rents from their position (to the disadvantage of other citizens), i.e., inflated monetary benefits, soft benefits, bribes and in how far institutions such as judicial independence can mitigate the rent-seeking problem.

Politicians respond to lobbying mainly for two reasons: first, a positive reply to the lobby groups demand can secure the politicians (indirect or direct) funding and votes to support their claim to power. Second, the politicians can gain access to information and knowledge when they communicate with lobby groups, with the apparent flaw that information is presented to them with a bias. This process has been analysed by Georg Stigler for the case of economic regulation.[42]

Obviously, the activity of lobby groups has a direct impact on the public budget. In a multi-tier union, local interest groups address the local government with demands for subsidies.[43] If the government of a local unit sees a good chance to lobby for horizontal or vertical transfers or bailouts, it can be more generous to give subsidies to its local interest groups and later on approach the central authority with a request for higher transfers. Similarly, the special interest representatives are aware that the costs of their privileges are not only shared by the community of their region but that the costs are shared by all local units within the transfer and bailout union, so that they are encouraged to ask for a privilege in the first place. Take the following example: If unit A was fully self-funded, the demands of, for instance, public employees for higher income and pensions could cause a conflict with taxpayers who might reject the public employees' demands. Similarly, subsidies to the private economy might be unpopular, so that the government would be rather cautious to grant special interest groups a privilege. If, however, unit A had a good chance to ask units B to Z for transfers or a bailout, the taxpayers in unit A and similarly the government of A should not have much of a problem to promise an increase of incomes and pensions to A's employees and to provide subsidies to the private economy of A. Citizens of A would be aware that the benefits are fully enjoyed in A while the costs are spread out across all regional units, so that the costs for A's citizens become less significant.

---

42 GEORGE STIGLER, 'The Theory of Economic Regulation' (1971) 2 (1) The Bell Journal of Economics and Management Science 3; GEORGE STIGLER, 'The Process of Economic Regulation' (1972) The Antitrust Bulletin 207.

43 In case of a transfer union of sovereign countries, the sovereign countries are understood as local units.

3.5 Rent-Seeking

The creation and distribution of public goods, funded by public budgets, is often not a question of wealth creation but of re-distribution. The government collects taxes and acquires debt in order to fund projects from which mostly special interest and regional groups will benefit. Only the benefits of a very few public goods (e.g., judicial infrastructure, law enforcement) are enjoyed by all citizens. Absent a stable rule for the creation and distribution of public goods/subsidies, the creation of public goods and the distribution of subsidies are the result of a competitive bargaining process. The process of lobbying itself is the prototype of such a competition. The lobby group makes a (transaction cost) investment to support its claim to the common pool. The 'applicant' for a rent adjusts its effort not to the market but to the privileges granted by public regulation. While many compete, some succeed, and the costs of this competition lead to a (partial) dispersion of rents. An analysis of the process of transfers and re-distribution in case of horizontal and vertical regional grants has, thus, to account for the costs of the competition for rents. The rent-seeking problem (as opposed to profit-seeking) has been brought to attention, prominently, by Tullock.[44]

In case of regional grants, a significant proportion of the actual subsidy received by the beneficiaries might have already been 'lost' in investments for lobbying and re-organisations necessary to fit within the (pre-)defined criteria for transfer payments. The lobbying effort is limited where the potential beneficiaries fear that other – quite similar – beneficiaries could free ride on their lobbying investment.[45] The higher the degree of organisation in a society, however, is, the more likely it is that special interest representatives bundle their efforts to lobby for a greater share from the common pool for their constituency.[46]

---

44 GORDON TULLOCK, 'The Welfare Costs of Tariffs, Monopolies, and Theft' (1967) 5 (3) Western Economic Review 224. See further: ANNE KRUEGER, 'The Political Economy of the Rent-Seeking Society' (1974) 64 (3) The American Economic Review 291.

45 MANCUR OLSEN, *The Logic of Collective Action* (Harvard University Press 1965).

46 MANCUR OLSEN, *The Rise and Decline of Nations: Economic Growth, Stagflation, and Social Rigidities* (Yale University Press 1982). For a more elaborate theoretical discussion of rent-seeking and for a practical example on lobbying/applying for rents in case of regional grants in Europe/Germany see: CHARLES BLANKART and DAVID EHMKE, 'Overcoming the Rent-Seeking Defect in Regional Policy: Time to Re-think the Institutional Design' (2015) 3 CESifo DICE Report 44.

III. Public Finances in a Multi-Tier Playing Field

1. *Preliminary Considerations*

This chapter begins with a review and analysis of the discussion about the costs, benefits, and risks of centralisation versus decentralisation in multi-tier unions in section III. 2. In section III. 3, the concept of institutional congruence will be presented. A theoretical framework will be developed which can be applied to the analysis of different sovereign and public entities. The underlying assumption is that institutional design matters more than the simple question of centralisation versus decentralisation. After a comparison of the market and central government control in section III 3.2, the optimal institutional design of a fiscal regime under the autonomy and integration model will be discussed theoretically in sections III. 3.3 and 3.4.

2. *Centralisation v Decentralisation*

2.1 Race to the Best Fit, to the Top, or to the Bottom?

A decentralised market economy outpaces a centrally planned economy because decentralisation offers an uncatchable information and knowledge advantage, according to Hayek. A central planner could hardly ever access and process highly dispersed information with the same precision as this information is generated and processed in countless decentralised market transactions.[47] The same idea of decentralisation can be transferred to the case of fiscal planning for sovereign/public units. Charles Blankart, for instance, applies Hayek's idea of the market as a discovery procedure to federalism:[48] decentralisation allows the local government to access and process the information about the local preferences more accurately as if the

---

47 FRIEDRICH AUGUST VON HAYEK, 'The Use of Knowledge in Society (1945) 35 (4) American Economic Review 519.

48 BLANKART (2017) 420–421 in reference to FRIEDRICH AUGUST VON HAYEK, 'Competition as Discovery Procedure' (2002, first 1969) 5 (3) The Quarterly Journal of Austrian Economics 9.

central government had to perform this job for multiple local units, i.e., had to collect and evaluate an excessive amount of complex information. More importantly, the information about the local citizens' distinct preferences would not even be generated if local units were not established to provide a tailor-made/attractive offer for (prospective) residents, i.e., if the local governments were not encouraged to search for and gather information about their (potential) residents' preferences, which are eventually expressed in the residents' choice to vote and/or exit. The competition for mobile taxpayers' and residents' support itself produces the information necessary for a 'best fit'-solution. Most famously, Tiebout formulated a model according to which individuals would choose their local unit so as to match their preferences for a package of public goods and services with their individual willingness/ability to pay the price in taxes and fees.[49] The optimal result from such a Tiebout-like competition would not only be a specialisation of the public service offer ('race to the best fit'), but also a race to the top, since every local units' government would not only compete with the quality of their product but also with the (tax) price.[50] Similarly, according to Wallace Oates' Decentralisation Theorem, decentralisation should generally yield a surplus in an optimal allocation of resources and thus be institutionally superior to centralisation; absent externalities in decentralisation and absent returns to scale in centralisation.[51]

The very same reason which is said to pave the way to heaven is also referred to as the route to hell: fiscal competition. The concern is that local units would compete mostly over the price instead of the speciality and quality of the public service offer, leading to an underinvestment in public goods. In particular where citizens' preferences for public goods are rather homogenous across local units, competition may lead to a 'race to the bot-

---

49 CHARLES TIEBOUT, 'A Pure Theory of Local Expenditures' (1956) 64 (5) Journal of Political Economy 416 discussed in BLANKART (2017) 438–443.

50 In this line, WALLACE OATES and ROBERT SCHWAB, 'Economic Competition Among Jurisdictions: Efficiency Enhancing or Distortion Inducing?' (1988) 35 (3) Journal of Public Economics 333 find homogeneity within (!) a local unit leads to a social optimal choice while heterogeneity within a local unit increases the probability of a socially suboptimal compromise when environmental standards have to be agreed upon.

51 WALLACE OATES, *Fiscal Federalism* (Harcourt, Brace, Jovanovich 1972) discussed by BLANKART (2017) 422. See the subsequent chapter for a discussion of returns to scale in centralisation.

tom' in taxation.[52] It is certainly true that the more homogenous the citizens' preferences are, the more similar the public service offer should be, so that comparability facilitates price competition. Nonetheless, the price and the quality should not race 'to the bottom'. Instead, the public good (of whatever quality the taxpayers/voters ask for) should be offered at the equilibrium price. Local residents can be expected to demand the right balance between quality and price, not the lowest price for whatever the quality may be. In some areas of public spending, a local unit's supply of public goods should be in competition with only the supply of public goods in other local units, while the local unit would be exposed to a rather tense competition were public goods could be easily substituted with private goods. A 'race to the bottom' is not feasible per se. What is widely perceived as the 'race to the bottom' may rather be that net contributors to a redistributive funding of public good have an incentive to move to another local unit when their net contribution exceeds their switching costs. Local units are, therefore, under pressure in fiscal competition to scale back on the re-distributional funding of public goods, which can certainly become a problem from a social point of view.

There is another widely recognised and studied risk in decentralisation, which may actually lead to a 'race to the bottom'. Many public goods are funded locally while their benefits spill over to other local units. The exhibit A for this case is the locally and publically funded university. While high quality university education benefits the entire economy, the costs are borne by the local taxpayers. The funding arrangement can incentivize the citizens of any local unit to opt for a reduction in expenditures for university education in the expectation to free ride on the expenses of other local units. The problem is underinvestment as a consequence of benefit spillovers.[53]

---

52 On this discussion see: JAN BRUECKNER, 'Fiscal Decentralisation with Distortionary Taxation: Tiebout vs. Tax Competition' (2004) 11 International Tax and Public Finance 133; GEORGE ZODROW and PETER MIESZKOWSKI, 'Pigou, Tiebout, Property Taxation, and the Underprovision of Public Goods' (1986) 19 Journal of Urban Economics 356.

53 For the German perspective on this problem see: BLANKART (2017) 432. Possible solutions to the underinvestment problem of universities include discriminatory access/funding, vertical or horizontal funding arrangements. For a more detailed discussion of this problem see: JOHN BOUND, JEFFREY GROEN, GABOR KEZDI, and SARAH TURNER, 'Trade in university training: cross-state variation in the production and stick of college-educated labor' (2009) 112 Journal of Econometrics 143; MICHAEL RIZZO and RONALD EHRENBERG, 'Resident and Nonresident Tuition and Enrollment at Flagship State Universities' in

A mirror-image risk of decentralisation to the underinvestment problem, or more precisely, a risk of a decentralised spending authority are overinvestment and oversupply. Local investments are first and foremost enjoyed by local residents. The costs, however, may be shared with other local entities and the central government. If this is the case, cross-subsidised expenditures become relatively cheap for the local residents, so that they order more than they would order and enjoy if they had to pay the bill themselves.[54] Problematically, it is not even guaranteed that the quality of the public product increases with more spending, since the local government's incentive to invest effort into governance reform in order to offer a high quality product at low costs decreases. A 'race to the bottom' in fiscal performance and in the ratio between quality and price will be a likely outcome if such negative externalities (spillover of costs) are not avoided by proper institutional design.[55]

2.2 Centralisation: Returns to Scale

While decentralisation has its advantages, history can tell many stories of nation-building and expansion. A plausible explanation for centralisation and expansion is offered by economies of scale. The citizens can share the benefits from cost-savings in centralisation/expansion when production costs for a public good per unit decrease with an increase of the total amount of units produced. Defense and foreign relations provide such examples where expansion and centralisation promise economies of scale. The cost-savings from an increase in production units, however, are not endless. At some point, an increase in the production of public goods can turn into an increase of production costs, often because the complexity of centralisation and expansion requires on additional investment into coordination and control (diseconomies of scale).

One may argue that economies of scale do not necessarily require a centralised regime if the decentralised units could contract to place an order

---

Caroline Hoxby (ed) *College Choices: The Economics of Where to Go, When to Go, and How to Pay For It* (University of Chicago Press 2004) 303; JAMES STRATHMAN, 'Migration, Benefit Spillover and State Support of Higher Education' (1994) 31 (6) Urban Studies 913.

54 See therefore the discussion in sections II. 3.4 and 3.5.

55 Institutions which should prevent such a 'race to the bottom' will be discussed in III. 3.3 and 3.4.

for public goods together. Possibly, one local unit assumes the responsibility to provide neighbouring units with a good for which they will share the costs, or several local units commission a third (private) party with this task. A problem with such arrangements will arise if one party has to make an upfront investment, e.g., for new machinery, for the training of specialised employees, or for the reorganisation of its administration. These costs are sunk, so that they will not be accounted for in future re-negotiations. Any self-commitment to deny service/supply in case that the initial investment will not be honoured ex post is not credible. Since the investor should be able to anticipate the hold-up strategy of other parties, the investment will not be made in the first place.

In order to encourage the investment, a binding and enforceable ex-ante agreement has to be reached in which the other parties commit to request a fixed/minimum amount of the respective product at a fixed/minimum price. Long-term contracts to regulate future events, however, are often incomplete. If the price/amount is fixed so as to account for the initial investment, the investor can still gain from a decline in quality; at least, the investor has no incentive to continuously innovate and improve the product. Certainly, more sophisticated contracts may implement a dynamic incentive scheme. If the quality of a product is easily observed, enforceable rules can guarantee a qualified standard. If, however, monitoring involves (prohibitively) high transaction costs, hold-up costs are likely to exceed the gains from shared production.[56]

A result from the sunk cost and hold-up conflict, especially in case of high costs for monitoring, is a pull towards the centralisation of functions with significant gains from an increase in scale. From a fiscal perspective, the question remains at which point the centralisation development stops. Studies of secessions suggests that stark differences in income between regions facilitate the drift towards separation, i.e., when the share of the gains from centralisation/unification received by the net contributors are

56 BLANKART (2017) 419–430. Charles Blankart discusses the here presented question of the optimal size of local government (at 419–430), of economies and diseconomies of scale (at 423), and in particular of the challenges and solutions to the case of contracting about public services; the latter point (at 425–428) in reference to GORDON TULLOCK, 'Federalism of Scale' (1969) 6 Public Choice 19. The 'sunk cost'- and 'hold up'-problem in (contract) negotiations has been profoundly analysed for private business activities by Oliver Williamson. See therefore: OLIVER WILLIAMSON, *The Economic Institutions of Capitalism* (The Free Press 1985), see especially 85–130.

not enough to compensate them for their transfer payments.[57] The recent developments in the European Union can be analysed from this perspective. While the union for peace and free trade enjoyed a high popularity Europe-wide, the trend towards a transfer union has harmed the European Union's popularity significantly; leading to the first successful vote for secession by the citizens of the United Kingdom, i.e., by the citizens of the second largest EU economy and by an important net contributor to the EU budget.[58]

2.3 Hercules and Hydra: The Political Architecture

The design of the political architecture affects the decision-making process about spending, taxation, and debt acquisition, i.e., about the allocation of resources, as already discussed in section II. 3. Under the assumption that political agents act opportunistically and possess superior information, the question of centralisation versus decentralisation has a Janus-face, which has been subject to quite extensive discussion and analysis. The question is as to whether and under which conditions, political agents will perform the Herculean task to realise the preferences of taxpayers and voters while they do not surrender to the temptation of excessive taxation, indebtness, and spending. According to Buchanan and Brennan, free trade and migration will 'keep Leviathan in check' if the power (and responsibility) to tax is decentralised.[59] While increased competition and comparability with neighbouring local units can, certainly, resolve an information problem and while it can hold politicians accountable, [60] a new menace becomes visible: if decentralisation is incomplete, i.e., if cost-shifting is a realistic option, the interaction of multiple local governments with autonomous

57 PATRICK BOLTON and GERARD ROLAND, 'The Breakup of Nations: A Political Economy Analysis' (1997) 112 (4) The Quarterly Journal of Economics 1057. Bolton and Roland add that perfect mobility would avoid separation since it should lead to homogenous income and tax rates. In JAMES BUCHANAN and ROGER FAITH, 'Secession and the Limits of Taxation: Towards a Theory of Internal Exit' (1987) 77 (5) The American Economic Review 1023, the authors find that a political and economic community may be best viewed as being ruled by a 'sharing coalition'. The goal of the 'sharing coalition' is to integrate/absorb the rich, a development from which the poor within the community will benefit. Nonetheless, the entry of the poor outside the community will be objected.

58 See chapter V.

59 BRENNAN and BUCHANAN (1980) Chapter 9 (at 166–183).

60 See therefore the discussion in II. 3.3 and III. 2.1.

spending authority and recourse to common pool financing can turn the fiscal organization into the many-headed beast of Hydra.

First, decentralisation certainly allows the regional electorate to closely monitor their political agents' performance, i.e., to reward and punish them for budget decisions, and thus to increase accountability and fiscal performance.[61] A good example for how the revenue-hungry Leviathan can be contained in its striving for more and more tax income and debt is the case of yardstick-competition.[62] Timothy Besley and Anne Case, for instance, found that voters compare the spending and taxation performance of their local government with that of neighbouring units. They demonstrated that politicians have an incentive to please their electorate in a 'race to the top' for a favourable ratio of public product and price.[63] Competition requires comparability and if politicians seek to gain their voters' support in order to stay in office, decentralisation has a positive impact on fiscal performance.[64]

If, however, the regional voters have no interest in an overall diligent budget policy because they themselves have an interest in excessive expenditures for a common pool-financed public good, a new problem will emerge. Since local politicians can be expected to act as special interest representatives of their local support base, decentralisation entails the risk of misallocation and overspending. Politicians can boost their reputation and their chances to be re-elected when they secure funds for their 'pork barrel.' In 'pork barrel' politics, regional politicians lobby for direct transfers or the support for projects of which the benefits remain local while the costs can be externalised across the multi-tier union. In such a constel-

---

61 See section II. 3.1 for asymmetric distribution of information and III. 2.1 for the application of this analysis for decentralisation in case of the best fit model for public goods.

62 ANDREI SHLEIFER, 'A theory of yardstick competition' (1985) 16 (3) Rand Journal of Economics 319.

63 TIMOTHY BESLEY and ANNE CASE, 'Incumbent Behaviour: Vote-Seeking, Tax-Setting, and Yardstick Competition' (1995) 85 (1) The American Economic Review 25.

64 In this line, Bordignon et al. concluded from a study of Italian cities, that effects of yardstick competition were measurable when mayors in neighbouring units would have to face re-election threats while a stable and strong majority or no chance for re-election (e.g. because of a time limit in office) would, logically, reduce the impact of yardstick competition. See therefore: MASSIMO BORDIGNON, FLORINA CEMIGLIA, and FEDERICO REVELLI, 'In Search for Yardstick Competition: Property Tax Rates and Electoral Behaviour in Italian Cities' (2002) CESifo Working Paper No. 644.

lation, the risk does not only come from opportunistic politicians, but from a complicity of regional voters and their political agents as special interest representatives. But who is to blame? Politicians and voters alike are trapped in a dilemma. Whoever stops to overfish the common pool may leave with an empty fish bucket while the costs of other local units' excessive spending will still be shared.[65]

Empirical research was undertaken to test the effects of decentralisation on the size of government, its funding, and the allocation of resources. Especially, research was conducted to test the Leviathan hypothesis. In a quite early study, Wallace Oates could not find any proof for Buchanan and Brennan's claim that decentralisation would keep Leviathan under control[66] while Jeffrey Zax, a few years later, found the Leviathan hypothesis confirmed when he showed that areas of larger counties, i.e., of relatively less decentralisation and competition, would correlate with a disproportionally large size of government.[67] Jonathan Rodden, later on, concluded from his empirical studies that there was no correlation between the size of government and decentralisation per se, but that local governments would be of a relatively small size if they had to be funded from local tax sources whereas they would grow larger, the higher the portion of funding for their local expenditures from transfers was.[68]

In a federation, cooperation on the federal level may actually increase the overspending problems when favours/transfers are being traded and shifted towards the regional units, so that the common pool is at a high risk to be overfished.[69] If, in this process and in case of a region-based voting system combined with a system of horizontal/vertical transfers, certain members are given a disproportionally large voting power, the assumption should hold that a disproportionally large voting power correlates positive-

65 THOMAS LANCASTER, 'Electoral Structures and Pork Barrel Politics' (1986) 7 (1) International Political Science Review 67.

66 WALLACE OATES, 'Searching for Leviathan: An Empirical Study' (1985) 75 (4) The American Economic Review 748. Further discussion: WALLACE OATES, 'Searching for Leviathan: A Reply and Some Further Reflections' (1989) 79 (3) The American Economic Review 578.

67 JEFFREY ZAX, 'Is there a Leviathan in Your Neighbourhood?' (1989) 79 (3) The American Economic Review 560.

68 RODDEN (2003).

69 BARRY WEINGAST, KENNETH SHEPSLE, and CHRISTOPHER JOHNSON, 'The Political Economy of Benefits and Costs: A Neoclassical Approach to Distributive Politics' (1981) 89 (4) The Journal of Political Economy 642; JÜRGEN VON HAGEN, 'Fiscal Rules, Fiscal Institutions, and Fiscal Performance' (2002) 33 (3) The Economic and Social Review 263.

ly with a disproportionally large share of the common pool.[70] In contrast, if a hostile party or a minimal-winning coalition with unevenly distributed regional links wins the federal government, funds are likely to be shifted towards the 'winning regions'. Since it is uncertain who is going to win the election, budget uncertainty cumulates with the misallocation problem in a competitive environment.[71]

A corollary from the previous considerations is that there is no clear answer to be found as to whether centralisation or decentralisation enhances fiscal performance. While decentralisation has the potential to improve on information, it can create perverse incentives where decentralised budgets cumulate with inter-regional cost-sharing in direct/indirect transfers and bailouts. Similarly, the incentive to collect and process information at the regional source so as to hold politicians accountable for their performance only arises where the effects of regionally linked decisions are internalised. The conflict between Hercules and Hydra cannot be resolved just with a decision for centralisation or decentralisation. Again, it is obvious that institutional design matters, which points to the discussion of institutional congruence.

2.4 Economic Performance in the Shadow of Federalism

While the previous three sections were primarily concerned with the question of the governments' fiscal performance as affected by the degree of centralisation versus decentralisation, this section will draw a line from the analysis undertaken to the governments' performance as the provider of a framework for private markets to thrive. A minimum consensus about the state's role, but also about the state's highest duty is certainly the protection of life, liberty, and property against (unlawful) violation.[72] In order for a market economy to prosper, the state, essentially, must be able to guarantee property rights; by law and by law enforcement. Underdeveloped and emerging countries often struggle to attract foreign investments

70 See the empirical study of the European Union voting system by JONATHAN RODDEN, 'Strengths in Numbers? Representation and Redistribution in the European Union' (2002a) 3 (2) European Union Politics 151.

71 TIMOTHY BESLEY and STEPHAN COATE, 'Centralized versus decentralized provision of local public goods: a political economy approach' (2003) 87 Journal of Public Economics 2611.

72 A failed state is a state unable to protect its citizens against outside and inside threats to their core rights of life, liberty, and property.

because they cannot credibly secure the investor's property and the fruits from the very same.[73] The question, therefore, is: how does centralisation versus decentralisation influence the state's economic performance? Barry Weingast, Yingyi Qian, and Gabriella Montinola have, most prominently, discussed this question in context of centralisation versus decentralisation, and formulated the hypothesis of market-preserving federalism.

The underlying idea of market-preserving federalism is that the strength of the government can be a fertile soil as well as a plague for markets. A state strong enough to protect property would be a state strong enough to seize property. Decentralisation, however, should offer an institutional solution to contain the government's destructive powers, since the local units have to compete for the market players' approval. If a local government took excessive action (e.g. for re-distributional purposes), the market players would exit to another local unit. Weingast, Qian, and Montinola present three case studies of eighteenth century England, nineteenth century USA, and contemporary China so as to illustrate how political and economic factors work together in limiting the central government's grasp and in strengthening the local governments' control over economic and financial affairs.[74]

The theory of market-preserving federalism is intentionally appealing. Certainly, competition amongst local units has an impact on the local government's financial and economic policy.[75] However, as Jonathan Rodden and Susan Rose-Ackerman have pointed out, competition alone cannot provide a global explanation for why a decentralised model has the potential to outpace a centralised model: Politicians are first and foremost moved by their reputation amongst the electorate. Exit threats play a role insofar as a declining economy has a negative impact on the politicians' chance to be re-elected. Nonetheless, history knows many examples of po-

---

73 On the problem of the weak/unpredictable enforcement of formal laws in transition economies see CHRISTIAN KIRCHNER and DAVID EHMKE, 'Staat und Recht' in Rainer Kollmorgen, Wolfgang Merkel, and Hans-Jürgen Wagener (eds) *Handbuch für Transformationsforschung* (Springer VS 2015) 455.

74 For the theory of market-preserving federalism see BARRY WEINGAST, 'The Economic Role of Political Institutions: Market-Preserving Federalism and Economic Development' (1995) 11 (1) The Journal of Law, Economics, & Organizations 1; YINGYI QIAN and BARRY WEINGAST, 'China's Transition to Markets: Market-Preserving Federalism, Chinese Style' (1996) 1 Journal of Policy Reform 149; GABRIELLA MONTINOLA, YINGYI QIAN and BARRY WEINGAST, 'Federalism, Chinese Style: The Political Basis for Economic Success' (1996) 1 World Politics 50.

75 For this discussion see section III. 2.1.

liticians who won elections with protectionist and anti-capitalist campaigns. If corruption is a problem, decentralisation can worsen the case, when the central government has no means to end corruption by an effective top-down rule. Investors would have to deal with political and bureaucratic rent-seeking on multiple levels. While competition on local levels can enhance the framework for market activity, it can also be exploited for cost-shifting, i.e., when a local unit internalises the benefits of an industry but externalises the costs. An example are environmental damages which are a consequence of local production but itself not contained to local borders.[76]

If, in this context, common pool financing is an option for the decentralised governments, and if the state is understood as a proactive designer of the framework within which economic activity takes place, decentralisation itself will carry a risk. This is precisely because the decentralised governments' option to fish in the common pool fundamentally decreases the governments' incentives to invest into governance reform. The beneficial effects of competition will only show under the condition that the governments' incentives to distinguish themselves in competition are upheld, i.e., under the condition that the benefits of reform are internalised.[77]

Eventually, the assumption underlying the theory of market-preserving federalism, that a central state strong enough to protect property is also strong enough to confiscate/(over-)tax property, is not inevitable. If one assumes that the citizens prefer a free market society over a planned economy, the protection of property rights constitutes the enforcement of a common belief against a few violators while the state's systematic violations of the citizens' private property is the enforcement of an authoritarian rule against the majority of the society. The latter case, thus, involves considerably higher enforcement costs. History shows that while capitalist and free market societies can survive with a relatively small government, socialist regimes have to invest heavily in the strength of the government so as to enforce the state's systematic violations of private property, until they eventually collapse. Hence, it requires a much 'stronger' state to systematically seize private property than to protect property.

---

76 JONATHAN RODDEN and SUSAN ROSE-ACKERMAN, 'Does Federalism Preserve Markets?' (1997) 83 (7) Virginia Law Review 1521, especially 1536–1546 (for the question of public choice and corruption) and 1555–1559 (for the question of externalities).

77 See the discussion of low interest rates for Greece and Puerto Rico and the temptation to delay governance reform if deficit-financing is cheaply available in sections II. 2.3 and IV. 2.5.2.

Some degree of centralisation, on the other hand, has certainly a beneficial effect on the development of private markets. Free trade and unified regulations (to reduce transaction costs) can be a boost for economic activity. The European Union as a free trade union is a good example thereof. A trade-off, however, remains. While centralisation should decrease transaction costs, it limits the opportunities from a competitive learning process in the decentralised model.

Again, it is pointless to call for centralisation or decentralisation as the single path to economic or financial success. The influence of the government on economic performance depends on the institutional design and the diversification and distribution of responsibilities in a multi-tier union. Decentralisation, if institutionally congruent, i.e, in case that benefits/costs are almost fully internalised, creates an incentive to race for a best fit solution in a learning process. Overregulation, the seizure of property, and excessive taxation are confined by competition and exit threats. Nonetheless, the centralisation of certain responsibilities, such as for free trade, standards, etc., as well as a uniform minimal framework of rules which regulate economic activity can create benefits for all market players.

3. *Institutional Congruence in Multi-Tier Playing Fields*

3.1 The Principle

Imagine yourself in a restaurant:

1. Constellation: You order the meal and the drinks you like, within the limits of your individual budget. Eventually you pay the cheque. Quite likely, you will have had an enjoyable dinner. Put differently, you will have chosen the best possible price/product-combination within your financial means. Costs and benefits of your choice are internalised!

On a different evening, the waiter approaches you and explains you the rather special rules of the restaurant:

2. Constellation: You order and enjoy whatever you like, the same as everyone else in the restaurant. At the end of the night, the costs for drinks and dinner will be split evenly amongst all guests. The restaurant is packed. You overhear the next table discussing their choice from the restaurant's vintage wine list. How will you proceed? Probably, it will not be your cheapest night out. The budget constraint is gone. You know that if you save, the impact on the final cheque you have to pay will be insignificant for yourself. So, why should you subsidise the feast for other guests while you make a second-best product choice. Most guest will order whatever they like without that they spare any thought on the price. Quite a few will order vintage wine instead of beer, even though they actually prefer beer, because they feel a displeasure if they believe that they did not receive their 'fair share' from the common pool funded order. The problem is clearly overspending.[78] The benefits of your choice are internalised, the costs are externalised (partly).

3. Constellation: Everyone will place an order, but the orders are mixed up randomly. You have to pay for whatever order is eventually presented to you (not for what you have ordered yourself). Let's assume everyone puts a decent amount of effort into their selection. There is a chance that you are pleasantly surprised with the dinner selection. You get to try something new. There is, however, a good chance that you are not happy with your dinner. You might even be upset. In the worst case, the vegetarian is presented with a steak and the reformed alcoholic with a splendid wine selection. You might get drinks and dinner served well above your budget (overspending problem), or someone has chosen the low-budget option for you while you were prepared to spend a lot for a really special evening (underinvestment problem). The main problem is misallocation.

4. Constellation: The same as in 3, except that the costs for all randomly assigned orders will be borne by the one who orders (*Constellation 4A.*) or that they are split evenly amongst all guests (*Constellation 4B.*). You hope to be allocated a good choice, the same as you may put some decent effort into your selection for someone else. However, you may not choose the most expensive product, since you will have to pay for your choice which benefits someone else (*Constellation 4A.*) or since you will have to share in the costs of an expensive order (*Constellation 4B.*). At the same time, the chance that you get to drink the most exquisite wine yourself because of an randomly assigned order is pretty low. The problem is misallocation. For example, many guests would have preferred to spend more for their own menu than to get served the 'low-budget version', but they might have placed themselves a 'low-budget' order because they expected that other guests would free ride on their generosity otherwise. There exists an under-

---

78 For some guests who care about the externalities of their choice and who would have been prepared to enjoy an exquisite and expensive dinner but now feel the need to restrict themselves, the problem might be underinvestment. For most guests, however, the problem should be overspending. See URI GNEEZY, ERNAN HARUVY, and HADAS YAFE, 'The Inefficiency of Splitting the Bill' (2004) 114 The Economic Journal 265–280.

investment problem. The benefits of your choice are externalised, the costs are (partly) internalised.

5. Constellation: This time, you have to agree on a combination of drinks and dinner. So, everyone will enjoy the same choice. The cheque will be split evenly amongst all guests. First, you will spend some time discussing the choice. Take this as coordination cost investment. Second, you will make a compromise. The final choice should allow all guests to realise their preferences to some extent; it will, nonetheless, be not their first best choice within the average budget constraint. The product mix is likely not the best possible choice for everyone (suboptimal choice problem) while the price should be within the range of the dinner guests' average spending power.[79] Since there is a uniform order, the restaurant grants a discount (economies of scale). Costs and benefits are internalised.

Transfer: The case of multi-tier unions of sovereign and public entities is not that different from our dinner constellations. The fundamental problem, which causes misallocation, underinvestment, and overspending, is always institutional incongruence, i.e., a disparity between the circles of decision-makers, beneficiaries, and payers.[80]

The transfer works quite smoothly:

Take the *1. Constellation*. Every guests orders, enjoys, and pays separately and individually. Similarly, in the autonomy model, every public/sovereign unit orders and enjoys the public good which will satisfy its taxpayers' preferences to the highest possible degree. The choice is limited by their budget constraint (best possible price-product-mix). Benefits and costs are fully internalised so that this model is correctly described as institutionally congruent.

The *2. Constellation*, in which everyone orders and enjoys without individual budget constraint on the costs of the common pool, reminds us of the mixed model with decentralised budgets and a transfer and/or bailout regime.

The *3. Constellation*, in which a third party decides about what someone else has to enjoy and pay for, is the mirror-image of any case where the subordinate entity is required to perform costly tasks assigned to it by a superi-

79 As a modification, we may assume that the rule is relaxed insofar as we allow for some flexibility (e.g., there is a meat/fish/vegetarian option) while the cheque is still split evenly. This will mitigate but not erase the misallocation problem.

80 See the references in footnote 1. For a graphical display of the principle of institutional congruence versus incongruence see BLANKART (2017) 431 and 433. See also Fig. 2 as a graphical differentiation of this principle in the here discussed constellations (1. to 5.).

or unit without that the superior unit assumes the funding responsibility. The misallocation reduces the quality of the public good in relation to the price. It may cause overspending or underinvestment.

In the *4A. Constellation*, the decision-maker has to pay while a random third party enjoys the benefits. Remember the example of the locally-funded public university in section III. 2.1. In the *4B. Constellation*, the decision-maker has to share-in the costs while a random third party enjoys the benefits. This example explains why residents of a local unit with the preferences and means to spend a lot for a high-quality local public good may be dissatisfied when decision-making and funding are centralised.[81]

The *5. Constellation*, eventually, is institutionally congruent, the same as the *1. Constellation*. The group of dinner guests decides collectively about the dinner selection and splits the bill. The selection should be within the average budget constraint. Coordination costs arise while economies of scale can be realised. The choice is not optimal, since everyone has to agree to a more or less flexible compromise. The choice is limited. It is, however, likely to be a better choice than in the *3.* and *4. Constellation*.

Limitation: There is one important limitation to the idea of institutional congruence in any multi-tier union of sovereign or public entities. Perfect institutional congruence is not a realistic assumption. Even in case of a local unit with a relatively small and homogenous population in the autonomy model, institutional congruence is not necessarily perfect. The circles of beneficiaries and payers for the local good often do not match perfectly: Unless each resident is taxed lump-sum, the individual taxpayers' contributions vary. Similarly, some residents will benefit over-proportionally, depending on the public good in question. Finally, and most significantly, the circle of decision-makers tends to be much smaller in practice than the circles of beneficiaries and payers unless all decisions are taken in direct democracy, which is quite unlikely.

In case of a representative democracy, a simple majority of voters delegates the decision-making power to a few political agents; i.e., they do not make specific spending decisions, but they appoint agents instead to decide about what public goods to order so that the principals may enjoy these goods and pay the cheque. Institutional congruence, however, remains a valuable principle and the models of autonomy and integration

81 One may argue that no one limits the local unit's residents to fund a regional publicly accessible good with private donations. However, differently from a local tax autonomy, such private funding campaigns are more likely to fail because of a free riding incentive.

provide an important orientation how to approach institutional congruence. The same as democracy is the closest possibly approximation to the principle of liberty, i.e., the smallest possible degree of coercion,[82] the fiscal models of autonomy and integration are the closest possibly approximation to the principle of institutional congruence. Naturally, the decision-making process involves some degree of delegation.[83]

---

82 HANS KELSEN, *Vom Wesen und Wert der Demokratie* (J.C.B. Mohr 1920) 9 describing the absolute majority principle as the closest possible approximation to liberty.

83 The situation is quite similar in context of a private firm. The decision-making power is delegated to the management while the shareholders are the main beneficiaries and payers. There are conflicts of interest, but an institutionally congruent system has proven to work better than an institutionally congruent system of 'soft budget constraints'. On soft budget constraints in a centrally-planned economy as opposed to a capitalist firm see: JANOS KORNAI (1979).

(Fig. 2) Institutional Congruence–Different Fiscal Models

Explanation:	Decision-makers	Beneficiaries	Payers
		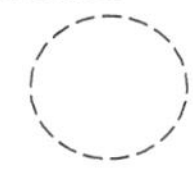	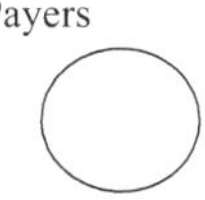

1. Constellation	Short-form analysis: ***Autonomy Model***
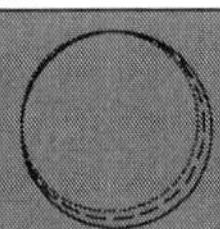	**(+) first best price-product choice**
2. Constellation	Short-form analysis: ***Mixed Model***
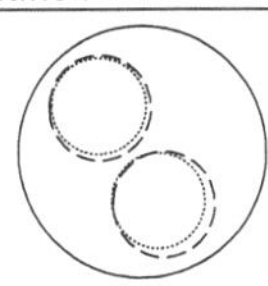	**(+) first best product choice** (in most cases) **(–) overspending problem overall**
3. Constellation	Short-form analysis: ***Mixed Model***
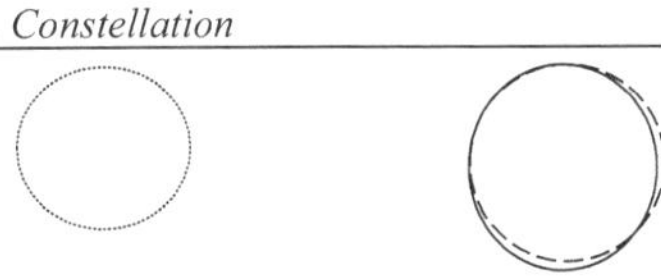	**(–) misallocation problem** (overspending/underinvestment possible, as a consequence of misallocation)
4A. Constellation	Short-form analysis: ***Mixed Model***
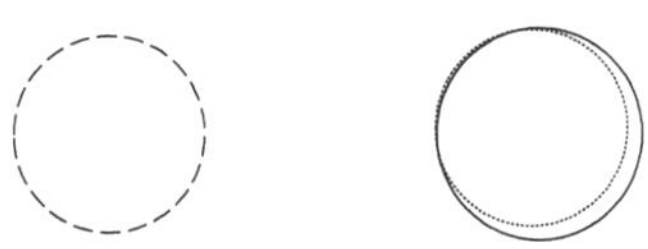	**(–) misallocation problem** **(–) underinvestment**
4B. Constellation	Short-form analysis: ***Mixed Model***
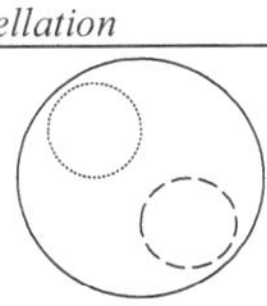	**(–) misallocation problem** **(–) underinvestment**
5. Constellation	Short-form analysis: ***Integration Model***
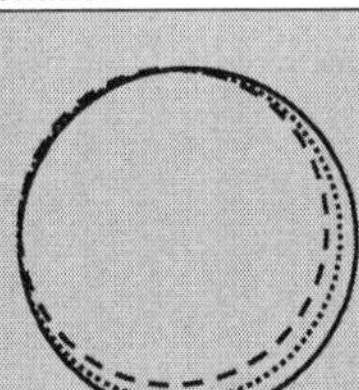	**(+) economies of scale** **(–) coordination costs** **(–) suboptimal choice=compromise** (The compromise should have a less negative impact than the misallocation problem, since making a compromise still involves the transmission of information and the participation in the decision-making process.)

The Principle: The degree of institutional congruence increases with the overlap of the circles of decision-makers, beneficiaries, and payers. A higher degree of institutional congruence correlates with the quality of the public good (measured as cost-benefit ratio) and a superior financial performance. A lower degree of institutional congruence correlates with an increased risk of misallocation/suboptimal choice, underinvestment, and/or overspending. A trade-off is apparent: The larger a (uniform) order is, the higher are the savings from economies of scale. However, the larger the circles of decision-makers, beneficiaries, and payers grow, the higher are the transaction costs for information gathering, communication, and negotiation, and the more likely it becomes that the product order diverts from the first best choice and develops to a suboptimal choice.

3.2 Market Control v Central Government Control

There are basically two ways to keep spending, taxation, and debt acquisition in balance; two ways, sustainable in the long-run, to increase a sovereign or public unit's fiscal performance: central government control and market control. Each debtor or each union of debtors, ultimately, has to face the market control mechanism. The question is: Will the market control the entire multi-tier union as one or every level and unit by itself? In a multi-tier union of multiple sovereign or public units, the members or the centre will have to make a fundamental decision if they want to create an efficient, i.e., institutionally congruent, financial regime: if they opt for the integration model, they will have to implement the institutions of central government control for an effective chain of commands top-down; if they opt for the autonomy model, they will have to establish the institutions that allow for effective market control.[84]

The creditors should be indifferent regarding the debtor's choice between the integration or the autonomy model, because they can simply adjust their monitoring activity and price expectations. The choice between integration and autonomy, however, has a significant influence on the (union of) debtors: It is a choice between independent decision-making and self-responsibility (autonomy) or the debtors' submission to central

84 Of course, the government can avoid this choice and factually design a mixed fiscal models; the consequences might be disastrous. Misallocation, underinvestment, and overspending are the likely outcomes–depending on the type of institutional incongruence.

government control and equalisation amongst the debtors via common pool financing as a consequence of the mutual debt insurance (integration).[85]

Market Control: In a nutshell, a sovereign/public debt contract is the debtor's promise to repay a specified amount upon maturity and a coupon in pre-defined intervals. The difference between the creditors' consideration (cash now) and the sum of accrued principal and interests promised by the debtor, consists of (i) the risk-free interest rate (capital opportunity costs) and (ii) the sovereign/public debtor's distinct risk premium. The debtor's distinct risk premium performs a pivotal role in market control. In a world, where all interest rates were equal, debt capital investors would offer their investment only to financially rock-solid borrowers. Borrowers with a less sustainable financial performance would be excluded from the debt markets; many public projects could not be realised. The moment when creditors distinguish by risk and demand a higher return on their investment from borrowers with a less than perfect financial performance is the moment of opportunity. No borrower is excluded from the markets per se, but the entry price varies. If a borrower is willing to pay the appropriate risk premium, i.e., a surcharge for its comparatively high risk of default, the deal is made.

If a borrower considers the risk premium to be too high, the borrower has an incentive to lower the risk, i.e., to improve its financial and economic performance so as to benefit from lower capital costs in the future.

85 In another scenario, the debtors may also opt for both, the autonomy and the integration model at the same time, and institute a model of choice. In such a model, different rules would apply to different members of the multi-tier union: While some members would be integrated, i.e., receive transfers and a debt insurance/bailout guarantee, for which they had to give up their autonomy and subject themselves to the central government's rule in exchange ("dependent members"), other member would be autonomous in their spending, taxation, and debt acquisition decisions without that they could resort to transfers or, ultimately, a bailout ("independent members"). The model of choice should not be confused with a mixed model which is the commingling of different elements of integration and autonomy within just one fiscal regime. In contrast, the model of choice is defined by the parallel existence of two institutionally congruent closed fiscal regimes within one multi-tier union. In a model of choice, central government control works for the dependent members while market control works for the independent members. Since the Model of Choice is, in essence, the co-existence of the two complete fiscal models autonomy and integration, it will not be discussed separately in this chapter. See therefore: CHARLES BLANKART and ERIK FASTEN, 'Schuldengrenzen im Föderalismus: Ein Optionsmodell für Vielfalt in Einheit' (2017, 3 March) 53 Frankfurter Allgemeine Zeitung.

The interest rate, and in particular the interest rate development, mirrors the market's prediction about how the borrower will perform in the future; not about how the borrower did perform in the past, even though past performance may form part of the analysis for future performance. The creditors, whose money is at stake, have an own and strong incentive to price the credit offer with at least the appropriate risk rate.[86] The borrower has to signal a diligent budgetary policy so as to convince its (potential) creditors from a lower than the present risk rate.

If creditors are accurate and ruthless monitors, their activity will have a positive externality of high value for the sovereign/public debtor's citizens. Market discipline creates an effective control mechanism for financial and political performance. In order to present the sovereign/public entity as reliable borrower, the political agents have to manage their citizens' tax money and the public good efficiently. If the markets demand a higher risk premium, this carries important information for taxpayers and voters about their political agents' performance. Empirical research has confirmed that the credit markets price the distinct risk for sovereign and public borrowers quite accurately,[87] so that the markets exercise control by way of creating an incentive scheme which rewards diligent and punishes weak political performance. In section III. 3.3, the core institutions for market control to function effectively will be introduced.

Central Government Control: If the centre or the members of a multi-tier union decide to be responsible for the debts of the union's members in case of financial distress, the market control mechanism collapses. Certainly, the union viewed as a transfer union will be subject to market control itself. It would, however, be irrational for the markets to monitor the individual parts of the union and to price them differently, since the credit default risk is ultimately not defined by the member's individual risk contri-

---

86 The sovereign/public debtor can be expected to possess superior information about its own finances, i.e., the sovereign/public debtor acts as agent. The principal creditors are aware of the agent's information advantage. Since they will anticipate the agent's opportunism, the chance of the agent to exploit the information advantage backfires on the agent itself, unless the agent can signal credibly enforced institutions which limit opportunistic action. See therefore also section VI. 2.3 and 2.5.

87 TAMIM BAYOUMI, MORRIS GOLDSTEIN, and GEOFFREY WOGLOM, 'Do Capital Markets Discipline Sovereign Borrowers? Evidence from the U.S. States' (1995) 27 (4) Journal of Money, Credit and Banking 1046. The authors examine 38 U.S. states for the time 1981–1990. See also: LISA FAIRCHILD and TIMOTHY KOCH, 'The Impact of State Disclosure Requirements on Municipal Yields' (1998) 51 (4) National Tax Journal 733.

bution but by the accumulated risk of all parts, i.e., by the risk that the multi-tier union defaults and that the union is unable to take responsibility for the debts of its subordinate units. As illustrated in sections III. 2 and especially III. 3.1, common pool financing creates a high risk of overspending (2. *Constellation*). The political agents in charge of a subordinate unit would have a strong incentive to overspend for an exquisite public good while they would have little incentive to tax their local electorate to pay the price. Similarly, the local electorate would have a strong incentive to vote politicians into office whom they believe to secure an as large as possible share from the common pool.[88]

In order to avoid 'a race to the bottom' in financial performance, credibly enforced rules have to be established. All rules implemented come down to the single principle of an effective chain of commands top-down.[89] The ultimate power to decide about spending, taxation, and debt acquisition must remain with the centre. This, however, does not necessarily mean that the subordinate units are without any power, since the decision-making process can be fashioned in a way that every member of the union has a (differently weighted) vote when a distribution key for common pool financed resources has to be agreed upon. Important is only that the members of the multi-tier union are bound to a central command, may this command result from a decision by the central government or by an assembly of all members. It is, moreover, not necessary that every single budget decision has to be approved by the highest central authority, the same as it is not necessary or even practical that the CEO of a firm reviews and approves every single budget decision. The key requirement in the effi-

88 The argument that an increase in transfers boosts a politician's chance for re-election has two sides: While one may criticize the politician for overfishing the common pool, the politician acts in the very interest of the local electorate. The local electorate has an incentive to choose an agent who promises to source as much "fish from the common pool" as possible, no matter the effect on the common pool/the effect on other regions. See the case study comparing Argentina and the USA by MARK JONES and OSVALDO MELONI and MARIANO TOMMASI, 'Voters as Fiscal Liberals: Incentives and Accountability in Federal Systems' (2012) 24 (2) Economics & Politics 135. See also sections II. 3.1, 3.2, 3.5.

89 BLANKART and EHMKE (2016), especially 45–46. An illustrative real life example of such an effective chain of commands top-down is the French case, in particular before the decentralisation reforms. See therefore section IV. 2.2. In RODDEN (2002), the authors takes "Fiscal restraint imposed by central government" (see e.g. Fig. 1 on page 673) as a determinant to evaluate the risk of fiscal imbalance in a federation. Such "fiscal restraints imposed by central government" qualify as part of the here discussed effective chain of commands top-down.

cient design of central government control is simply that the centre has to bear the final budget authority and responsibility, and therefore, must have the power (and enough information to exercise this power) to command each subordinate part of the multi-tier union to act in a certain way.

3.3 Autonomy Model

3.3.1 No Bail-Out Regime

A merchant who grants a penniless bon viveur the right to buy in his shops on credit without limitation might be considered a fool. If, however, you were told that the mother of this young man is known to be the richest woman in the country, you might want to reconsider your opinion about the merchant. First, the mother might have given the merchant a guarantee to clear her son's debts. This is in no way different from an explicit bailout guarantee in a multi-tier union of several debtors. Second, she might have not guaranteed the merchant to repay her son's debt, but the merchant concludes from previous experiences that whenever her son was past due his liabilities, his mother would clear the debt; one motivation would be to protect the family's good name. This is the same as if the markets expect for good reasons that a multi-tier union will stand together in distress. Indicators might be the threat of spillover effects, the absence of a credible no-bailout regime, a history of bailouts, or at least no history of defaults/restructurings. The disciplinary force of market control requires a credible no-bailout regime, reflected in different risk premia for different debtors. Analytical and empirical research supports this conclusion.[90]

A no-bailout regime may be established by explicit rules which prohibit a bailout of any kind. These rules must build a fence without loopholes in order to protect the no bailout principle against rescuers, who fear the short term impact of a crisis spillover, and against the distressed debtor, who tries to shift the burden of distress. Even if a no-bailout rule exists, this does not say that it will hold against any 'unlawful' violation. A rule

---

90 See the empirical research undertaken by RODDEN (2002) and by BAYOUMI, MORRIS, and WOGLOM (1995). See further LANS BOVENBERG, JERON KREMERS, and PAUL MASSON, 'Economic and Monetary Union in Europe and Constraints on National Budgetary Policies' (1991) 38 (2) IMF Staff Papers 374. Bovenberg et al. argue in favour of a no-bailout principle and a conservative central bank policy as pillars for a successful European Monetary Union.

must be armed with an enforcement mechanism. Its execution must be credible.

In order to be credible, first, members of the multi-tier union following the autonomy model have to be independent in their budget and tax decisions, as it will be discussed in more detail in section III. 3.3.2. Second, if they are largely independent in their budget and tax decisions, they might still be interconnected by a bailout regime as the case of institutionally incongruent mixed systems shows. Important, however, is that the no-bailout principle has been and will be executed. Otherwise, it will be a lifeless rule like Artt. 123 (1) and 125 (1) TFEU, which were firmly established in the law books but bluntly ignored in reality.[91]

More important than the enactment of the no-bailout principle is its credible execution over a sufficient period of time, i.e., a no-bailout history. Charles Blankart describes the no-bailout principle as "dynamically developing credence capital good" and provides the following definition: "This means the belief that the policy will be followed grows through its application over time, and debases itself when it is disregarded. Each application of the no-bailout rule strengthens the expectation that it will be applied in the future."[92] Bailouts which may not debase the no-bailout principle are bailouts which form an extraordinary exception and which unburden the debtor from a debt out of the debtor's control such as a bailout following a natural catastrophe. Robert Inman demonstrates how the no-bailout principle evolved by way of application since the 1840s in the US.[93] If the no-bailout principle has been applied in multiple cases of distress, the multi-tier union following the no-bailout principle will have built up a reputation value: Creditors will assume that the multi-tier union will stick to its principles, and therefore, creditors will monitor the individual units, price them differently, and create an incentive scheme to reward the strong

---

91 Artt. 123 (1) and 125 (1) Treaty on the Functioning of the European Union. If, however, the no-bailout principle was never credible in the first place, there is no comparative loss from a violation of the no-bailout principle in the second place; rather a forfeited chance to establish a credible no-bailout principle. For a discussion of the credibility of the EMU no-bailout principle see section V. 3.5.2 and 3.5.3.

92 CHARLES BLANKART, 'What the eurozone could learn from Switzerland' (2015, 18 May) Institute of Economic Affairs.

93 ROBERT INMAN, 'Transfers and Bailouts: Enforcing Local Fiscal Discipline with Lessons from U.S. Federalism' in Jonathan Rodden, Gunnar Eskeland, and Jennie Litvack (eds) *Fiscal Decentralisation and the Challenge of Hard Budget Constraints* (Massachusetts Institute of Technology 2013) 35, especially 56–61.

and to punish the weak performing debtors. If, now, the union decided to make a U-turn and to break with the no-bailout principle, it would confuse the markets and devalue the credence capital good which it has acquired in the past. If creditors adjusted their expectations after a bailout, so that the capital cost of all units plateau around a common pool level, without that the members of the multi-tier union give up their independence and subject themselves to central government control, the costs of institutional incongruence would fall upon the multi-tier union.[94]

3.3.2 Tax and Budget Autonomy

In order to function autonomously, any sovereign or public entity has to have the power to decide about expenditures and about taxation 'on its own.' Budget autonomy requires the sovereign/public entity to make spending decisions independently, i.e., without command or approval of a central government or other members of the union. This, certainly, does not exclude the option that the sovereign/public entity commits itself to contribute to a commonly funded task, or to perform a public service/ provide a public good according to an agreement of the members of the union.[95] Tax autonomy is a key element for institutionally congruent fiscal decentralisation. Thereby, tax autonomy does not mean that the sovereign/ public unit receives/has a right to a tax share, but that the sovereign/public unit has the authority to determine the tax rate independently, i.e., without command or approval from another entity.[96]

The reasons for budget and tax autonomy are quite intuitive. If a sovereign/public unit shall be responsible for its budget, it must be in a position to manage its budget, to raise funds, and to decide about its expenditures (unity of decision-makers and payers). Budget autonomy prevents burden-shifting. Tax autonomy allows the sovereign/public unit to tax its residents for what they did enjoy as a public good. If a sovereign/ public unit had no tax autonomy, the only way to fund an excess above the delegated tax revenue would be the acquisition of more debt. Without sharp saving cuts in the following years, the sovereign/public unit would

94 See therefore sections III. 3.1 and 3.2.

95 The collection of a federal tax, or the contribution towards tasks which are supposed to remain with the centre, i.e., defense, are good examples therefore.

96 RODDEN (2003). See chapter IV. 1, and especially (Switzerland) 2.4 and (USA) 2.5 compared to 2.3 (Germany).

probably fall into the debt trap. The central government or the other members of the multi-tier union, naturally, will be under severe pressure to bailout the distressed debtor. If, however, they can refer the debt transgressor to raise taxes in order to pay for what was enjoyed in the past, a no-bailout regime becomes credible.[97] Eventually, an internally tax-funded debt repayment instead of an external bail-out creates an incentive for taxpayers/voters to correctly value the financial performance of their government, and thus to incentivize the political agents to invest effort into a diligent budget policy.

3.3.3 Self-Imposed Borrowing and Deficit Constraints

A sovereign or public entity may subject itself to a borrowing or deficit constraint, i.e., not to have a higher deficit than X per year or not to accumulate more debt than Y. In the autonomy model, such a deficit constraint may be the result of a plebiscite or of a representative vote. Borrowing and deficit constraints, primarily, perform two functions:

First, borrowing and deficit constraints legally bind a government to adhere to certain budget principles, which are considered to improve financial stability. The higher the requirements for an amendment of the borrowing/deficit rules are, the more credible they are. A simple majority borrowing/deficit constraint which can also be altered with a simple majority, may easily fall victim to short-term political interests. If the borrowing/deficit constraint is embodied in the constitution or made subject to a super-majority requirement for modifications, this will support its survival. Borrowing/deficit constraints enacted by plebiscite, additionally, are strengthened by the voter's explicit support. Even though the parliament might be formally entitled to modify a borrowing/deficit constraint by a vote, the parliament would position itself in direct opposition to the people's will if it neglected the plebiscite. Another question is how a violation of the borrowing/deficit constraint will be punished. One possibility is that there is no legal consequence to a breach. In that case, the principle is name and shame. A directly (and automatically) exercised punishment would be a prohibition to carry over the deficit to the next period so that

97 JÜRGEN VON HAGEN and BARRY EICHENGREEN, 'Federalism, Fiscal Restraints, and European Monetary Union' (1996) 86 (2) The American Economic Review 134; RODDEN (2002); RODDEN and WIBBELS (2002).

the government would have to cut spending or raise taxes, which should cost the government popularity in the next election cycle.[98]

Second, the borrowing/deficit constraint is implemented to send out a signal to the markets. The higher the barriers for its amendment and the harsher the punishment upon its violation, the more credible the sovereign/public debtor can signal to the markets a diligent budgetary policy. Especially since creditors find themselves in a relatively weak bargaining position when the sovereign/public debtor's debt has to be renegotiated, and because security for sovereign/public debt is an extraordinary exception, borrowing and deficit constraints are a prudent strategy for sovereign/public debtors to convince their creditors of a safe investment. The difficulties which creditors face in case of the sovereign/public debtor's distress will be explored in more detail in Chapter VI. Conditional upon their credibility, borrowing and deficit constraints have a favourable impact on the debt capital costs for the sovereign/public debtor.[99]

3.3.4 Rules for Restructuring and Governance Reform

If a sovereign or public debtor has reached an unsustainable debt level so that a debt restructuring becomes necessary (provided there is no bailout to be expected), the debtor will regularly face severe collective action problems. While it often would be in the interest of all creditors to cooperate, individual creditors might have a perverse incentive to hold out and to free

98 HENNING BOHN and ROBERT INMAN, 'Balanced Budget Rules and Public Deficits: Evidence From U.S. States' (1996) NBER Working Paper 5533; JAMES POTERBA, 'Balanced Budget Rules and Fiscal Policy: Evidence from the States' (1995) 48 (3) National Tax Journal 329 (on self-imposed borrowing constraints in the US). For a comparison of debt and deficit constraints see: ROEL BEETSMA and MARCOS POPLAWSKI RIBEIRO, and ANDREAS SCHABERT, 'A Comparison of Debt and Primary-Deficit Constraints' CEPR Discussion Paper No. DP6897. The Maastricht Treaties' debt and deficit rules provide an example for a debt and deficit constraint which holds no credibility. See especially deficit/debt constraints in sections IV. 2.4 and 2.5 (in consequent *Autonomy* models) and V. 3.4 and 3.7 (in the EMU) for a comparison of differently strong debt/deficit constraints.

99 LARS FELD, ALEXANDER KALB, MARC-DANIEL MOESSINGER, STEFFEN OSTERLOH, 'Sovereign bond market reactions to fiscal rules and no-bailout clauses: The Swiss experience' (2013) ZEW Discussion Papers, No. 13-034; CRAIG JOHNSON and KENNETH KRIZ, 'Fiscal Institutions, Credit Ratings, and Borrowing Costs' (2005) Public Budgeting & Finance 84.

ride, since this could lead to a higher individual payoff than cooperation. Individual opportunistic behaviour, however, can result in a collectively suboptimal payoff for the creditors.[100] If the sovereign/public debtor has implemented a debt crisis resolution scheme, the no-bailout principle becomes more credible, since the multi-tier union cannot be blackmailed with the threat of a disorderly debt crisis. Essentially, rules for restructuring and governance reform in case of distress help to reduce (i) the probability of distress, and (ii) the costs of distress, so that the outcome should be a win-win-situation for the debtor and its creditors.[101]

3.3.5 Ratings

Market control works ex ante. The market has to adjust its credit cost expectations constantly to the default risk of the sovereign/public debtor; otherwise, the disciplinary effect of credit costs would not exist. In order to accurately price the debtor, the creditors need information about the debtor's financial performance. In case of a concentrated creditor structure with substantial debt capital investments per creditor, the creditors may perform this task individually or share the costs, as for instance in a syndicated inter-creditor loan agreement.

If, however, the credit structure is dispersed, monitoring is too costly for individual creditors and cost-sharing is no realistic option. The moment that a creditor with market expertise and a large holding invests into monitoring and takes action based on newly acquired information, the information is revealed by the monitoring creditor's market action and other creditors can free ride. In anticipation of the free riding effect, all creditors hold out and the debtor alone holds the information advantage. In such a situation of asymmetrically distributed information, there is no seperating equilibrium. Creditors price the debtor based on a calculation of the average debtor's default risk, so that high-quality debtors have no interest to make an over-priced debt offer. They leave the market. The creditors' price expectation goes up, the quality goes down. Akerlof describes this phenomenon as Lemon Market.[102] Since there is quite a lot of high-quality information about sovereign and public debtors publicly available, a single

100 See therefore VI. 2.
101 See section VII. 3.
102 GEORGE AKERLOF, 'The Market for "Lemons": Quality Uncertainty and the Market Mechanism' (1970) 84 (3) The Quarterly Journal of Economics 488.

pooling equilibrium is unlikely, i.e., that the United States of America are priced at the same rate as Ukraine. It is, however, likely that seperating equilibria emerge in quite broad clusters, i.e., that several pools of certain types of debtors (e.g. rural municipalities in country X) exist and that each pool constitutes a small lemon market.

The debtor, therefore, has an interest to overcome the asymmetry of information, since the costs will ultimately fall back on the debtor itself. Rating agencies emerge so as to concentrate the monitoring efforts. Since it would be pointless to sell the information to the creditors in a dispersed credit structure, because the information would be revealed with the first sale and other creditors would free ride subsequently, the debt issuer pays. The rating agency backs the rating of the debtor's credit risk with its reputation. While rating agencies had come under harsh criticism for their ratings of structured financial products, being accused of biased ratings ("rating shopping/catering"),[103] this problem does not exists to a similar extent for ratings of sovereign/public debtors; mostly, because sovereign/public debt ratings are more transparent as a consequence of easily accessible high-quality information about the sovereign/public debtor's performance.[104] With better information about the sovereign/public debtor's financial performance, the credit rating allows the markets to adjust their credit cost expectations and to exercise control over the debtor, as described in section III. 3.2.

103 For a discussion see: PATRICK BOLTON, XAVIER FREIXAS, and JOEL SHAPIRO, 'The Credit Ratings Game' (2012) 67 (1) The Journal of Finance 85; JOHN GRIFFIN, JORDAN NICKERSON, and DRAGON YONGJUN TANG, 'Rating Shopping or Catering An Examination of the Response to Competitive Pressure for CDO Ratings' (2013) 26 (9) The Review of Financial Studies 2270; VASILIKO SKRETA and LAURA VELDKAMP, 'Ratings shopping and asset complexity: A theory of ratings inflation' (2009) 56 (5) Journal of Monetary Economics 678.

104 On sovereign debt ratings see: ANTÓNIO AFONSO, 'Understanding the Determinants of Government Debt Ratings: Evidence for the Two Leading Agencies' (2003) 27 (1) Journal of Economics and Finance 56. On the link between currency crisis and default in sovereign debt ratings: CARMEN REINHART, 'Default, Currency Crises, and Sovereign Debt Ratings' (2002) 16 (2) The World Bank Economic Review 151. See also: ERIK FASTEN, 'Two-Sided Certification: The market for Rating Agencies' in *Financial Markets and Public Finance* (Nomos 2012) 86.

3.4 Integration Model

3.4.1 Top-Down Directives

The integration model works under the assumption that the central authority has the ultimate funding responsibility. To be institutionally congruent, the centre must have the final say when it comes to decisions about spending, taxation, and debt acquisition. While the subordinate parts of the integrated multi-tier union may make spending decisions, collect taxes, and acquire debt within the limits set by the central government, the central government must have the right to interfere whenever the central government considers intervention to be necessary, i.e., the power to limit the subordinate units' authority and to take the driver's seat instead; quite generally, the central government must have the authority to set the guidelines and principles for spending, taxation, and debt acquisition. In practice, the subordinate parts may appear to act quite independently, as they are guided by soft and informal pressure, i.e., they are aware that the centre will interfere if they overstep the mark and become a financial burden for the multi-tier transfer union. The main legislative power has to be centralised, the same as the centre must possess oversight rights and the option to assume control whenever this is necessary to secure financial stability.

While the centre has to have the right to manage the subcentral budgets, the central government needs to collect information and oversee the subordinate units' performance. The markets will not take on the responsibility to assess the financial performance of individual parts of the multi-tier union. For the markets, only the accumulated risk of the multi-tier union as one is of interest.[105] The central government may oversee the subordinate units constantly and closely, or it may give them more scope of action and lead by setting the right incentives. The central government may force subordinate units, which got into trouble because of a wasteful policy in the past, to cut down heavily and painfully on spending and/or it may reward the good efforts of subordinate units with a successful financial policy and allow them more flexibility under the central government's rule.[106]

---

105 See section III. 3.2 with further references.

106 An interesting proposal comes from MASSIMO BORDIGNON, PAOLO MANESSE; and GUIDO TABELLINI, 'Optimal Regional Redistribution Under Asymmetric Information' (2001) 91 (3) The American Economic Review 709. The authors suggest that re-distributional grants should be adjusted to the fiscal effort shown by the local units. If a local unit raises taxes to improve on its financial situation, the grant should be increased correspondingly.

Contra-productive would be a central government's policy by which wasteful budgetary decisions are rewarded with transfers to make good for the sins of the past, cross-subsidised by those units which did well in the past.[107] The central government, thus, can monitor and control and/or it can install an incentive scheme so as to align the subordinate government's interests with the collective interest of the multi-tier union.

3.4.2 Cooperative Budget-Rules

While a centralised decision-making process is inherent to the integration model, the decision-making process itself may be designed differently. The most consequently centralised approach would be a legislative and executive body elected via a party-list in a proportional election system (without regional links). The soon as regional links are established in a majority election system, the regional representatives have an incentive to lobby for a disproportionally large share from the common pool for their constituency. In case of a state house as second chamber, the regional interests gain additional weight. If the voting power assigned to the regions is disproportional, i.e., if certain regions have a higher voting share than other regions in relation to the size of the regional electorate, they will have an increased chance to receive a disproportionally large share from the common pool. While a strongly centralised decision-making process without regional links can curtail rent-seeking and logrolling for the pork barrel, regional links in the decision-making process allow for the collection of information about regional preferences.[108] In the end, the integration model is characterised by the power of the central government and/or the legislative assembly of regional representatives to set the guidelines for spending, taxation, and debt acquisition for the subordinate units and to command fiscal actions.

The question of the threshold for decision-making becomes an issue of importance for the integration model in case that the regions are represented in the decision-making process. A higher than a majority threshold

---

107 For the case of distorted incentives as a consequence of intergovernmental transfers to compensate for a weak performance in the past see: BLANKART and EHMKE (2014); BLANKART and EHMKE (2016); RODDEN (2002); RODDEN (2013). As a practical example thereof see especially the German case in section IV. 2.3.

108 See section III. 2.3. BESLEY and COATE (2013), RODDEN (2002a).

works in two directions: If borrowing/deficit constraints are implemented with a high threshold requirement for modifications, this will strengthen financial stability. If transfers to the regions are guaranteed with a high threshold requirement for modifications, this will, in the long-run, increase spending, as the favoured regions are unlikely to give up their privileged position unless they are offered new transfers. Logrolling and rent-seeking games are likely to be the consequence. The rule of unanimous consent to a modification of previously agreed upon rules, finally, stands in stark contrast to the idea of the integration model, as the regions gain a veto power which frees them effectively from the central government's command.[109]

3.4.3 Vertical and/or Horizontal Transfers

Transfers may flow vertically, i.e., from the central government to the subordinate parts of the union, or horizontally, i.e., from the subordinate parts to each other. The difference is often rather technical, especially in case that the central government collects proportionally from the regions and re-distributes disproportionally top-down. In this case, the vertical equalisation is a horizontal equalisation 'in disguise', as the following example may illustrate.

> ***Example: Horizontal = Vertical Transfers***
> Imagine federation F with local units A and B with each the same population size. A has a financial capacity of 125, B of 75.

109 The principle of unanimity is integral part to the very definition of sovereignty in international law. A modification is regularly only possible where the sovereign has committed itself to follow a different voting rule, e.g., in an international organization, for specific and pre-defined questions. While unanimity is the rule in international law, several authors have argued in favour of a more flexible choice of rules: NOBMAN HILL, 'Unanimous Consent in International Organization' (1928) 22 (2) The American Journal of International Law 319; ANDREW GUZMAN, 'Against Consent' (2012) 52 (4) Virgina Journal of International Law 747. In JAMES BUCHANAN and GORDEN TULLOCK, *The Calculus of Consent* (University of Michigan Press 1962), the authors conclude that the lower the threshold, the higher are the external costs, i.e., the costs that someone can else impose on you without your consent. To put it differently, the higher the threshold is, the better someone can defend a favourable position.

1. Constellation (vertical):
The accumulated level of local taxation in A and B is 20 per cent. The accumulated level of federal taxation is 30 per cent. The local tax rate (%) is fixed. Thus, A collects 25 in local taxes, B collects 15 in local taxes, and F collects 60 in federal taxes. With the goal to equalise the public service standard nationwide, F creates an equalisation fund equipped with 10. The fund will be distributed so that all local units will eventually possess the same financial endowment for the public budget on a per capita basis. B receives 10.
Post-Equalisation Result: A and B have each a public budget of 25 and F of 50. The nationwide tax burden equals 100.
2. Constellation (horizontal):
The accumulated level of local taxation in A and B is 25 per cent and the accumulated level of federal taxation is 25 per cent. The local tax rate is fixed. A collects 31.25 in local taxes, B collects 18.75 in local taxes, and F collects 50 in federal taxes. With the goal to equalise the public service standard nationwide, A has been obliged to contribute 6.25 to a scheme of which B will receive 6.25.
Post-Equalisation Result: A and B have each a public budget of 25 and F of 50. The nationwide tax burden equals 100.
Inference: If we take a closer look at both constellations, we will see that one is a mirror-reflection of the other. In both constellations, citizens of A shoulder a tax burden of 62.5, and citizens of B carry a tax burden of 37.5. The public budgets of A, B, and F are eventually the same in Constellation 1. and 2.
The only difference is that in case of a vertical equalisation scheme (1. Constellation), the federal government levies an extra tax of 6.25 from A and of 3.75 from B. In a second step, the federal government gives B 'its contribution' of 3.75 back and channels A's contribution of 6.25 to B (via the equalisation fund).
In case of a horizontal equalisation scheme, the federal government does not have to fund an equalisation scheme, so that it can levy less taxes. However, A and B will charge a higher tax: A has to fund its direct transfer to B (6.25) and B has to raise a fund of 3.75, instead of that the federal government raises the same tax in order to transfer it to B.

More importantly than the direction of the transfers is their size and the conditions on which they are provided. Typically, the central government provides matching grants to support specific projects on the regional level. If the coordination function rests with the central government, as in the integration model, such matching grants can be a way to encourage investments in the interests of the multi-tier union; a soft type of command. The downside of matching grants can be a dispersion of rents in a rent-seeking game, especially in case that the central government runs an open application[110] as well as matching grants may increase regional spending overall if they are used to substitute for regional expenses which were already budgeted for the respective project ("flypaper effect").[111]

Matching grants, however, can provide a good solution to overcome the underinvestment problem in case of local projects with nationwide positive spillovers, of which the local university is a good example.[112] Another good example for the use of matching grants is an inter-state traffic way. The costs for building such a traffic way and the benefits of its use can vary significantly by state/subordinate unit. Costs and benefits are not at all correlated. Transit-states, especially with a difficult landscape for construction, would have high costs and little benefits while import and export states would collect most of the benefits.[113] If a matching grant promises a value-maximisation, it makes sense for the central government to provide such intergovernmental matching grants.[114] While matching grants are not an inherent element of the autonomy model, they might function very well with the autonomy model.

Another type of transfers is provided with the intention to equalise the living standards across the multi-tier union. Equalisation schemes are established to improve on fairness, social integration, and quite generally to lift the average welfare standard. While the question in how far equalisation schemes can achieve a higher welfare standard is certainly interesting, this project will concentrate on the question in how far equalisation schemes have an (unintended side-)effect on the financial performance of the (potential) contributors and receivers under the scheme. Equalisation transfers diminish the incentive to invest effort into a diligent budgetary

110 Example: European regional development programme. See section II. 3.5.

111 See section II. 3.2.

112 See section III. 2.1.

113 For a discussion of the US highway programme see: HARRY MEYERS, 'Displacement Effects of Federal Highway Grants' (1987) 40 (2) National Tax Journal 221; EDWARD MILLER, 'The Economics of Matching Grants: The ABC Highway Program' (1974) 27 (2) National Tax Journal 221.

114 On intergovernmental matching grants – also compared to lump-sum grants – see: DAVID BREDFORD and WALLACE OATES, 'Towards a Predictive Theory of Intergovernmental Grants' (1971) 61 (2) The American Economic Review 440.

policy at the subordinate level since they siphon off the gains from the strongest and fill up the gap for the weakest of the multi-tier union. The higher the targeted minimum equalisation standard is (e.g., 95% of the average, 80% of the average, et cetera),[115] the lower the subordinate unit's incentive to apply a diligent budgetary policy is, and the greater the need for top-down budgetary regulation becomes. To put it differently, the less room for manoverous the subordinate units have because of a restrictive top-down regime, the more plausible equalisation transfers are, since the plus or minus on the subordinate unit's accounts becomes less correlated with their own effort. Since equalisation transfers are provided unconditionally, the citizens of a 'receiver unit' are less likely to experience the transfer in a tax reduction, but possibly in an extra supply of public goods.[116]

3.4.4 Bail-Out Guarantee/ Shared Debt Responsibility

In a multi-tier union following the integration model, the centre or the union are typically responsible for the debt of the subordinate parts. This requires an effective chain of commands (top-down) so that the link between decision-making and funding responsibility functions. A bailout guarantee/shared debt responsibility without an effective chain of commands top-down opens the doors for declining financial performance as a result of the wrong incentives set by common pool financing.[117] The central government's right to manage the subordinate entities' budgets without a bailout guarantee is similarly a misconception. Certainly, the central government can temporarily delay the bailout, shift the burden of costs and debt to the subordinate governments, and present itself as diligent housekeeper. This game, nonetheless, has to come to an end when the subordinate units' debt level becomes unsustainable.

Even though direct vertical and/or horizontal transfers, as discussed in the previous section, are quite typical for a multi-tier union following the integration model, they are not an inevitable part of its construction. The absence of such direct transfers, however, does not mean that the units

115 Compare the equalisation schemes in sections IV. 2.1 (Canada), IV. 2.3 (Germany), and IV. 2.4 (Switzerland).

116 The same considerations as for matching grants/the flypaper effect apply. See section II. 3.2.

117 See section III. 3.2 with further references.

fund themselves autonomously until the point that they have reached an unsustainable debt level and that they are bailed out. When creditors anticipate a bailout, because of an explicit or implicit bailout guarantee/shared debt responsibility, they will price the different debtors of the transfer union at (almost) the same level.[118] As a consequence, indirect transfers flow from the stronger parts of the union, which have to pay for a risk premium higher than their incremental risk rate, while weaker parts of the union can acquire debt at a risk premium lower than their own incremental risk rate. Weaker parts may do not receive direct transfer payments, but they receive the bailout privilege to acquire debt capital at a subsidised rate, so that indirect transfers flow constantly.[119]

3.4.5 Imposed Borrowing and Deficit Constraints

Similar to self-imposed borrowing and deficit constraints in the autonomy model, the central government of a multi-tier union following the integration model may opt for centrally imposed borrowing and deficit constraints. The same considerations for constraints on political actions, for different thresholds for modifications, and for the signalling effect apply as in section III. 3.3.3. Different is only that the borrowing/deficit constraint may be implemented without unanimous approval of all subordinate units. Essentially, the imposed borrowing and deficit constraint is nothing else than a quite visible control device in form of a top-down directive. However, since especially the subsidy for risk rates encourages weaker parts of the union to borrow, an explicit, less negotiable constraint on borrowing and deficit is a sensible solution for an integrated multi-tier union.[120] If the borrowing and deficit constraints are tight enough to avoid that the subnational units even accumulate an unsustainable debt burden, the integration model will not even require a bailout guarantee.

---

118 See section III. 3.2 and III. 3.3.1.

119 See therefore especially the country-analysis in chapter IV. and the EMU analysis in chapter V.

120 See the French case as a good example thereof in section IV. 2.2.

3.5 Summary: Autonomy, Integration, and Mixed Models

The following table shall summarize the main findings from section III. 3. See the Institutional Congruence Index (Fig. 3) in III. 3.6 for a description of the autonomy and the integration model:

(Tab. 1) Summary: Autonomy, Integration, Mixed Models

Model	Control	(+)Chance/(–)Risk/ (→)Solution
Autonomy Model	hard budget constraints by market control	(+) first best price-product choice within budget constraint (–) benefit spillover possible
Integration Model	hard budget constraints by central government control	If compared to the Autonomy Model: (–) second best price-product choice within budget constraint (–) higher information /coordination costs (+) economies of scale
Mixed Models	soft budget constraints	(–) overspending, as a consequence of moral hazard (–) misallocation of resources (–) burden-shifting (–) suboptimal choice result: declining financial performance (→) solution: implement institutions to support central government OR market control

In short:

In the autonomy model, each sovereign/public unit operates independently and is ultimately responsible for its debt. The no bailout principle correlates directly with market discipline.

In the integration model, the budget authority is centralised. Sub-ordinate units operate within the framework set by the central government. The bailout/debt responsibility is typically shared, unless the right to borrow and to run deficits is strictly and tightly limited.

The question as to whether a multi-tier union should favour the autonomy or the integration model depends on: (i) the surplus of the first best price-product choice over the second best price-product choice (β), (ii) the extra costs for monitoring and coordination in case of a larger unit (θ), (iii) the savings from economies of scale in case of a larger administrative unit (λ), so that the

> ***Autonomy model*** should be implemented **if $\beta > \lambda - \theta$**, and that the
> ***Integration model*** should be implemented **if $\beta < \lambda - \theta$**.

In mixed models, institutions of autonomy and integration are 'mixed up'. From a financial perspective, the result is always inferior to an alternative institutionally congruent regime, because of overspending, misallocation of resources, burden-shifting, and a suboptimal price-product choice for the public good in the mixed model. The exit route can only be: the implementation of the autonomy or the integration model (III. 3.2) so that stability may be achieved by market and/or central government control.

3.7 Institutional Congruence Index

The theory of institutional congruence will be presented schematically in Fig. 3. The institutional congruence index shall give some orientation on the degree of institutional congruence/incongruence of a fiscal regime. The institutional congruence index will be applied to an analysis of those countries presented in Chapter IV and for the European Monetary Union in Chapter V. The index here developed, however, should be transferable and thus applicable for an analysis of any fiscal regime in a multi-tier union of public/sovereign debtors.

Fig. 3 (Institutional Congruence Index)

Autonomy Model ← **Mixed Model** → **Integration Model**	
Elements of Autonomy	**Elements of Integration**
1A.Aut. No Bailout Principle AND Definition: no extraordinary financial assistance in case of distress.	**1A.Int. Bailout Guarantee AND/OR 1B.** Definition: extraordinary financial assistance in case of financial distress in form of transfers, loans, and/or guarantees (well below market price).
1B.Aut. Borrowing Autonomy AND Definition: no top-down constraints on borrowing; self-enacted and self-enforced borrowing constraints possible.	**1B.Int. Top-Down Borrowing Constraints AND** Definition: top-down commanded constraints enforced by an effective mechanism of review, veto, and/or deterring sanctions; borrowing constraints comprise rules for the matter of debt acquisition (e.g. only capital investments), for supervision (e.g. only with qualified approval top-down), rules for the max. debt level, and/or rules for the budget (e.g. balanced budget requirements, deficit limits).
2.Aut. Spending Autonomy AND Definition: as a corollary of own legislative and own administrative competences, the power to use the available resources according to an individual budget.	**2.Int. Top-Down-Controlled Spending Authority AND** Definition: centralised legislative authority to define the scope of administrative action plus central administration or centrally supervised local administration.
3A.Aut. Tax Autonomy AND Definition: autonomy to choose tax bases and set tax rates individually, i.e., not collectively.	**3A.Int. Top-Down Controlled Tax Authority AND** Definition: shared or delegated tax income, i.e., the tax base chosen and the tax rate set by a collective or central body; individual public units have no or only insignificant latitude to occupy an alternative tax base and to set a higher/lower tax rate.
3B.Aut. Tax-Funded Budget Definition: budget is funded by own (i.e. not by shared/delegated) taxes.	**3B.Int. Transfer-Funded Budget** Definition: budget is funded by shared/delegated tax income and/or transfers.

IV. Lessons from Subnational Fiscal Experiments

1. *Institutions Matter*

It is finally time to road-test the theory of institutional congruence and apply it to a variety of different countries. In the following sections, an institutional analysis of five different multi-tier unions will be conducted. The analysis will include an analytical review of the institutions governing the fiscal relations in each of the five countries. The purpose of this chapter is not to present a broad-scale empirical analysis of institutionally congruent versus institutionally incongruent fiscal regimes but to provide an in-depth institutional analysis of selected fiscal regimes which cover the range from integration (e.g. France) over mixed models (e.g. Germany) to autonomy (e.g. USA).

The underlying proposition is that institutions matter and that the combinations of institutions which make up the integration model[121] or the autonomy model[122] promote a superior financial performance if compared to the institutionally incongruent mixed models. The key to financial sustainability is effective market or central government control.[123]

This proposition may also be derived from broad-scale empirical studies on the combination of different institutions. In an empirical study of 43 countries, Jonathan Rodden shows that a good fiscal performance and a balanced budget require that the subnational units are subject to effective borrowing constraints (as in the integration model) or that borrowing autonomy comes along with tax autonomy (as in the autonomy model). In contrast, borrowing autonomy without tax autonomy (as in the mixed model) would cause unsustainable budgets.[124] In another empirical study of 44 countries dealing with Buchanan and Brennan's Leviathan-hypothesis, Jonathan Rodden demonstrates that a decentralised spending authority is associated with less government spending if funding comes from taxes

121 These institutions are: bailout guarantee and/or strict borrowing constraints, spending constraints, top-down controlled tax authority, and transfer-funded budget.

122 These institutions are: no bailout principle and debt autonomy, spending autonomy, tax autonomy, and tax-funded budget.

123 See section III. 3.2.

124 RODDEN (2002).

on which the subnational units can decide independently (as in the autonomy model). However, according to Rodden, spending autonomy will lead to higher spending if subnational budgets are primarily funded with shared taxes and transfers on which the subnational units have no influence individually (as in the mixed model).[125]

This way, the riddle can be resolved about why empirical research has regularly shown very different results when investigating as to whether decentralisation or centralisation produces superior financial performance, less spending, less taxation, or less indebtness. Rodden points out that often research which did not focus on the concrete design of decentralisation, but on decentralisation in any form, would show an ambiguous image of the benefits and flaws of decentralisation.[126] Consistent with the theory of institutional congruence, empirical research which focused on decentralisation on the subnational level within countries that clearly fit the description of the autonomy model (e.g. Switzerland and USA) would show very positive effects of decentralisation.[127] Similarly consistent with the theory, studies focusing on countries with an institutionally incongruent fiscal design would show a negative picture of decentralisation.[128]

So, the question must not be centralisation or decentralisation but how to centralise or how to decentralise. The goal of this chapter, therefore, is to take a closer look at the concrete institutional design in five distinct federations to eventually draw lessons from this observation on how a fiscal structure of a multi-tier union (of subnational or sovereign units) may be evaluated according to the standard of institutional congruence. For this purpose, country studies of Canada, France, Germany, the USA, and Switzerland are presented in sections IV. 2.1 to 2.5, with a comparative

125 RODDEN (2003).

126 Rodden refers here to the famous study conducted by OATES (1985).

127 Rodden refers here to an unpublished work by Feld, Kirchgässner, and Schaltegger, later on published as LARS FELD, GEBHARD KIRCHGÄSSNER, and CHRISTOPH SCHALTEGGER, 'Decentralized Taxation and the Size of Government: Evidence from Swiss State and Local Governments' (2010) 77 (1) Southern Economic Journal 27 (evaluating the Swiss case) as well as e.g. to a study by MICHAEL MARLOW, 'Fiscal decentralisation and government size' (1988) 56 Public Choice 259 (evaluating the US experience). See also ZAX (1989).

128 Rodden refers here to a study by ERNESTO STEIN, 'Fiscal Decentralisation and Government Size in Latin America' (1999) 2 (2) Journal of Applied Economics 357 (evaluating a sample of Latin American countries). See also: TAO ZHANG and HENG-FU ZOU, 'Fiscal decentralisation, public spending, and economic growth in China' (1998) 67 Journal of Public Economics 221.

summary in section IV. 3. The analysis, thus, comprises five highly developed economies of which one country quite closely resembles the integration model (France), one provides the exhibit A for a mixed model (Germany), while three other countries fit the definition of the autonomy model, with one country (Canada) showing some relevant deviations towards institutional incongruence and two countries (Switzerland and USA) being the almost perfect representation of an institutionally congruent autonomy model.

2. Country-Specific Analysis of Different Fiscal Concepts

2.1 Canada

Canadian federalism is challenged to integrate quite different parts of the federation while at the same time it is challenged to encourage a beneficial competition between the subnational units. The fiscal landscape of a profoundly heterogeneous, multi-linguistic, multi-cultural, and multi-ethnic society, traditionally seen to be divided by association to either the English or French heritage, is characterised by a stark contrast in nation-wide income distribution per subordinate unit, as well as by a division between natural resource-rich and –poor regions. The Canadian solution for how to strike the balance in federalism may be summarized with the following formula: strong provincial autonomy in decision-making and social integration through a nationwide high welfare standard.[129]

Provincial autonomy in decision-making is pronounced in a wide area of joint, and especially exclusive provincial legislative powers. The executive power and therewith the spending authority and responsibility follows in principle from the legislative power; nonetheless, the federal government has the right to (co-) fund projects attributed to provisional legislative/ executive power.[130] For the funding of their expenses, the provinces and the federal government each may occupy all potential tax bases at the same time. With the exception that resource and property taxation practically

129 For a good overview of the distribution of spending, taxation, (and debt acquisition authority) in the first-to-second tier relation from a comparative perspective see: ROBIN BOADWAY and RONALD WATTS, 'Fiscal Federalism in Canada, the USA, and Germany' (2004) 6 IIGR Working Paper, Queen's University.

130 BOADWAY and WATTS (2004) 2–7. The distribution of legislative powers between the federal parliament and the provinces is established by Artt. 91–95 of the Constitution Act 1867.

rests with the provinces and municipalities, any relevant tax base is typically utilised by the federal and the provincial government at the same time.[131] While the federal tax rate applies nationwide, the provinces may choose their own tax rate upon their discretion; a process which has led to quite some diversification regarding the actual tax level in different parts of the country.[132]

The situation is different for the third-tier of government. The sub-provincial municipalities are subject to the legislative and executive order of their province.[133] In the spirit of decentralisation and in the provinces own right, the municipalities, however, regularly perform important public services, especially in the areas of education, policing, and transportation.[134] For this purpose, they are typically entitled by the law of their respective province to raise specified taxes and to charge user fees. A great share of their revenues, nevertheless, comes from transfers. Municipalities are often constraint to run deficits, i.e., to acquire debt in order to fund the gap between expenditures and revenues. Debt acquisition is typically limited to capital investments. Local debt acquisition regularly requires the province's approval. In order to balance its operating budget, the municipal government may be required to cut expenditures, to adjust delegated taxes/fees, or to negotiate for larger transfer payments from the province.[135]

As far as to this point, the Canadian fiscal regime presents itself twofold: the relation between the federal government to the provinces (first-to-second-tier) shows a high degree of decentralisation and autonomy for decision-making on spending, debt acquisition, and taxation. The province's extensive legislative and executive powers as well as their autonomous spending, taxation, and debt acquisition authority could make the Canadi-

131 BOADWAY and WATTS (2004) 7. Art. 91, No. 3 Constitution Act 1867 grants the federal legislative comprehensive tax authority. Art. 92, No. 2 Constitution Act 1867 grants the provincial government comprehensive tax authority within its territory.

132 See Canada Revenue Agency's website: http://www.cra-arc.gc.ca/tx/ndvdls/fq/txrts-eng.html. Tax harmonisation as the definition of upper/lower tax limits is not enforced by top-down commands but agreed upon in negotiations between the sub-national governments. See BOADWAY and WATTS (2004) 7, 13–14.

133 Art. 92 No. 8 Constitution Act 1867 grants the provinces exclusive legislation over the municipalities.

134 JEAN-FRANCOIS TREMBLAY, 'Fiscal Federalism and Public Service Provision in Canada' (2007) 3 (1) Public Policy Review 51 at 64 and 66.

135 RICHARD BIRD and ALMOS TASSONYI, 'Constraints on provincial and municipal borrowing in Canada: markets, rules, and norms' (2001) 44 (1) Canadian Public Administration 84 at 91–99.

an model of fiscal federalism an object lesson for decentralisation. The relation between the provinces and the municipalities (second-to-third-tier) instead is best described as controlled decentralisation within the integration model. The municipalities act within the boundaries of the province's top-down directives. Consequently, they may not expand their scope of action beyond their financial means by excessive debt acquisition. The requirement of a balanced budget at the municipal level follows logically from the ultimate funding responsibility of the provincial government.

The story in the first-to-second and second-to-second tier relation between the federal government and the provinces and between the provinces amongst each other gets more complicated once the welfare state is introduced. The Canadians have made a fundamental policy decision that they would guarantee every Canadian citizen, regardless of their income and their regional link, a minimum living standard. They have decided that they would provide equal opportunities for the younger generation by way of free and good quality education. Since the constitutionally agreed upon distribution of responsibilities mandates the provinces with the core welfare functions of education, welfare (social security), and health, and since the provinces are quite differently wealthy on a per capita basis, the risk exists that the public welfare offer would vary significantly across the different provinces, which could erode the principle of an equally high welfare standard across the nation. The principle of equalisation so as to overcome regional disparities is embodied in Art. 36, No. 1 of the Constitution Act 1982, according to which the "government of Canada and the provincial governments, are committed to (a) promoting equal opportunites for the well-being of Canadian; (b) furthering economic developments to reduce disparity in opportunities, and (c) providing essential public services of reasonable quality to all Canadians".

The federal equalisation strategy takes three forms: First, all provinces receive conditional transfers as subsidy for health and social welfare through the federal programmes Canada Health Transfer and Canada Social Transfer. Second, an unconditional equalisation programme exists to mitigate the horizontal 'fiscal imbalance'. As pointed out previously, the provinces are independent to set their own tax rates, so that not the actual tax revenues but the fiscal potential for taxation is the right comparator to determine which provinces are more or less capable to fund public services at a nationwide standard. The federal government makes equalisation payments to provinces which would yield a revenue below the ten provinces' average from five sources of income (specific taxes and natural resources revenues), assumed that taxation levels at the national average.[136] The receiving provinces have the privilege that 50% or 0% of their natural resource revenues is accounted for as their revenue, whatever yields the higher equalisation transfer payment. There is a cap to the equalisation payments. The budgets for transfers may not increase to a higher percentage than the national GDP growth as well as no receiving province will receive transfers of an amount so that it eventually stands better than the poorest non-receiving province.[137]

Third, even though not formally guaranteed/agreed upon, all provinces with a higher than average risk of default if they were standing 'on their own' receive a constant credit cost subsidy, since creditors can reasonable expect bailout transfers in case that one province will be unable to meet their credit obligations in the future. The bailout expectation has been tested empirically. An early study by Stuart Landon and Constance Smith found that provincial credit ratings are significantly negatively affected by a rising debt accumulation at the federal level. If the markets expect the federal government to bailout the provinces, the question of the federal government's ability to do so is crucial for the creditworthiness of the provinces; otherwise, it would be of less interest.[138] More pronounced, re-

---

136 The four taxes out of this calculation are the personal and the business income tax, the consumption tax, and the property tax.

137 Art. 36 (2) Constitution Act 1867 provides: "Parliament and the government of Canada are committed to the principle of making equalization payments to ensure that provincial governments have sufficient revenues to provide reasonably comparable levels of public services at reasonably comparable levels of taxation." For a short explanation of the functioning of the Canadian equalization scheme see: ÉDISON ROY-CÉSAR, 'In Brief: Canada's Equalization Formula' (2013) Library of Parliament, Publication No. 2008-20-E, 10 November 2008, Revised 4 September 2013. For a political/historical review of the Canadian equalisation scheme see: ANDRE LECOURS and DANIEL BELAND, 'Federalism and Fiscal Policy: The Politics of Equalisation in Canada' (2010) 40 (4) Publius 569.

138 STUART LANDON and CONSTANCE SMITH, 'Government debt spillovers and creditworthiness in a federation' (2000) 33 (3) Canadian Journal of Economics 634. Landon and Smith find that a high debt level of the central government has a significant negative impact on the province's creditworthiness. This finding is consistent with the bailout assumption. The higher the central government's debt, the lower is its own capacity to fund a bailout programme for the provinces. For the provinces, Landon and Smith find a negative, however, small debt spillover effect with the remarkable exception of Ontario. They find that if the largest province Ontario's debt level rises, this will have a positive impact on the credit rating of other conferences, and vice versa, which they explain with lenders measuring creditworthiness by yardstick competition.

garding the question of a federal bailout expectation, are the empirical results presented by Marc Joffe. Joffe shows that, despite different ratings, wealth, debt level, and risk structure, the provincial interest rates are almost the same. In rating and risk-adjusted calculations, the author can demonstrate that the interest rates would divert substantially from the actual interest rates if there did not exist an implicit bailout guarantee.[139] Past rescue transfers to ease the financial burden of distressed provincial debtors and the federal government's commitment to secure a comparatively high welfare standard for all Canadians across the country contribute to the market's bailout expectation.[140]

With every step taken towards developing a high-quality welfare standard on a nationwide comparative level, the Canadian fiscal regime takes a step back from the realisation of an institutionally congruent model of fiscal autonomy. The first step, the Canadian Health Transfer and the Canadian Social Transfer programmes, causes little distortion. The subsidy is conditional and provided equally across the country. The performance incentives of the provincial governments in relation to each other are not affected. This is different with the second step, the federal equalisation programme: The equalisation programme is provided unconditionally and it is directly related to the financial/economic performance of the provinces in so far as one can assume that the provinces' government can influence the wealth in their region, and thus the financial capacity, by creating a framework for the economy to prosper. In so far as this assumption holds, the programme punishes strong and rewards weak performers. Since, however, the programme does not take the provincial government's actual budget balances but the financial capacity of the province as the comparator, the equalisation programme does not create the perverse incentive to spend excessively, to tax little, and to run deficits so as to benefit from the common pool. While the equalisation programme is certainly not part of an institutionally congruent autonomy model, and while it has the potential to cause conflicts between comparatively rich and poor regions, the step away from the fiscal autonomy standard is small.

139 MARC JOFFE, *Provincial Solvency and Federal Obligations* (Macdonald-Laurier Institute 2012).

140 KYLE HANNIMAN, 'Provinces in the Credit Market: Market Discipline and the New Classic Federalism' in Bruce Doern and Christopher Stoney (eds) *How Ottawa Spends* (Queens-McGill University Press 2013) and JOFFE (2012), especially 39–43 (for past bailouts during the 1930s).

The last step towards a bailout union, however, is a quite significant step away from the autonomy model. The benefit received (i.e. the interest rate subsidy) is negatively correlated to the financial performance (i.e. the default risk). The weaker a province's financial performance is, the higher is the interest rate subsidy received; and the stronger a province is, the higher is its contribution towards the interest rate subsidy received by weaker parts of the union. Market control vanishes with the pooling equilibrium of credit capital costs.

The Canadian fiscal regime is torn between the striving for two distinct goals in the first-to-second tier relation: provincial financial (and political) autonomy and provincial social integration. While both goals can be accomplished up to a certain degree, at least the goal attainment for either financial autonomy or social integration has to be incomplete in a multi-tier federal union. Fiscal autonomy builds on self-responsibility and competition. Social integration is intended to flatten stark differences and to introduce reciprocal responsibility. In particular, the absence of a no-bailout regime in the presence of provincial spending, tax, and debt acquisition autonomy threatens the financial performance. The overall picture of the first-to-second tier relation in Canadian federalism, thus, shows an autonomy model with a quite significant tendency towards the mixed model. Interestingly, the provinces did not copy the first-to-second tier budget rules for their relation to the municipalities, and implemented an integration model instead. While many municipalities might appear to work quite independently, they are still subject to the superior authority of the provincial government with ultimate funding responsibility. Debt acquisition is strictly constrained. The provinces can tighten the reins if necessary and desirable to strengthen the municipalities' financial performance.

2.2 France

France is widely regarded as the prime example of a centralist state, with all strings being pulled in Paris. This has changed. The process of decentralisation picked up speed under the Presidency of Francois Mitterand. Important legislative changes, conceptionalised by interior minister Gaston Defferre, were brought on their way in the 1980s. Most importantly, they would grant locally elected representatives the administrative power to manage their own affairs. Priorly, the prefect, the central state's representative, i.e., Paris' agent, was equipped with vast powers to decide upon matters of local governance in the départements. With the decentralisation reforms, Paris loosened its reins, but the central government and legislator still holds the reins in its hand and has the final responsibility for fiscal management.

The French Constitution guarantees the subnational entities (1st subnational level: regions, 2nd subnational level: départements, 3rd subnational level: municipalities) an original area of self-governance[141] for those matters which may be best managed at the local level. Different from any other country in the country-specific analysis of this chapter, the French Constitution does not grant the subnational entities any original legislative authority.[142] While the subnational entities may manage their own affairs, they do so within the limits of the laws as they are enacted in Paris.[143] The prefect acts as Paris' agent to monitor and control the local governments.[144] The prefect's main responsibility is to evaluate as to whether the acts of the local governments confirm with the national laws. Since the central government defines the framework of administrative action for the subnational entities by its national laws,[145] and since spending authority is naturally linked to the local governments' administrative authority, Paris defines the limits within which local spending may be managed independently by the local authorities. Subnational representatives, nonetheless, have influence collectively by initiating and influencing legislation in the Senate, the upper house of the French parliament, which assembles representatives elected by local officials across the country.

While the subnational entities in France enjoy some autonomy when it comes to spending, they have very little influence on the revenue to cover their ongoing budgetary expenses. Article 72-2 of the French Constitution says that "Tax revenue and other own revenue of territorial communities shall, for each category of territorial community, represent a decisive share

141 Article 72 Constitution of France of October 4, 1958.

142 In a federalist state, the constitution typically prescribes which level of government may enact laws for which matters; regularly, with the default rule that subnational entities have legislative authority for all possible areas of law-making not explicitly delegated to the federal government.

143 Article 24 Constitution of France of October 4, 1958 says in its first sentence: "Parliament shall pass statutes."

144 The correct terminology is *préfet de region* for the prefect of the regions, *préfet* for the prefect of the départements, and *sous-préfet* for the prefect of the municipalities.

145 Article 72-2 Constitution of France of October 4, 1958, 1 sentence 1 says: "Territorial communities shall enjoy revenue of which they may dispose freely in the conditions determined by statute".

of their revenue." The Constitution, however, does not grant the subnational entities original tax authority. The subnational entities shall receive own and/or shared taxes and grants which shall be sufficient to cover the costs of their delegated administrative responsibilities.[146] The Constitution does not establish rights to specific taxes. The central legislator can design and also modify the revenue package of taxes and grants for regions, départements, and municipalities. The subnational entities may modify the rate of selected taxes but only if a statue has authorized them to choose a rate and only within the range as it is defined by the statue. Other revenues, such as fees collected for the use of local services, make up only for a small portion of the total revenues necessary to cover the local responsibilities.[147] Eventually, it is fair to say that the revenue available to cover the ongoing local budgetary expenses is largely determined in Paris.

So, it is only consequential that the Constitution requires the central legislator to install an equalisation scheme.[148] While it makes a lot of sense to allow local entities to enjoy higher revenues if their revenue is influenced by their choice and effort, there is little reason not to re-distribute if high or low revenues are mostly the result of coincidence, i.e., if the subnational entities have little influence on the revenue side. The equalisation scheme in France, nonetheless, is of relative minor importance, e.g., if compared to the enormous equalisation scheme in Germany, which is mostly because of a relatively even distribution of wealth across the local communities.[149]

So far, the French fiscal strategy resembles quite closely the integration model. Local budgetary decisions are controlled top-down by the central government/legislator. Significantly, the latitude for spending is defined by the revenue on which the local authorities have little influence, at least concerning taxation and grants. Additional funds may only be sourced from debt financing. In the integration model, the central authority has generally two choices: First, the central government can allow the local governments to raise debts without a qualified limit and without further

146 Article 72-2 Constitution of France of October 4, 1958, sentence 6 and 7 say: "Whenever powers are transferred between central government and the territorial communities, revenue equivalent to that given over to the exercise of those powers shall also be transferred. Whenever the effect of newly created or extended powers is to increase the expenditure to be borne by territorial communities, revenue as determined by statute shall be allocated to said communities."

147 VIOLA JULIEN, 'Französische Gebietskörperschaften' (2012, 5 October) Helaba Volkswirtschaft/Research 2–4.

148 See section III. 3.4.3.

149 JULIEN (2012) 5–6.

conditions and it can guarantee the locally acquired debt with a bailout promise so as to lower the interest rates for debt finance. If this, however, is the case, the central government will have to tighten the strings if the central government wants to avoid a situation of overspending and overindebtness. It has to monitor and, as the case may be, it has to intervene, i.e., control and correct spending decisions. Second, the central government can establish tight rules for debt acquisition. In this case, the central government can loosen the strings. If the spending budget cannot be increased by debt, the risk of burden shifting is contained. Thus, the central government can relax monitoring and let the local governments dispose freely of their allocated revenues in taxes and grants. The French have opted for the second alternative, which allows decentralisation of spending authority without creating perverse incentives to overfish the common pool.

The local governments are prohibited from acquired debt to finance a possible budget deficit. They are required by law to present an annually balanced budget. The only reason for which they may acquire debt are capital investments (similar as it is the case for municipalities in Canada). The costs of debt repayment have to be accounted for as compulsory expenditures in the annual budget. Thus, an increase in borrowing forces the local government to cut spending elsewhere unless revenues from taxes, grants, or fees increase.[150]

Compliance with the budget rules is enforced by a supervisory system: The subnational entities deposit their cash in a central account. A local representative in charge of local budget decisions, e.g., the mayor, makes a payment order. A civil servant of the central government, the public accountant, checks if the payment confirms with the budget rules and rejects the payment order otherwise. The public accountant is personally liable to perform this duty with due care. The local representative may overrule the public accountant's decision but assumes personal liability in this case.[151] The annual local budget, which has to list all expenditures and revenues, is reviewed by the prefect. If the prefect finds a violation of the budget rules, importantly, the balanced budget rule, an adjustment process sets in. The case is submitted to the Regional Chamber of Accounts. The local government can modify the budget in this process. Eventually, a revised budget

---

150 LILI LIU, NORBERT GAILLARD, and MICHAEL WEIBEL, 'France's Subnational Insolvency Framework' in Otaviano Canuto and Lili Liu (eds) *Until Debt Do Us Part* (The World Bank 2013) 230 and 238–240.

151 LIU, GAILLARD, and WEIBEL (2013) 236–238.

may be approved or the prefect will implement a budget with recommendations made by the chamber, overruling the local budget as it was originally planned and approved by the local authorities.[152]

The French model may be best compared to a single firm with multiple regional branches which has adopted a policy of decentralised management. Each regional branch may be managed by its regional director. The board, however, will set out guidelines within which the regional directors manage the affairs as it best fits the particularities of the region in which they operate. A control system is established to check as to whether the regional directors comply with this guidelines. A regional branch may operate quite independently, one may say 'autonomously' but its 'autonomy' is conditional upon being in line with the board's guidelines. In France, that is quite similar. The legislative authority is in Paris and Paris sets the frame within which the subnational entities manage their own affairs. The spending budget is limited by the expected taxes, grants, and fees. Debt is only available for capital investments. Since debt repayment and interest costs are accounted for as compulsory expenses, debt acquisition forces spending cuts or an increase in taxes insofar as the local governments are entitled by statue to adjust the tax rate. Prefects, the Regional Chambers of Accountants, and public accountants supervise the local budgetary process together. As a consequence thereof, the debt levels of the subnational entities remain very modest and only account for a small portion of the aggregated government debt.[153] Thereby, the tight budget rules allow the subnational entities some 'autonomy' in making budget decisions with the available resources. This is especially notable in comparison to the neighbouring country Germany (see IV. 2.3).

While the French fiscal architecture origins from the integration model, there are some deviations. First of all, while the French have managed the decentralisation process in a way which allows the local governments to allocate resources available as it best fits the local needs but which contains the risk of overspending and overindebtness quite well with tight budget rules, the French could have done even better. Prior to the reforms targeted towards decentralisation, the prefect had to authorise debt acquisition and check as to whether it would be in the local and national interests (not only as to whether it is lawful, as today). Debt was acquired from a central government authority at favourable interest rates. The decentralisation reforms of the 1980s abolished the tight oversight without appropriate re-

152 LIU, GAILLARD, and WEIBEL (2013) 230–236.

153 JULIEN (2012) 6–7.

placement. Several subnational entities manoeuvred themselves into serious financial distress within the next years.[154] As reaction to this, new budget rules were introduced, of which the most important rules were discussed in this section.[155] It would, however, have been better to reinstate the old regime for borrowing with a central debt agency and the prefect as the central government's agent with wide discretionary power. This would have best fit the fiscal regime which so closely mirrors the integration model. A second glitch in the design of the fiscal architecture is the multiplying of responsibilities between the four levels of government (central, region, département, municipality) in many areas. If responsibilities are not clearly assigned to one level of government, this causes unnecessary coordination costs, possibly unnecessary spending for double/triple/quadruple functions, and it also weakens the accountability for a diligent budget.[156]

Institutional congruence as the mainstay of financial sustainability is within close reach. A few adjustments towards a tighter debt regulation with central debt authority and responsibility would make for an institutionally congruent design. The subnational entities may still allocate their resources from grants and (adjustable) taxes towards the best local use, so as to offer a public good which best corresponds with the local preferences. The example of the firm with self-governance conditional upon intervention top-down illustrates how decentralisation works smoothly in the integration model. Alternatively, France could make a bold move towards actual decentralisation, abolish the budget rules and allocate original tax rights sufficient to cover all expenditures to the subnational entities, ideally accompanied by an insolvency regime for subnational public debtors. This, however, would turn the French fiscal architecture upside down. An easy and effective solution instead would be to take the last few steps towards an institutionally congruent integration model.

---

154 LIU, GAILLARD, and WEIBEL (2013) 246.

155 For the development of subnational debt, (risks of) financial distress, debt adjustments, and budget rules in France see LIU, GAILLARD, and WEIBEL (2013), especially 238–253.

156 For the problem of an diffuse distribution of responsibilities see: PETER GEY and BENJAMIN SCHREIBER, 'Frankreich: Wird der Staat jetzt umgebaut?' (2014) Working Paper Friedrich Ebert Stiftung.

2.3 Germany

The German model of federalism is elusive. At least the commonly used terms 'centralisation' and 'decentralisation' do not really describe German federalism. That was different for a long time. History shows a tradition of strongly autonomous German states connected via a loose federation, eventually united in the German Empire in 1871.

After WWII, the first proposal by the 'Herrenchiemseer Verfassungskonvent' for post-WWII Germany envisioned a consequently decentralised federation while the second proposal by the parliamentary council, soon thereafter, would have meant a strong concentration of important fiscal competences at the federal level; an ambition, which did not please the Allied Powers. A compromise was found which would eventually become the German Basic Law (Grundgesetz) and which did neither fulfill the institutional requirements of a consequently decentralised nor of a consequently centralised fiscal regime. The result was a hybrid to the core.[157]

In Germany, the legislative power is highly concentrated at the federal level. Even though Art. 70 (1) Basic Law states that the legislative power rests with the Länder unless the federal government is especially empowered, the following articles make clear: the legislative power has been largely allocated to the federal level.[158] The Länder, notably, maintain exclusive legislative authority in the areas of public safety, education, and culture.

Nonetheless, the Länder governments play an important role in the law-making process at the federal level. The Länder governments are represented in the state house (Bundesrat) with between three to six votes each. Dependent delegates of the Länder governments (not independent representatives) vote. Several laws at the federal level require the approval in both the national parliament (Bundestag) and the Bundesrat. For other laws, the Bundesrat may interpose its veto, but the veto may be rejected by a (qualified) majority in the Bundestag.[159]

With the exception of some minor taxes and tariffs, the major tax laws require the approval in both the Bundestag and the Bundesrat for their enactment and modification.[160] The tax rates for the most important personal income, corporate, and sales tax are set at the national level. They are uniform across the country with no option for the Länder to divert from

157 BLANKART (2017) 471–473.

158 Artt. 73, 74, and 105 (for taxes) Basic Law.

159 Art. 77 (3) and (4) Basic Law.

160 Artt. 105, 106 Basic Law.

the single national path and to levy a higher/lower/additional tax on the centrally determined tax bases. Regarding legislative and taxation authority, the German fiscal model shows a very high degree of centralisation; with the particularity that the decentralised units (the Länder) are part of the centralised decision-making process; a decision-making process which eventually results in a uniform solution for the entire country.

When it comes to the execution of the centrally enacted laws, however, the German approach is the direct opposite. The Länder execute the federal laws 'as their own affair', except in specially prescribed cases where the federal government, naturally, has the executive power (e.g., national defense, foreign relations).[161] The Länder have wide discretion regarding the application of the law as it fits best for their special purpose. The execution of the federal law is under federal supervision and subject to top-down directives only in so far as the federal government is especially entitled to such powers by the Basic Law. An important case thereof is Art. 104 (3) Basic Law, which provides that the Länder execute federal laws under the supervision of the federal government if the law creates pecuniary entitlements and if the federal government bears at least half of the costs. The rule, however, remains that the Länder administer and concretise the federal laws in practice and that each level of government (federal or Länder government) has to pay the expenditures of their own administration.[162] Matching grants, i.e., conditional transfers, shall only be made in the cases pre-determined by the Basic Law (joint-tasks, administration under federal supervision).[163] The prohibition of additional matching grants shall prevent the federal government from influencing the Länder by ruling, as it is commonly said, with "golden reins".[164]

In order to fund their expenditures, the federal government, the Länder, and the municipal governments have to collect taxes. While there are some taxes which are exclusively received by the federal government,[165] the

161 Artt. 86, 87 Basic Law.

162 For the rule see: Art. 30 and Artt. 83, 84 Basic Law. For the funding rule: Art. 104a (1) and (5) Basic Law and Art. 109 (1) Basic Law.

163 For the exceptions see: Art. 85 Basic Law for administration under federal supervision, and 104a (2), (3), and (4) Basic Law; Artt. 91a to 91e Basic Law and 104a (4) Basic Law for cooperative federal and Länder administration.

164 For a discussion of the German federalist regime before the federalism reform II see: THOMAS DÖRING and STEFAN VOIGT, 'Reforming Federalism German Style: A First Step in the Right Direction' (2006) July/August, Intereconomics 201.

165 Art. 106 (1) Basic Law.

Länder governments,[166] and the municipal governments,[167] taxes which yield the most significant tax returns are uniform across the country and shared amongst the three levels of government: the personal income tax, the corporate tax, and the sales tax.[168] The Länder' and municipalities' share of the shared taxes is calculated according to the place of residence or operating business site, respectively. This is different for the sales tax. The German equalisation scheme already begins with the distribution of the Länder/municipal share of the sales tax. Three quarters are distributed on a per capita base whereas one quarter is distributed disproportionally according to a key which favours the Länder with a below than average tax income (in a calculation excluding the sales tax income).[169]

In a next step, the actual financial endowment, calculated as tax revenue per capita of every Land and 64 % of tax income of its municipalities is compared to the average financial endowment per capita across the Länder. This formula is modified in so far as the population of some Länder, notably of the federal city states Berlin, Bremen, and Hamburg, is calculated with a favourable multiplier. Those Länder with a below than average financial endowment are entitled to receive equalisation transfers. Those Länder with an higher than average financial endowment are obliged to pay equalisation transfers. The amount received from or paid to the equalisation scheme in horizontal transfers is calculated according to a formula which varies with the positive or negative difference between the Land's actual and the average financial endowment.[170] The horizontal

166 Art. 106 (2) Basic Law.

167 Art. 106 (3) Basic Law: Most importantly, the municipalities can collect the property and local business tax and, in principle, set their own tax rates therefor. The municipalities tax autonomy has, however, been heavily curtailed by case law. In consequence, the municipalities can only set their own tax rates within a narrow scope. This issue was raised in a case, where a municipality had set the tax factor down in order to attract businesses. The court ordered that the municipality had to raise a certain tax minimum. See the discussion of Decision of the German Federal Constitutional Court, BVerfGE 125, 141 (27 January 2010) in BLANKART (2017) 442–443.

168 Art. 106 (3) to (5a) Basic Law.

169 Art. 107 (1) Basic Law. See the Law about the Financial Equalisation between Federation and Länder § 1 and § 2.

170 See the Law about the Financial Equalisation between Federation and Länder § 4 to § 10.

equalisation scheme has a very significant effect on the Länder budgets.[171] 77.5 per cent of the (relatively small) difference to 99.5 per cent of the mean financial endowment which remains after the horizontal equalisation transfers have been executed is filled up with vertical equalisation transfers. East German Länder receive additional transfer payments for their structural development.[172] In the end, all Länder have fairly the same financial endowment.[173]

In 2020, the current equalisation scheme shall be replaced by a new, so-called 'vertical' equalisation scheme. The share of the Länder in the distribution of the sales tax shall be increased (approx. 4 additional bn euros p.a.). The sales tax shall continue to be distributed on a per capita basis with the current favourable multiplier for certain Länder in the per capita-calculation. The Länder' share from the sales tax pool shall be adjusted to the Länder' financial endowment, calculated on a linear base of 63 per cent. The tax revenue of the municipalities will be accounted for with 75 per cent instead of 64 per cent. The federal government will increase its commitment furthermore and fill up the difference to 99.75 per cent of the mean financial endowment with 80 per cent of the difference, after the first step of equalisation via the sales tax transfers will have taken place.

---

171 In CLEMENS FUEST and MICHAEL THÖNE, *Reform des Finanzföderalismus in Deutschland* (Stiftung Marktwirtschaft 2009), the authors illustrate (at page 46) the effect of the horizontal financial equalisation scheme. While the financially strongest Land would have 120 % of the average financial endowment per capita available before it has to pay its contribution and while the financially weakest Land would have 67 % of the average financial endowment per capita available before it receives its equalisation transfer, the financially strongest Land would have 107 % and the financially weakest Land would have 90 % of the average financial mean after the transfers have been effected.

172 See the Law about the Financial Equalisation between Federation and Länder § 11 (2) and (3) and (3a). Smaller Länder (10 out of 16) receive an additional transfer to compensate them for relatively high overhead costs. See the Law about the Financial Equalisation between Federation and Länder § 11 (4).

173 For an empirical investigation of the German tax-revenue sharing and equalisation scheme see: RALF HEPP and JÜRGEN VON HAGEN, 'Fiscal Federalism in Germany: Stabilisation and Redistribution Before and After Unification' (2010) ZEI Working Paper B 02. The authors examine the period 1970 to 2006 and find a significant re-distributive effect. In TIMM BÖNKE, BEATE JOCHIMSEN, and CARSTEN SCHRÖDER, 'Fiscal Federalism and Tax Administration: Evidence from Germany' (2013) DIW Discussion Paper 1307, the authors discuss the distortion that the equalisation scheme brings to the incentives of the German local units when it comes to making investments for an efficient tax enforcement.

Moreover, the federal government will directly channel funds to the municipalities and fill the gap from the respective municipality's financial endowment to 80 per cent of the mean municipal financial endowment with a contribution of 53.5 per cent (of the difference). Federal funds for structural development, with new funds for research promotion, will continue to flow in order to especially benefit financially weak Länder.[174]

The complex German equalisation programme currently pulls all Länder close to 100 % of the mean financial endowment. The new equalisation scheme is unlikely to make a significant difference. The simple fact that formal horizontal and vertical equalisation will be replaced by formal vertical equalisation is likely to be nothing than a new label for the same product. As discussed in III. 3.4.3, vertical equalisation is horizontal equalisation in a different colour, since all tax resources are first raised regionally and then re-distributed disproportionally in order to achieve the desired equalisation.

If a Land, eventually, wants to spend more than it receives in own taxes, shared taxes, and equalisation transfers, the Land will have to acquire debt. While the formal equalisation scheme is designed to equalise present revenues, the German system of common pool financing in debt acquisition allows subnational governments which have performed comparatively weak in the past to partly shift the debt burden towards other subnational units and towards the federal government. If all subnational units were exclusively responsible for their debts (no bailout expectation), the risk-adjusted costs of debt capital for the outstanding debt would still have to be subtracted from the (equalised) tax revenue stream; i.e., there would be an incentive to avoid excessive debts and overspending.

The rules of the game are, however, entirely different in the presence of a strong bailout expectation. First, the cost of debt capital are not adjusted to the individual risk of any subnational unit but to the accumulated risk of the multi-tier union. In case of Germany, this means that also the worst public debtor benefits from the strong creditworthiness of the entire union which guarantees its debt. Debt becomes an temptingly cheap option. Second, the hard budget constraint vanishes. If a Land wants to spend more than it receives in (shared) taxes (minus present debt payments), it can do

174 See BUNDESREGIERUNG, 'Neuregelung des bundesstaatlichen Finanzausgleichs 2020' (Pressemitteilung 369, 14 October 2016); LARS FELD, CLEMENS FUERST, JUSTUS HAUCAP, HEIKE SCHWEIZER, VOLKER WIELAND, and BERTHOLD WIGGER, 'Für eine echte Reform der Bund-Länder-Finanzbeziehung' (2016) 62 Kronberger Kreis, Stiftung Marktwirtschaft 31–41.

so by acquiring additional debt. And this is pretty much an accurate description of the German model of equalisation via bailout subsidies. In 1992, the Federal Constitutional Court ordered the bailout of the Länder Bremen and Saarland when their debt level became unsustainable.[175] In 2006, the Federal Constitutional Court rejected the Land Berlin's request for a bailout. While it is arguable as to whether the Federal Constitutional Court has increased the requirements for a bailout request, it is without doubt that the Federal Constitutional Court did not weaken the bailout expectation. Berlin was not in default and the court made clear that Berlin had to take more serious measures before it could request a bailout as an 'ultima ratio'. As the court pointed out, the budgetary situation of Berlin was taunt but not a case of budgetary emergency. Berlins per capita expenses in many areas of public spending were disproportionally high if compared to other (comparable) Länder. So, there was no reason why Berlin should not first undertake measures itself to balance its budget.[176]

The design of the German federal fiscal architecture is an open invitation for high debt levels. The Länder have little influence on the tax revenue stream. If they need to/desire to increase spending, they have to raise further debts, which are cross-subsidised by a strong bailout expectation to the advantage of the financially weak Länder. In order to keep indebtness within limits, the Basic Law was modified to include a debt brake which would bind the federal government and the Länder, i.e., a self-binding rule for the federal government and a top-down imposed rule for the Länder. Art. 109 (3) Basic Law regulates that the federal budget and the Länder budgets have to be balanced in so far as the expenditures shall not exceed the tax income. Federal and Länder governments may debt-finance part of their expenditures in order to adjust their budget to the business cycle. Deficits from times of cyclical downturns have to be compensated for by savings in times of cyclical upturns. An exception from this rule is provided for natural catastrophes and crises. The federal government has the privilege to add a 'structural component' to the calculation, so that debt income of 0.35 per cent of the GDP may be added to the tax revenue to balance the expenditures. This option does not exist for the Länder.[177] The re-

175 Decision of the German Federal Constitutional Court, BVerfGE 86, 148 (27 May 1992).

176 Decision of the German Federal Constitutional Court, BVerfGE 116, 327 (19 October 2006).

177 Art. 115 Basic Law concretises Art. 109 (3) Basic Law for the federal budget. The accumulated deficit as a result of anti-cyclical debt acquisition may not exceed 1.15 per cent of the BIP.

quirements set by the debt brake are mandatory for the federal budget from 2016 onwards and for the Länder from 2020 onwards.

The third-tier level of government has a constitutionally guaranteed right to manage its local affairs 'autonomously' with own funds.[178] The German municipalities regularly perform tasks in local administration which they find themselves or which are assigned to them by the Länder. Such tasks include, for example, the operation of schools, cultural institutions, and transportation. They are subject to top-down directives in so far as they perform tasks on behalf of the Land. In order to fund their expenditures, municipalities receive a share of the personal income tax and the sales tax. They levy the property tax and additional taxes under the condition that the tax base is not already occupied by the federal or Länder governments (e.g. tourism tax), as well as they can charge user fees for public services. A significant share of their revenues comes from transfers received from the superior government of the Land. The law of the Länder vary to the degree of equalisation in horizontal/vertical transfers for the municipal finances.[179]

In practice, most German municipalities struggle with empty coffers. An often heard complaint is that the Länder transfers are not sufficient to cover the costs of mandated public services. While not sustainable in the long run, this might reveal a burden-shifting strategy of the Länder to window-dress their budget, quite likely under the pressure of the debt brake. In case of a municipality's factual insolvency, nevertheless, the superior level of government will have to carry the burden of a bailout. The possibility of a municipal insolvency procedure has been explicitly ruled out.[180] In case of deep financial distress, a municipality may be deprived of its autonomy in administration and it may be made subject to forced administration by the Land.

Measured against the institutional congruence standard, Germany is a mess. While the legislative power is highly concentrated, the direct opposite is true for the executive authority. The Länder concretise the law and perform essential public services. They are truly autonomous when making spending decisions. The Länder have, however, no latitude when it

---

178 Art. 28 (2) Basic Law.

179 CHRISTIAN BARETTI, 'Wird gute Standortpolitik bestraft? Die Anreizeffekte des kommunalen Finanzsystems' (2002) 7 ifo Schnelldienst 10.

180 BLANKART and EHMKE (2014). See also § 12 (1) No. 2 InsO (German Insolvency Law) allows the Länder to exclude the option of insolvency for their third-tier units. This option has been used by all German Länder.

comes to taxation. The major taxes are uniform across the country and determined at the federal level. There is no tax competition and no effective way to balance increased spending by correspondingly adjusting the tax rate. The Länder can only influence their budget by cutting expenditures or by acquiring debt. A complex and tight equalisation scheme is targeted to eradicate almost all performance differences. The bailout guarantee for the Länder creates a strong incentive to regulate the budget via indebtness. The combination of autonomy in spending and debt acquisition with a centralised tax authority is toxic. As to whether the newly introduced debt brake can function as a bulwark against indebtness is very questionable. Creative accounting is likely to be expected. The federal budget does not account for the guarantees and loans granted to Greece with the actual default probability. It remains to be seen how creative the 'political accountants' will be when presenting future budgets. The temptation to 'manipulate' the accounts so as to fulfill the conditions of the debt brake is high. [181]

While the German approach, in fact, can equalise the conditions of public services across the nation, it fails to promote financial performance. The lower levels of government are autonomous in making spending and debt acquisition decisions while the safety net of the bailout guarantee allows them to behave carelessly. Those who will have to pay the costs of a bailout, the union of the Länder and the federal government have little to no influence to prevent individual members of the union not to exploit the opportunities of common pool financing to the disadvantage of the entire multi-tier union. Considering that the German fiscal system fits the very definition of institutional incongruence, gradual reforms are of little help. The German fiscal architecture requires a remoulding. The way towards integration as well as towards autonomy is long. If the Germans do not want to abandon the federalist system and opt for the integration model in a centralist state, the only way towards financial sustainability is the way back to the ideas of the 'Herrenchiemseer Verfassungskonvent'; the ideas of a federal union with consequently decentralised tax, spending, and debt autonomy.

181 Bremen, for instance, presented a budget for 2016, where the costs associated with the care for refugees were excluded from the budget. See FREIE HANSESTADT BREMEN, Bericht der Freien Hansestadt Bremen vom September 2016 zur Umsetzung des Sanierungsprogramms 2012/2016. This attempt to 'windowdressed' the budget was heavily criticised by the other Länder and the Stability Council.

2.4 Switzerland

The history of Switzerland is the story of the successful striving for autonomy. It is a story with three dimensions about Switzerland as a small but autonomous country amongst the European super-powers, about the Swiss model of democracy as the archetypical example for the bottom-up rule by the people in direct democracy, and about the Swiss federal system organised according to the principle of 'subsidiarity'.[182]

The principle of 'subsidiarity' is firmly established in the Federal Constitution of the Swiss Confederation (hereinafter, Constitution). The legislative power rests with the 26 cantons (second-tier) unless it has been explicitly delegated to the federal level (first-tier) by the constitution.[183] Moreover, the execution of federal laws is principally assigned to the cantons. The cantons shall be granted an as high as practically possible scope of action to model the 'best fit' administrative solution for their residents.[184] The decision-making power and, naturally related to this, the spending authority are assigned to the federal level or the cantonal level according to the principle that legislative and executive power is best decentralised to the cantonal level, unless centralisation to the federal level promises to yield a surplus to the Swiss citizens. The Constitution does not guarantee a uniform autonomy standard to the Swiss municipalities (third-tier of government). The Constitution, however, obliges the federal government to consider the impact of its policy on the Swiss municipalities and to recognise their autonomy "in accordance with cantonal law".[185] While the degree of autonomy varies by canton, the principle of 'subsidiarity' is widely understood as a constitutive principle also in the second-to-third tier relation, so that municipalities often perform important public services on the local level on their own.

In order to fund their expenditures, the federal, the cantonal, and the municipal governments may raise taxes and acquire debts. The federation's, cantons', and municipalities' power, respectively, to fund their expenditures by taxation and debt acquisition, however, is not without lim-

182 For a theoretical analysis of the Swiss model see: CHARLES BLANKART, 'An Economic Theory of Switzerland' (2011) 3 CESifo DICE Report 74. See also BLANKART (2017) 485–495.

183 Art. 3 Swiss Constitution and Art. 5a Swiss Constitution as amended by referendum in 2004. See further: Artt. 42, 43, 43a Swiss Constitution.

184 Art. 43 Swiss Constitution.

185 Art. 50 Swiss Constitution.

its. The Swiss federal architecture incorporates varies institutions 'to keep Leviathan in check':

On the federal level, the Constitution specifies which kind of taxes the federal government may levy. Importantly, it sets an upper limit for many taxes, such as for the federal personal income and federal business income tax of 11.5 and 8.5 per cent, respectively.[186] The federal government's option to resort to debt financing as an alternative to taxation is limited as well. The federal debt/deficit brake, implemented by a nationwide referendum, prohibits the federal government to run deficits over the course of a business cycle. The federal government may not spend more than it raises in tax revenues. The expenditures may not exceed the projected tax income adjusted to the business cycle [i.e., estimated revenues × (real trend GDP ÷ actual GDP)]. So, the government can spend and tax anti-cyclically, i.e., generate a surplus in times of a boom and run a deficit in times of recession. Deficits which may occur as a consequence of projection errors or of a violation of the debt brake have to be compensated for in future budgets.[187] The debt brake is fortified by the fact that it was established by a referendum. A government violating the debt brake would position itself in direct opposition to the articulated will of the people.[188]

For the cantons, there is no limit to taxation and debt acquisition in the Swiss Constitution. This follows logically from the principle of autonomy. If the citizens of a cantons wish to limit their government's power to tax and to acquire debt, they may enact a debt brake or an upper tax limit themselves. Many cantons have made use of this strategy to curtail excessive spending, taxation, and debt acquisition.[189] Typical for the Swiss model and of even more significance than formal limitations to taxation and indebtness, taxation is limited by inter-cantonal tax competition as well as indebtness is kept under control by the no bailout principle:

First, while the cantons are in principle free to set their own tax rates, the tax may be best understood as a price for the cantonal public good. Every citizen can make a calculation as to whether the comparative benefit of another canton's price-product mix minus the switching costs yields a sur-

186 Art. 128 Swiss Constitution.

187 Art. 126 Swiss Constitution.

188 LARS FELD and GEBHARD KIRCHGÄSSNER, 'On the Effectiveness of Debt Brakes: The Swiss Experience' in Reinhard Neck and Jan-Egbert Sturm (eds) *Sustainability of Public Debts* (MIT Press 2008) 223, especially 241–244.

189 GEBHARD KIRCHGÄSSNER, 'Fiscal Institutions at the Cantonal Level in Switzerland' (2013) 149 (2) Swiss Journal of Economics and Statistics 139. See also: FELD and KIRCHGÄSSNER (2008).

plus, so that he/she could gain from an exit. The cantonal government has an inherent incentive to conduct the same calculation and estimate how much taxation its citizens will accept as a price for the public good before they exit or elect another government. The exit threat is even more convincing, since high taxes on high incomes could also be backed by a middle-to-low income majority in elections if there was no exit threat. The tax competition in Switzerland becomes especially tense with the large number of cantons on relatively small geographical space, which indicates relatively low switching costs.[190]

Second, the cantonal governments cannot easily circumvent the natural tax limits by raising debt so as to shift the tax burden to future generations. To put it differently, they cannot circumvent the tax limits by way of 'fiscal illusion.' While there has been no federal bailout of a canton as well as there has been no default of a canton, it is fair to say that the market's expectation is that there will be no bailout in case of a default. When several cantons got into serious financial distress, the question of a federal bailout was not considered as a feasible option. This follows logically and convincingly from the broad spending and tax autonomy of the cantons, i.e., their own-responsibility for their debts and their own capacity to raise revenues to pay off their debts.[191]

Eventually, the no-bailout principle, as it was confirmed by the Federal Supreme Court of Lausanne[192] for the second-to-third tier relation between cantons and municipalities, must apply to the first-to-second tier relation between the federal government and the cantons, following the *a fortiori*-argument: A canton may set the standard between integration and autonomy for its municipalities by its own law. While the cantons often grant their municipalities substantial rights to manage their budget autonomously, they typically retain a right of last action to intervene. If even in such a relation of controlled or conditional budget autonomy the no-bailout principle applies, it must apply all the more in a case of unconditional autonomy, which is profoundly the description of the first-to-second tier relation between the federal government and the cantons in Switzerland.

190 On tax competition in Switzerland see: LARS FELD, *Braucht die Schweiz eine materielle Steuerharmonisierung?* (economiesuisse 2009).

191 On the established no-bailout expectation in Switzerland (e.g. no assistance to financially distressed cantons/no bailout of the insolvent municipality Leukerbad) see: CHARLES BLANKART, 'Swiss Role–What the Eurozone Could Learn from Switzerland' (2015) 2 CESifo Forum 39.

192 *Leukerbad v Valais*, 2C.4/2000 (3 July 2003, Federal Supreme Court).

For the municipal level, the limitation to taxation and indebtness comes from two distinct sets of formal/informal institutions. The first kind of formal institutions comprises cantonal laws. The cantons can make laws which allow the municipalities to raise taxes and fees within the limits defined by the canton. There is no original municipal power to do so, but only a mandated power. The question as to whether and under which conditions the municipalities are entitled to run deficits and to acquire debts is, similarly, a matter of discretion for the cantonal legislator. Many cantons have opted for a model of controlled or conditional autonomy. The municipalities would be given rights to tax so as to raise sufficient funds for their own expenditures while they could alternatively acquire debt. Budget autonomy would be the principle while it would be controlled and conditional in so far as the cantonal government would retain a supervision and intervention right. The insolvency of Leukerbad, a case which was decided by the Supreme Court of Lausanne, is an excellent example for the principle of subsidiarity applied also to the lowest level of regional government. It illustrates the functioning of the no-bailout principle and market control. At the same time, it exemplifies the idea of controlled autonomy as a final reaction to a municipality's insolvency with the institution of cantonal intervention in form of 'Beiratschaft.'

The story of Leukerbad's insolvency goes as follows: The government of the small municipality Leukerbad, with less than 2000 residents, had big dreams. The goal was to play in the first league of tourism in Switzerland. Massive investments in luxurious facilities, such as a new thermal bath, soon overreached the financial capacity of the small municipality, which ended up with approx. 350 million CHF debt. Up until to the point of Leukerbad's factual insolvency, Leukerbad had managed its budget autonomously. It had made investments, and since it could not raise enough taxes for that purpose, it acquired debt instead. This was a risky bet and the creditors did participate in this speculative venture. Eventually, the investments did not pay off and Leukerbad was in default. The punishment came twofold: First, the government of the canton Valais placed the municipal Leukerbad under forced administration (Beiratschaft). Leukerbad lost its budget autonomy and, from now on, it was subject to central government control. The condition (default) upon which conditional autonomy would turn into a regime of supervision and intervention materialised. Second, the government did not step in to relief Leukerbad from its financial burden. The cantonal government pointed out that Leukerbad made its deals autonomously with its creditors, and once the investments did not yield the hoped-for returns, it remained the debtors' and the creditors' responsibility to assume the losses. The Federal Supreme Court in Lausanne confirmed the no-bailout decision of the canton Valais on these grounds. Consequently, the municipal Leukerbad and its creditors were forced to negotiate a debt restructuring deal; a bailout was not feasible. The creditors accepted a major haircut of approx. 80 per cent and Leukerbad was bound to a repayment plan which still requires deep cuts in the municipal budget.[193]

As a reaction to the Leukerbad case, i.e., as a reaction to the confirmation of the no-bailout principle in the second-to-third tier relation, a significant positive effect on the cantons' debt capital costs could be measured, which reflects the markets' now firmly established expectation that the cantons are responsible for their own but not for their municipalities' debts.[194] In Switzerland, each public debtor is responsible for its own debt. No bailout can be expected. Creditors adjust their price expectation to the individual debtor's risk. Different from the ECB in the Eurozone, the Swiss National Bank does not try to manipulate the market. As it will be further discussed in sections V. 3.5.2 and 3.5.3, the ECB has made enormous investments in government bonds issued by its member states. This way, the ECB has become the main creditor to many European governments. As a main creditor, lender of last resort, and crisis manager alike, the ECB has manoeuvred itself in a dangerous conflict of interests. In contrast, the Swiss National Bank buys/holds only insignificant assets in Swiss franc bonds of the federal, cantonal, municipal governments. The debts of the federal, cantonal, and municipal governments remain primarily funded by private market investments. The Swiss National Bank is at no danger to push for a bailout for official debtors so as to protect its own position as a creditor.[195]

Naturally, the informal and formal institutions which contain taxation and debt acquisition, and, consequently, spending on the federal, cantonal, and municipal level set a limitation to re-distribution at the same time. Nevertheless, the public good generally has a high quality in Switzerland, the same as the Swiss citizens enjoy a high welfare standard in form of social security, education, and health.[196] The goal of social integration, i.e.,

193 BLANKART (2017) 489–491; BLANKART and KLAIBER (2006).

194 See the empirical paper by FELD, KALB, MOESSINGER, and OSTERLOH (2013).

195 BLANKART (2015); SWISS NATIONAL BANK, 109th Annual Report 2016, e.g. 78–82, and 155.

196 FELD (2009) 49–53.

the goal to guarantee a public good of nationwide high quality, is inscribed in the Constitution[197] and reflected in the federal architecture in form of an equalisation scheme.[198] The Swiss equalisation scheme is designed as a vertical-horizontal hybrid. Cantons with a below than average financial capacity receive equalisation payments so that their financial capacity may reach a level of 85 per cent of the national average. The financial capacity is calculated based on the taxable income and wealth of the canton's citizens and on the taxable corporate earnings. The federal government contributes to the equalisation payments (vertically) and cantons with a higher than average financial capacity provide an amount between two-thirds and four-fifths of the federal government's contribution (horizontally). Moreover, the federal government makes hardship payments to support cantons which have especially high expenses because of their topographical-geographical or their socio-demographic situation.[199] While the federal government provides matching grants so as to (co-)fund projects of national interests, which may be executed by the cantons, such funds are not designed to particularly favour financially weak cantons. The equalisation concept has been adopted in different shades for the second-to-third and third-to-third tier relations between cantons and municipalities.[200]

The Swiss fiscal regime in federalism comes very close the autonomy model. The distribution of spending, taxation, and debt acquisition authority according to the principle of 'subsidiarity' is institutionally congruent in its design. Some deviations from a model of strict self-responsibility are due to the constitutionally articulated goal of social integration, i.e., to provide a comparatively high standard of the public good nationwide. Notably, the equalisation scheme is implemented to perform this task. While one could argue that the equalisation scheme partly erodes the incentive of the cantonal government to invest into governance reform for economic performance, this effect should be small considering the target standard of 85 per cent of the average. Most importantly, despite the mutually agreed upon equalisation, there will be no bailout. The scope of transfer payments is predictable and limited. Individual members of the multi-tier union cannot spend excessively on the costs of other members so that, albeit some

197 Artt. 41, 43a No. 4 Swiss Constitution.

198 Art. 135 Swiss Constitution.

199 Gesetz über den Finanz- und Lastenausgleich 2003.

200 BLANKART (2017) 491–494. For a discussion of the Swiss welfare concept see: CARLO KNÖPFEL, 'Sozialstaatliche Rahmenbedingungen in der Schweiz' in B Wütherich et al. (eds) *Soziale Versorgung zukunftsfähig gestalten* (Springer 2015).

concessions in favour of social integration, the Swiss model achieves a quite high degree of institutional congruence.

2.5 United States of America

2.5.1 Fiscal Architecture

'E pluribus unum' ('Out of many, one') is the heraldic motto in the Great Seal of the United States of America. Out of many former colonies, out of independent states first loosely related in a confederation, one united federation should emerge in 1787. Independence from the European/British rule was won in battle. Unity was achieved by contract. A contract as the product of unanimous consent requires the parties' belief in its mutual benefit.

While the federation should guarantee its citizens' freedom, it was also expected to support their striving for prosperity. This applies, first, to the (legal) framework which the federation and each state of the federation would create for private activities of business and trade. Justice Louis Brandeis trenchantly pointed out that "It is one of the happy incidents of the federal system that a single courageous State may, if its citizens choose, serve as laboratory; and try novel and economic experiments […]".[201] This applies, second, to the fiscal design of the federation, i.e., to the first-to-second, second-to-second, and second-to-third (and third-to-third) tier relation of federal government, states, and municipalities. The governments' financial performance on different levels is defined by the quality of the public good and the price which the citizens have to pay in tax money. The mutual benefit of a prudent fiscal strategy is characterised by a model which reflects quite perfectly the idea of autonomy in a multi-tier union.

For matters of decision-making, the federal architecture in the first-to-second tier relation in the United States of America is designed according to the principle of subsidiarity. Where there is no gain from centralisation, the rights of legislation (and administration) are decentralised. Also the process of decision-making itself is shaped by the federal spirit, especially by a representation of each state–regardless of its population size–with two senators in the second chamber of Congress. The Tenth Amendment to the United States Constitution expresses the idea of decentralisation: "The Powers not delegated to the United States by the Constitution, nor prohib-

201 NEW STATE ICE CO. V. LIEBMANN, 285 U.S. 262 at 311 (1932).

ited to it by the States, are reserved to the States respectively, or to the people." Congress' rights are enumerated, most importantly, in Art. 1 Section 8. In particular, the Commerce Clause (Art. 1 Section 8 Clause 3) and the Necessary and Proper Clause (Art. 1 Section 8 Clause 18), however, have allowed Congress to extend its power. The Constitution declares the federal power to "lay and collect" taxes in Art. 1 Section 8 Clause 1 with the requirement that the federal tax may be uniform across the country. The Sixteenth Amendment to the US Constitution clarifies that the federal government is empowered to collect an income tax.[202]

As a consequence thereof, the federal government has delegated and the state governments have original powers in legislation and administration. This allows and requires them to make spending decisions for which they need to raise taxes and/or debt. The states have an independent tax authority and generally occupy the major tax sources (or co-occupy them with the federal and/or local government). This combination of autonomous spending and tax authority makes separate and independent budgets credible. Typically, the states collect a state income, a state corporate tax, and a sales tax. Since they are able to adjust the tax rate, they can react to financial shocks. During its tense financial crisis, California, for instance, increased taxes to lower the deficit and to approach a financially more sustainable future.[203]

On the third tier level of government, the scope of decision-making power about spending and revenue collection differs from state to state. The third tier of government in the USA comprises general-purpose districts (e.g. municipalities, townships) and special-purpose districts (e.g. school, water, energy supply, health and care districts). The degree to which these general and special-purpose districts can make spending decisions independent from the state government's direction and to which extent they can raise funds (taxes and debts) on their own without being transfer-dependent is not uniform across the country and varies by state. For general purpose-districts, competences as well as responsibilities differ. This depends, amongst others, on the question as to whether the state applies the home rule or the Dillon's rule in its second-to-third tier relation

---

202 The Sixteenth Amendment follows the Supreme Court's decision in *Pollock v Farmers' Loan & Trust Co.*, in which it was ruled that income taxes as direct tax (in this case a property tax) had to be "apportioned among the several States", according to Art. 1, Section 2, Clause 3 of the Constitution. See POLLOCK V FARMERS' LOAN & TRUST CO. 157 U.S. 429.

203 DAVID SKEEL, 'When Should Bankruptcy be an Option (for People, Places, or Things)? (2014) 55 William & Mary Law Review 2217, 2232–2233.

with the districts. The home rule says that the third tier of government has original and unalienable rights of self-governance. The local units can set the legal framework and release administrative orders to govern their own affairs, i.e., decide about expenditures and revenues out of their own right. In contrast, the Dillon's rule says that a local unit may only have the powers expressly granted to the local unit by the state's legislator. According to the Dillon's rule, the power emanates from expressive delegation.[204] That a state employs the Dillon's rule, however, does not necessarily mean that the third level of government is confined to the narrow path of top-down rule in the integration model. The local governments have to bargain with the state about their status of more or less dependent or independent budgetary governance.[205]

The US fiscal system in the first-to-second tier and second-to-second tier relation entails no formal equalisation mechanism. Neither does the federal government nor do the states contribute to an equalisation fund. Vertical transfers do not flow with the explicit intention to flatten inequalities in the states' financial capacity. Quite generally, vertical transfers are conditional and granted in order to support projects of national interest. From a financial/economic perspective, this has several significant advantages: First, the states' incentives to invest into a diligent budgetary policy are not distorted to the same extent as if the states could rely on unconditional equalisation transfers. Positive and negative effects of budgetary decisions are internalised. Second, if transfers are conditional for specific projects, there is not the same flypaper effect to fear as if the transfers were directly channelled to the general budget. Transfers come with a commitment to specific investments. Third, matching grants allow the federal government to encourage projects with a positive net present value for the country which, otherwise, would have not been undertaken.[206]

---

204 Originally own powers may then only be power which are necessary for the core function of the local unit.

205 On home rule and Dillon's rule see: CLAYTON GILETTE, 'In Partial Praise of Dillon's Rule, or, Can Public Choice Theory Justify Local Government Law' (1991) 67 Chicago-Kent Law Review 959; JESSE RICHARDSON, 'Dillon's Rule is from Mars, Home Rule is From Venus: Local Government Autonomy and the Rules of Statutory Construction' (2011) 41 (4) Publius: The Journal of Federalism 662; JON RUSSELL and AARON BOSTROM, 'Federalism, Dillon Rule and Home Rule' (2016) January, White Paper, American City County Exchange 1. See the Dillon's rule applied in the Supreme Court ruling in HUNTER v PITTSBURGH 207 U.S. 161 (1907).

206 See section III. 3.4.3.

(Conditional) federal funds, however, have primarily two downsides: First, depending on the distribution procedure, a rent-seeking game may result in a dispersion of rents. Second, there is a risk that federal transfer do not benefit the national but primarily the local interests despite the fact that the project itself has a negative net present value. Such an outcome may be the consequence of the regionally based majority voting system for both houses of Congress. In order to boost their chance for re-election, a Congressman/-woman or Senator has every incentive to lobby for federal funds to benefit his/her 'pork barrel'–may the subsidised project actually be benefical to the nation or not. Third, the dependency on federal funds increases the federal governments' influence. This becomes in particular problematic when the federal government does not only provide funds for the financing of selected projects but when the federal government attaches (only distantly related) conditions to its transfers. The federal government's influence on local governments is marred with an information problem. The federal government cannot be expected to possess similarly good information about the local residents' preferences as the local government. It is, eventually, debatable as to whether and to which degree matching grants have an equalisation effect. It is plausible that funds, i.e., directed to support a basic welfare standard, favour poor states disproportionally. It is, nonetheless, fair to say that the equalisation effect of matching grants in the USA does not compare to the equalisation schemes which are designed to lift all regions below the national average (close) to the national average; as this is, for instance, the case in Canada and especially in Germany.[207]

As previously discussed, even in the absence of a formal equalisation scheme, equalisation may be achieved through the back door by way of an explicit or implicit bailout (guarantee). A bailout guarantee would not only achieve equalisation by way of ex post rescue transfers but by a constant interest rate subsidy which would allow financially weak debtors to borrow at the rate of the pooling equilibrium, i.e., on the cost of the financially strongest parts of the union. In the first years of the United States, bailout was the rule. The federal government's bailout commitment in these early years can be viewed as a strategy to strengthen the young nation in unity as well as it can be justified in light of the financial burden which

207 On matching grants, federal assistance to the provision of local public goods in the US see: ROBERT INMAN, 'Federal Assistance and Local Services in the United States: The Evolution of a New Federalist Fiscal Order' in Harvey Rosen (ed) *Fiscal Federalism: Quantitative Studies* (University of Chicago Press 1988) 33.

the nation and its parts had to assume in defense against outside aggression. In the 1840s, the federal government took a bolt move and rejected the request of several members of the union for a bailout. Since then, no state or territory has ever been bailed out. Financial assistance as for the district/capital Washington D.C. in 1997 in a comprehensive bailout and in form of a (relatively minor) interest rate subsidy for a short-term loan in case of New York City in 1975 form the rare exception.[208] The no-bailout rule has strengthened since the 1840s with every default, with every no-bailout, with every private ordering debt restructuring agreement, and with every public ordering debt restructuring procedure. Since the enactment of Chapter 9 in 1934, there have been hundreds of municipal insolvency procedures. The no-bailout expectation is reflected in interest rates adjusted to the individual risk of different subnational US public debtors.[209]

The consequent application of the no-bailout principle for autonomous public debtors has contributed towards a solid financial and economic performance of public entities in the United States. Since the US states are financially self-responsible, i.e., since they cannot expect a bailout, they have widely imposed self-binding budget rules on themselves so as to signal a diligent budgetary policy to the markets.[210] However, where there is fiscal autonomy, there is the chance of success and the risk of failure, just as business activity of autonomous players comes naturally with the risk of insolvency. The USA have found a unique tool to deal with the problems which public debtors in distress and their creditors encounter.

Under Chapter 9 US Bankruptcy Code, an insolvent municipality, i.e., a general-purpose or special-purpose district or public entity on the sub-state level, may enter an orderly insolvency procedure with the authorization of its state. While some states, such as California, have empowered their municipalities to file for insolvency themselves without further review by the state, other state governments retain the right to approve or to veto their

---

208 See INMAN (2013), especially 56–61.

209 BAYOUMI, GOLDSTEIN, and WOGLOM (1995); FAIRCHILD and KOCH (1998).

210 On budget rules in the US see: BOHN and INMAN (1996); THOMAS GARRETT, 'State Balanced-Budget and Debt Rules' (2011) 33 Economic Synopses, Federal Reserve Bank of St. Louis; BYRON LUTZ and GLENN FOLETTE, 'Fiscal Rules, What Does the American Experience Tell Us? (2012) Finance and Economics Discussion Series, Working Paper 2012-38, Federal Reserve Board, Washington D.C.

municipalities' request for the acceleration of Chapter 9 case by case.[211] Chapter 9, in essence, copies the corporate debt restructuring procedure of Chapter 11 with certain modifications. Importantly, there is no threat of liquidation for the public debtor (as in Chapter 7 for the corporate debtor), the petition may only be filled voluntarily by the debtor (not by its creditors),[212] and the court as well as the creditors may not assume political control (and e.g. order higher taxes, specific cuts).[213]

The limited power of the court in municipal insolvency has contributed towards the understanding that Chapter 9 would be first and foremost a debt restructuring device but not an instrument to induce governance reform. This limitation, however, is a lost chance since insolvency is seldom a blow of fate but the consequence of governance mistakes of the past. Especially in the absence of a liquidation alternative, which should encourage the debtor to convince its creditors of the going-concern surplus, governance reform should become an utterly important feature of municipal insolvency. A governance reform oriented approach would not only benefit the creditors in their expected payoff, it could benefit the debtor, especially the debtor's taxpayers, in so far as it would facilitate financial performance ex-ante and ex post.[214]

For the purpose of the (acute) management of a debt crisis, nonetheless, Chapter 9 provides some key institutions: The municipal debtor may borrow money as an administrative expense (i.e. with high priority in the ranking of claims) so as to secure the inflow of liquidity throughout the process.[215] The debtor's proposed plan may become binding for all creditors without unanimous consent, conditional upon that all classes[216] or at

211 § 109(c) Bankruptcy Code, Chapter 1.

212 §§ 303, 901(a) Bankruptcy Code, Chapter 3 and 9.

213 § 903 Bankruptcy Code, Chapter 9.

214 For this criticism on the commonly understood limitation of Chapter 9 to the ex post debt adjustment and for a strong plea in favour of expanding the understanding of Chapter 9 to governance reform see: CLAYTON GILETTE and DAVID SKEEL, 'Governance Reform and the Judicial Role in Municipal Bankruptcy' (2016) 125 The Yale Law Journal 1150. The authors suggest, moreover, that the court's power in plan confirmation based on several conditions and in particular on the condition that the plan has to be 'feasible' would allow the court to encourage governance reform. See therefore pages 1195 to 1202.

215 §§ 364(c), 901(a) Bankruptcy Code, Chapter 9 and 11.

216 §§ 943(b), 901(a), 1129(a)(8) Bankruptcy Code, Chapter 9 and 11. Acceptance requires that creditors half in number (headcount) of a class holding two-thirds in value accept the plan, § 1126(c), Bankruptcy Code, Chapter 11.

least one impaired class of creditors (cram-down)[217] has accepted the plan, and that other criteria, importantly, that the 'plan is in the best interest of creditors and that it is feasible' are fulfilled. This way, collective action problems and prisoner dilemma situations in case of an insufficient pool of assets available for distribution can be resolved.[218] The debtor, moreover, may restructure its obligations under collective bargaining agreements with its employees, the same as the debtor may restructure pension agreements. Together these obligations often amount to a significant if not the overwhelming present and future portion of the debtor's obligations.[219]

That a municipal debtor is not treated as an ordinary debtor but that a municipal debtor enjoys several privileges is further exemplified by the case of Detroit's insolvency. The city of Detroit mastered a so-called 'Grand Bargain' in order to secure the city's great art collection and to protect its employees' pensions, for social and political reasons. The Detroit Institute of Arts was sold to a non-profit foundation legally committed to keep and present the Art in Detroit for 816 million dollars; a deal without competing bids (allowed) and arguably way below the actual market value of the art collection. The proceeds from the sale were pledged to solely benefit Detroit's pensioners, despite the fact that this would give pensioners a considerably higher payoff than other similarly (unsecured) general creditors. It is fair to say that such a 'bargain' would have not survived an ordinary bankruptcy procedure; neither the sale below market value without competing bids nor the significantly positive discrimination in favour of one class of creditors.[220]

The fiscal architecture in the United States of America provides an example par excellence for the autonomy model. The states as well as the federal government are equipped with an autonomous authority for taxation, spending, and debt acquisition. There is no comprehensive equalisation scheme and the no-bailout principle is firmly established. The positive and the negative effects of fiscal policy are internalised in a decentralised approach. Fiscal discipline is enforced by the markets. The principle of autonomy regularly also applies to the relation of the states and the third tier of

217 §§ 943(b), 901(a), 1129(b) and 1129(a)(10), Bankruptcy Code, Chapter 9 and 11.

218 See section VII. 2.

219 DAVID SKEEL, 'Can Pensions be Restructured in (Detroit's) Municipal Bankruptcy? (2013) ILE Research Paper No. 13-33.

220 On the Detroit case see: DAVID SKEEL, 'From Chrysler and General Motors to Detroit' (2015) 24 Widener Law Journal 121, 136–148. For repayments on bondholder v pension claims see: YVETTE SHIELDS and KEELEY WEBSTER, 'Why Pensions Beat Bonds in Bankruptcy Court' *The Bond Buyer.* (17 August 2016).

government–with a varying degree due to the specific state law. For the case of a municipal debt crisis, Chapter 9 provides an orderly restructuring procedure, which itself inspires the debate about the design of a sovereign insolvency procedure. In order to fully achieve institutional congruence, Chapter 9 could and should be advanced to be a debt restructuring tool and a governance reform mechanism alike as well as it should be available not only to municipalities, but also to states and territories. The legal framework (PROMESA) enacted for the purpose to resolve the Puerto Rican debt crisis provides a model for how such a state insolvency regime could look like.

2.5.2 Puerto Rico Case Study

Chapter 9 is the presently most convincing example for how to deal with the debt crisis of an official public debtor 'on its own.' Unfortunately, there does not exist a (Chapter 9 like-) insolvency regime which is available to all US states and territories.[221] Nonetheless, the USA has shown an impressively strong commitment to the principle of autonomy when the US territory Puerto Rico reached an unsustainable debt level. As it has already been argued, and as it will be further discussed in Chapter VI., an autonomous fiscal architecture logically requires a debt crisis resolution mechanism. Consequently, Congress enacted a law (PROMESA) especially designed to deal with the current Puerto Rican debt crisis, i.e., an insolvency law for the single case. While PROMESA is likely to be the best feasible solution of this time, it would be advisable to create a permanent and predictable debt restructuring mechanism for municipalities, states, and territories alike so that the markets can price in the probability of default under a credibly enforced law.[222] For now, PROMESA may be seen as a test-run

221 For a criticism of the lack of an orderly insolvency procedure for US states and/or territories see: JONATHAN RODDEN, 'Sovereignty and Orderly Defaults' (12 July 2016 Library of Law and Liberty); DAVID SKEEL, 'Is Bankruptcy the Answer for Troubled Cities and States?' (2013) 50 (4) Houston Law Review 1063; DAVID SKEEL, 'States of Bankruptcy' (2012) 79 (2) The University of Chicago Law Review 677. For a plea in favour of an orderly bankruptcy procedure for Puerto Rico: CLAYTON GILETTE and DAVID SKEEL, 'A Two-Step Plan for Puerto Rico' (2016) Research-Paper No. 16–3.

222 For a more in-depth discussion of insolvency laws for the second-tier of government in a federation see section VI. 3.5.

for a such a more permanent insolvency regime and as a robust confirmation of the US no-bailout principle.

Puerto Rico constitutes a special case in the USA: A former Spanish colony, no US state but a US territory (with limited political rights), Puerto Rico's problem of excessive spending and debt acquisition has often been attributed to political mismanagement. The economic slowdown, which hit Puerto Rico on the revenue side, is certainly due to a lack of political reforms but also due to the abolishment of federal tax laws which had benefitted US corporations doing business in Puerto Rico with significant tax exemptions up until the year of 2006 in order to create incentives for investments in Puerto Rico.[223]

An investigation into the subject of why political mismanagement could continue over decades, of why necessary reforms were delayed, and of why excessive spending was possible on a regular debt income stream shows an interesting similarity of Puerto Rico and the distressed debtors in the European Monetary Union (EMU). With the strong bailout expectation in the EMU, the debt costs for EMU member states levelled off at a pooling equilibrium price. This gave especially financially weaker countries within the union a great incentive to cheaply acquire cross-subsidised debt capital as well as the availability of low-cost debt capital relieved these countries from market pressure to conduct necessary economic reforms. The favourable accounting regulations to treat high-risk sovereign bonds from Eurozone member states as zero-risk assets added fuel to the flames (and explain why especially European private banks turned out to be Greece's main creditors before the debt was rolled over to official creditors).[224] For Puerto Rico, there was no bailout to be expected. However, the US tax laws created a dangerous temptation for creditors to over-invest into Puerto Rican bonds. The income from Puerto Rican bonds is triple-tax exempt, i.e., there is no federal, state, or local tax on interests to be paid for debt issued by Puerto Rico. Therefore, Puerto Rico has traditionally had an easy access

223 SCOTT GREENBERG and GAVIN EKINS, 'Tax Policy Helped Create Puerto Rico's Fiscal Crisis' (2015, 30 June) Tax Foundation, section I; LARRY ROHTER, 'Puerto Rico Fighting to Keep Its Tax Breaks for Businesses' (1993, 10 May) The New York Times. MARRY WILLIAMS WALSH, 'Puerto Rico: A Debt Problem That Kept Boiling Over' (2017, 5 May) The New York Times.

224 JACK EWING, 'Is Greek Debt Risk-Free? European Banking Officials Think So' (2011, 21 July) The New York Times.

to debt capital[225] – with an effect comparable to the interest rate subsidy for the financially weaker member states of the EMU.[226]

Puerto Rico's debt level kept rising, with no prospect of economic growth to bolster the income stream from taxes. Especially because corporate investments significantly decreased since the tax exemptions for corporations had been scaled back and finally abolished in 2006, Puerto Rico came under more and more pressure to fill the income gap with further debts. After the rating agencies had downgraded Puerto Rico's debt to junk level and Puerto Rico had first defaulted on its bond payments in August 2015,[227] Congress took action in a bi-partisan effort to create an orderly and protected debt adjustment procedure for the Puerto Rican debt crisis and enacted PROMESA, which provides for a financial oversight and management board and a debt restructuring mechanism. In mid-2017, Puerto Rico had about 75 billion dollars outstanding in bond debt and about 50 billion dollars in unfunded pension liabilities.[228]

Financial Oversight and Management Board: PROMESA establishes an oversight board, which importantly is not a partisan representation of the debtor nor the creditors but an independent committee of experts. The board's main functions are (i) to oversee the debt adjustment procedure and (ii) to review, approve, and/or demand amendments to the budget and fiscal plan as presented by the government of Puerto Rico.[229] The board is not only responsible to manage the debt restructuring procedure but also to guide the process of financial and economic rehabilitation. It is quite common that US states establish a municipal oversight board for their distressed municipalities. Cantons in Switzerland have similar rules ("Beiratschaft") for their municipalities. The troika managing the Greek debt crisis, in apparent contrast, is not an independent board but a parti-

225 GREENBERG and EKINS (2015) section II; MARRY WILLIAMS WALSH, (2017).

226 See the discussion in section V. 3.5.3.

227 MARRY WILLIAMS WALSH, 'Puerto Rico Defaults on Bond Payments' (2015, 3 August) The New York Times.

228 MARRY WILLIAMS WALSH, 'How Puerto Rico is Grappling With a Debt Crisis' (2017, 16 May) The New York Times.

229 Puerto Rico Oversight, Management, and Economic Stability Act (hereafter, PROMESA) of 2016, signed to become law with effect on June 30, 2016. For the Oversight Board see: Title I, Sections 101 to 109 (Establishment and Organization) and Title II, Section 201 to 212 (Responsibilities). PROMESA follows closely the proposal by GILETTE and SKEEL (2016).

san representation of the official creditors, which hold almost all of Greece's debt by now.

The Financial Oversight and Management Board has taken an active role in fashioning a plan for the financial rehabilitation of Puerto Rico. After an initial plan had been rejected by the board, and after the board had demanded further amendments, a fiscal plan was finally approved with amendments as proposed by the board on 13 March 2017. The fiscal plan builds on a ten year financial projection and sets out important "Fiscal Reform Measures"[230] on "Revenue Enhancement" such as tax reforms and tax compliance improvements,[231] "Government Right-sizing",[232] "Reducing Healthcare Spending",[233] and "Pension Reform"[234] as well as "Structural Reform Measures" such as reforms to support business activity and economic growth in Puerto Rico (e.g. deregulation, labour market reforms)[235]. The fiscal plan, moreover, includes a debt sustainability analysis and a proposal for how the Puerto Rican government plans to approach the debt restructuring procedure.[236]

Debt restructuring: PROMESA offers two options for an orderly debt adjustment. According to Title VI, a debt adjustment may be undertaken in 'creditor collective action'. Importantly, a binding debt restructuring under Title VI requires the approval of all creditor groups.[237] Title III allows for a Chapter 9-like court supervised procedure with the option of a cramdown, i.e., a procedure with less hold-out potential.[238] Eventually, PROMESA provides for a stay which was initially set to expire on the day after 15 February 2017 but which was extended by the board to expire the day after 1 May 2017.[239]

230 GOVERNMENT OF PUERTO RICO, *Fiscal Plan for Puerto Rico* (San Juan, Puerto Rico, 13 March 2017) 16–21.

231 GOVERNMENT OF PUERTO RICO (2017) 18.

232 GOVERNMENT OF PUERTO RICO (2017) 19.

233 GOVERNMENT OF PUERTO RICO (2017) 20.

234 GOVERNMENT OF PUERTO RICO (2017) 21.

235 GOVERNMENT OF PUERTO RICO (2017) 22–24.

236 GOVERNMENT OF PUERTO RICO (2017) 25–28.

237 See Section 601(m)(1)(A) PROMESA. A creditor group or pool, by the terminology of PROMESA, is said to have approved the debt restructuring proposal if creditors voting and holding two-thirds of the outstanding debt within their voting pool and holding at least the majority of the outstanding debt for their pool approve the proposal.

238 See Title III, Sections 301 to 317 PROMESA.

239 See Section 405 PROMESA. The extension was granted in accordance with section 405(d)(1)(B) PROMESA.

The goal was that a 'voluntary creditor agreement' under Title VI. would be achieved. The debt restructuring negotiations, however, failed and several creditors went to court immediately after the stay was lifted, so that Puerto Rico asked the oversight board to initiate the court supervised insolvency procedure under Title III. The Title III procedure started on 3 May 2017.[240]

The debt restructuring is in particular complicated because of an unresolved issue of how to rank the outstanding claims, i.e., how to regulate the inter-creditor relations with different recovery quotas. Prominently, this is a conflict between the holders of general obligation bonds and holders of so-called Cofina bonds. For the general obligation bonds, Puerto Rico's Constitution guarantees that "available revenues" shall first be pledged to the repayment of these bonds, i.e., they are backed by a promise to the tax income of Puerto Rico.[241] The Cofina bonds instead are backed by a promise to be repaid from the sales tax revenues collected by Puerto Rico.[242] Once the debt restructuring plan will be finally confirmed by the court, the Puerto Rican debt restructuring case will be the largest single insolvency of an official public debtor to be conducted in an orderly insolvency procedure in public ordering by then.

3. *Institutional Congruence: Comparative Review*

In section III. 3.6, an institutional congruence index was presented, according to which the institutional congruence of a multi-tier fiscal architecture can be evaluated. After an elaborated discussion of the fiscal architecture of five distinct multi-tier unions was conducted in sections IV. 2.1 to 2.5, the findings shall be compared in this section:

---

240 MARRY WILLIAMS WALSH, 'Puerto Rico Declares a Form of Bankruptcy' (2017, 3 May) The New York Times.

241 Article VI, Section 8 of the Constitution of the Commonwealth of Puerto Rico reads: "In case the available revenues including surplus for any fiscal year are insufficient to meet the appropriations made for that year, interest on the public debt and amortization thereof shall first be paid, and other disbursements shall thereafter be made in accordance with the order of priorities established by law.".

242 MICHAEL CORKERY and MARY WILLIAMS WALSH, 'Message of Puerto Rico Debt Crisis: Easy Bets Sometimes Lose' (2017, 7 May) The New York Times.

(Fig. 4) Cross-Country Comparative Summary

Autonomy Model ◄── Mixed Model	──► Integration Model
USA SWITZERLAND CANADA GERMANY	FRANCE
Elements of Autonomy	Elements of Integration
1A.Aut. No Bailout Principle AND	**1A.Int. Bailout Guarantee <u>AND/OR 1B.</u>**
USA SWITZERLAND	CANADA GERMANY
1B.Aut. Borrowing Autonomy AND	**1B.Int. Top-Down Borrowing Constraints AND**
CANADA SWITZERLAND USA GERMANY	FRANCE
2.Aut. Spending Autonomy AND	**2.Int. Top-Down-Controlled Spending Authority AND**
CANADA GERMANY SWITZERLAND USA	FRANCE
3A.Aut. Tax Autonomy AND	**3A.Int. Top-Down Controlled Tax Authority AND**
CANADA SWITZERLAND USA	GERMANY FRANCE
3B.Aut. Tax-Funded Budget	**3B.Int. Transfer-Funded Budget**
USA SWITZERLAND CANADA	FRANCE GERMANY

Explanation:

1.A.Aut. No Bailout Principle versus 1.A.Int. Bailout Guarantee: The USA has clearly the longest and most stable no-bailout tradition established in a credible execution of the no-bailout principle since the 1840s. The no-bailout expectation is confirmed by several financial crises, which the official debtors had to deal with 'on their own'. It is strengthened by the existence of an effective and regularly used bankruptcy mechanism (Chapter 9) as well as by Congress' reaction to the Puerto Rican debt crisis (PROMESA). In Switzerland, the no bailout expectation is reflected in the risk-adjusted credit costs per individual official debtor, and prominently by the case Leukerbad. However, the implementation of an insolvency law for official debtors could certainly strengthen the no-bailout expectation in Switzerland. In Canada, creditors generally expect a bailout. The bailout expectation is reflected in credit costs which are not appropriately adjusted to the risk of individual official debtors. While a no-bailout principle could be credibly established considering the provinces' capacity to source funds from own taxes and react to financial crises this way, the strong preferences for equality and a high welfare standard make a bailout quite likely. The bailout expectation in Germany, finally, is cast in stone. The German Länder (and Gemeinden) have little to no possibility to adjust their revenue stream if not by debt income. The German law explicitly rules out the insolvency option for official debtors and the equalisation scheme largely eliminates financial differences between the Länder. Bailouts have taken place in the past and creditors expect the bailout to be the rule. Therefore, they do not demand an individual risk-premium from official creditor.

1B.Aut. Borrowing Autonomy versus 1.B.Int. Top-Down Borrowing Constraints: In the USA, Canada, and Switzerland, the federal/central level does not impose borrowing constraints on the subordinate public units. Borrowing constraints and budget rules, if applicable, are self-imposed and – enforced for the first- and second-tier of government. The relation between the second- to third-tier of government differs per province, state, and canton. Germany has a constitutional debt brake agreed upon between the first- and second-tier of government. As to whether the debt brake will hold in the future is questionable. The constitution itself does not require the federal government to approve the Länder budgets. There is no automatic sanction for the case that the budget rules are ignored. France, in contrast, provides the example for how effective top-down borrowing and budget constraints are enforced. The local budget is subject to a review process. If the balanced budget requirement is not fulfilled, the budget may be cancelled and replaced. Payments are checked by a central authority. Debt acquisition is only possible for capital investments and debt costs are deducted from the operating budget. With such strict borrowing and budget constraints, there is no question of a bailout.

2.Aut. Spending Autonomy versus 2.Int. Top-Down Controlled Spending Authority: In Canada, Germany, Switzerland, and the USA, the first- and second-tier of government each have their own legislative and administrative competences (with some variation). Each level of government manages its spending budget autonomously. The French subnational units have received considerable autonomy for their spending budget since the reforms of decentralisation in the early 1980s. However, the French subnational units have no constitutional right to specific administrative competences and their spending decisions are taken within the framework of the law. The law, eventually, is made in Paris.

3A.Aut. Tax Autonomy versus 3A.Int. Top-Down-Controlled Tax Authority: In Canada, Switzerland, and the USA, the subnational units (especially of the second level) have original tax rights to choose their tax base and to set their tax rate. They regularly occupy the main tax sources. In Germany, the main taxes are all decided upon centrally/collectively. The Länder receive their share of tax income, but they have little room to adjust their tax income stream individually. They may only choose a tax base or adjust the tax rate for relatively minor taxes. In France, the subnational units may only modify the tax rate within the frame set by the central law-maker. Theoretically, the French subnational units' present rights to (minor) taxes are subject to the central law-maker's discretion while the German Länder have (minor) original tax rights. In practice, however, the situation is not much different from the German situation.

3B.Aut. Tax-Funded Budget versus 3B.Int. Transfer-Funded Budget: In the USA, the revenue to fund the budget has to come almost entirely from own taxes (or debt, for which the subnational units are liable with future taxes, unless the debt burden is reduced in orderly insolvency). Federal matching grants form an exception to this rule. In Canada and Switzerland, the budget is mostly funded from own tax income. However, federal transfers and transfers from a national equalisation scheme are an important additional source of income for many subnational units. In France and Germany, shared taxes and transfers form the most important source of income to fund the budget.

Final result:

- USA: The USA is the prime example for the autonomy model reflected in a credibly executed no-bailout principle, an orderly insolvency procedure for municipalities and Puerto Rico, borrowing, spending, and tax autonomy, and budgets almost entirely funded from own taxes. The most apparent improvement possible would be a permanent insolvency law for states and territories.
- Switzerland: Switzerland follows closely. Small deviations from the pure autonomy model are the lack of an orderly insolvency regime and the existence of an equalisation scheme. Such deviations do, however, not cause significant distortions from the ideal of institutional congruence.
- Canada: The link of borrowing, spending, tax autonomy, and primarily tax-funded budgets would place Canada only a few steps away from the completion of an institutional congruent autonomy model if the bailout expectation would be rejected, e.g., by an insolvency law or future no-bailouts in case of distress. (The USA turned the scale in the 1840s from bailout to no-bailout expectation.) The Canadian equalisation scheme, of relative more volume/importance/a higher equalisation target than in Switzerland, however, would still exist as a deviation from the principle of autonomy.
- Germany: Germany is right between autonomy and integration, i.e., it is the example of institutional incongruence, the example of the mixed model. Spending autonomy comes along with a bailout guarantee and borrowing autonomy (and only a weak framework for top-down borrowing constraints). A no-bailout principle, however, would not be credible at all as long as major taxes are controlled top-down and as long as the subnational units' budget is mostly funded from shared taxes and transfers. In order to establish institutional congruence, Germany could work towards centralisation (e.g. by equipping the debt brake with effective sanctions) or towards decentralisation (e.g. by granting the Länder tax autonomy for relevant taxes and establishing an insolvency regime for subnational debtors).
- France: France still closely resembles the integration model, albeit decentralisation reforms. Strict and effective top-down borrowing constraints work smoothly with spending autonomy (within the framework of Paris' laws), with a top-down controlled tax authority, and with a primarily transfer-funded budget.

There is not just one solution for financial sustainability. The question is not simply to be decided between decentralisation and centralisation. The key question to be answered is: how should decentralisation or centralisation be organised in order to be institutionally congruent?

In order to create institutional congruence, a multi-tier union organised according to the principle of integration must provide for a framework with an effective chain of commands top-down. In the French fiscal architecture, as an example par excellence, the central government has established tight oversight rules to avoid that subnational governments engage in excessive spending funded with debts which may eventually be shifted to the common pool. If a multi-tier union instead wants to activate the benefits of decentralisation such as information generated and evaluated bottom-up, competition, transparency, and regional accountability, the union must be ready to enforce the ultimate consequence: in a competition where each candidate has the means to master its own fate (i.e. tax and spending authority), financial distress has to be resolved in orderly insolvency. The US provides an impressive example thereof, as in particular the Puerto Rican case demonstrates.

V. The Challenge of Integration: The European Monetary Union

1. *Preliminary Considerations*

The European Monetary Union (EMU) is the presently unique experience of a single currency to unite multiple sovereign countries; unique by its shire volume, commitment, and challenge.[243] Past attempts of monetary integration, such as the Bretton Woods system, a pure exchange rate regime,[244] were ambitious but not of the same significance and commitment as the EMU, which is the abundance of distinct currencies for a single currency, the euro. Eventually, Bretton Woods failed[245] and the future of the euro project is unsettled. The goal of fiscal integration constantly gained importance in the EMU, especially during and after the financial crisis, when a gigantic bailout mission for distressed Eurozone member states was set on track. The EMU constitutes the presently single experiment of a fiscal regime with significant elements of integration on the level of sovereign states. This chapter will deal with the exceptional case of monetary/fiscal integration in the European Union/EMU. After a short historical review of the EMU and European Union's origin, the EMU will be analysed according to the criteria of the institutional congruence index.

---

243 As of 2017, 19 EU member states are also Eurozone member states. With the exception of the United Kingdom and Denmark, all other EU member states have committed to introduce the Euro once they have fulfilled the convergence criteria. Sweden has delayed this process for its own currency without significant opposition in the EU.

244 The participant countries in the Bretton Woods system agreed to keep their currencies adjusted to the US dollar within pre-defined limits. The dollar to gold exchange rate was fixed to $35/ounce.

245 On the Bretton Woods system see: MICHAEL BORDO, 'The Bretton Woods International Monetary System: A Historical Overview' in Michael Bordo and Barry Eichengreen (eds) *A Retrospective on the Bretton Woods System: Lessons for International Monetary Reform* (University of Chicago Press 1993) 3.

2. *The Prelude to the European Monetary Union*

A Contract for Peace and Trade: The European integration began as a project of unity after times of devastation, war, and chaos. It would soon develop into a remarkably successful contract for peace and trade by way of de-nationalising the European economies. After WWII, it was a major concern how to secure peace in Europe while the former aggressor Germany was re-emerging as an European super-power. In this spirit, the European Coal and Steel Community was formed in 1951 to place the industries relevant for armament and warfare under a common supervision and regulation. Aa publicly managed cartel was formed, quite the opposite of free markets and trade, but a first step towards cooperation after times of confrontation.[246]

A few years later, in 1957, the European Economic Community (EEC) and the European Atomic Energy Community were established with the Treaty of Rome. In particular, the ECC was a milestone towards the creation of a single market with the abolishment of national tariffs in favour of a costums union with outside tariffs; a second important step towards integration, this time by liberalisation. Several areas of economic activity were placed under a single regulatory authority so as to facilitate cross-border trade within the union. The process of economic integration was set on track. The idea of a single market, i.e., of integration driven by the cross-border pursuit of prosperity, was further developed from a single market for goods to a single market for goods, capital, services, and labour throughout the years and decades to come; potentially, for the benefit of every incorporated business and every citizen of EU member state.

Meanwhile, the organizational integration was moving forward. With the Treaty of Brussels (1965), the Single European Act (1986), the Treaty of Maastricht (1992), i.e., the founding treaty of the European Union, and the Treaties of Amsterdam (1997), Nice (2001), and Lisbon (2009), the policy areas of regulation to which the European institutions were empowered by delegation were extended and unified under the umbrella of the European Union. Importantly, the European Commission, as the administrative and regulatory body, the European Parliament as the legislative body, and the European Council as the representation of the sovereign member states evolved as the European Union's main players in the decision-making pro-

246 The six founding countries were: Belgium, France, Germany, Italy, Luxembourg, Netherlands.

cess. In many areas, the requirement of an unanimous consent of all (sovereign) member states was replaced by a majority rule.

Conflicting Ideas about Monetary Integration: While economic integration was moving forward, the design of monetary integration with a single currency remained cloudy. A first step towards monetary integration was taken with the European Monetary System (EMS). After the downfall of Bretton Woods, several (but not all) members of the European Community established or later on joined the EMS, which came with a commitment of its participants to keep their exchange rates within a fixed range of +/- 2.25% to the European Currency Unit (ECU), a basket of the currencies of all participating countries. If the currency of one member state was about to appreciate or depreciate beyond the +/- 2.25% currency band, the member state with the currency about to sheer out was forced to act. The respective member state had to lower/raise the central bank's interest rate or it had to sell/buy the appreciating/depreciating currency. Financial assistance to perform a short-term adjustment was available in form of loans limited in their amount to a maximum of 22bn ECU. Any member state finally unable to keep its currency within the currency band was forced to leave the EMS, as Italy and the United Kingdom did in the early 1990s. In reaction to a currency crisis in the early 1990s, the currency band was widened to +/- 15%. Since the Deutsche Mark was clearly the strongest currency in the EMS, it became the anchor currency similar to the US dollar in the Bretton Woods era, which factually forced the EMS members to follow the lead of the Bundesbank in their monetary policy. The "diktat of the Bundesbank" (German central bank) was a constant bone of contention for other member states of the EMU.

The EMS was heading towards reform and the plan for of a single currency took shape. For the design of the euro in a future European Monetary Union (EMU), however, there existed two entirely distinct ideas: The 'French version' envisaged a European central bank as a common reserve pool from which the member states could draw funds to balance their deficits with the printing press. The capital exports/imports from the surplus to the deficit countries would result in an average inflation rate and burden-sharing across the member states. The 'German version' instead was a European central bank designed after the model of the Bundesbank. Independent from political influence/directions, the central bank should be first and foremost devoted to the goal of price stability. This would force the deficit countries to make substantial adjustments to their budgets; the printing press was off the table.

The finally agreed upon version of the euro/EMU, as specified by the Treaty of Maastricht (1992), looked very much like the 'German version.' The newly established European Central Bank (ECB) was obliged to secure price stability and it was prohibited to monetarize the public debts of its stakeholder. The member states of the EMU had to avoid excessive deficits as well as they were bound to the no-bailout principle. The operating code of the EMU was: 'Every member on its own.' As the analysis in V. 3 will show, the EMU in reality looks quite different from the EMU on paper.[247] The restrains on excessive deficits, the no-bailout principle, and the ECB's commitment to secure price stability and to abstain from socialising debts via the printing press, however, were sacrificed to short-term political interests. The 'German version' of the EMU turned out to have no teeth. The rules or a regime of budgetary discipline were lacking an enforcement mechanism which could effectively prevent common pool financing.[248]

The Integration Project in Danger?: While the European project could be described as a phenomenal success: peace, free trade, prosperity, and the EU's role as a super-power in world politics which would hardly be the same if every nation had to act on its own and represent itself, the continued existence of the EMU and the EU is not without doubt. The vote by the British people to leave the EU (BREXIT) has shaken the union to its core. Since the onset of the European sovereign debt crisis, anti-European parties are on the rise. While especially in Southern Europe the top-down directives which command strict austerity programmes as part of the rescue mission have mobilised millions to protest the EMU/EU on the streets and in upcoming elections, the dissatisfaction with the bailout/transfer payments is also a heavy burden for the EMU/EU in the rescuing member states.[249] The institutional incongruence in the fiscal architecture of the EMU has now the potential to threaten the further existence not only of the EMU but also of the EU contract for free trade and peace.

---

247 On the EMS, the conflicting ideas of a 'French version' and a 'German version' for the EMU, and the development from the law in the books to the law in reality see: CHARLES BLANKART, 'Oil and Vinegar: A Positive Fiscal Theory of the Euro Crisis' (2013) 66 (4) Kyklos, International Review for Social Sciences' 497.

248 On the European integration process, the financial/monetary integration, and the long way from the EMS to a transfer union see BLANKART (2017) 451–463 and BLANKART and EHMKE (2014).

249 Certainly, the refugee/immigration crisis, which followed shortly after the debt crisis had started to develop, has been another serious threat to the European project, as there is not a single explanation for the current crisis of the European Union.

3. *An Institutional Analysis: Defining the Character of the EMU*

3.1 Preliminary Considerations

Certainly, neither the European Union nor the EMU form a country such as other countries around the world. The EMU/EU members are fully sovereign countries bound to play by the rules of contract. If the sovereign of a member state decides to leave the union, it may do so without that a 'supreme power' of the union could hinder the move towards separation. Nonetheless, the EU and the EMU in their relation to their members and the member states in their relation to each other resemble a federalist architecture, especially since the rescue mission for distressed member states was officially announced. In this section, the EMU will be analysed through the lenses of the institutional congruence index.

3.2 Decisions about Spending

In the EMU/EU, each member state, in principle, has maintained its full sovereignty in matters of government spending. The only noteworthy exceptions are the EU's restrictions for government subsidies. These restrictions are a necessary pre-condition for fair competition in a single market. No government shall 'artificially' give its national businesses a leg-up.[250] Other than for this exception, the national governments are free to decide how they want to spend their income from tax and debt. Transfers from the EU budget,[251] nonetheless, may come at a condition for a specific investment or they may be distributed directly to beneficiaries at the subnational/sub-governmental level.

Especially if compared to other multi-tier unions/federations, it is fair to say that the EMU/EU member states enjoy a very high degree of spending autonomy. If spending autonomy comes hand in hand with an independent debt and tax authority and in the absence of a transfer and bailout regime, one should expect resources to be directed to their best possible use. If, however, spending autonomy is paired with a transfer and/or bailout regime, the government of a potential beneficiary country has a perverse incentive to increase spending for the sake of consumption on the costs of other member states.

---

250 See therefore Artt. 107, 108, 109 TFEU.

251 See section V. 3.5.1.

3.3 Decisions about Taxation

Each EMU/EU member state is in principle free to choose its own tax base and to set its own tax rate within its own territory. Each state may collect as much or as little taxes from corporate and natural personas as the government desires (with the support of its people). An exception applies for indirect taxes, importantly, the VAT tax. According to Artt. 110 and 113 TFEU and the VAT tax directive, the VAT tax has to be the same for every comparable product in the country of destination, regardless of the country of origin. A regular minimum VAT tax of 15% and a reduced minimum VAT tax of 5% applies EU-wide.[252] The idea behind this regulation is not (primarily) tax harmonisation but fair competition, i.e., the functioning of the single market.[253]

For a truly autonomous country, tax autonomy is the only right (and logical) choice. Any restrictions on a government's ability to levy taxes makes a no-bailout regime not credible, as the German experience of the Länder shows.[254] Without the option to adjust the tax revenue stream, a country is dangerously dependent on debt income and debt relief by bailout. In case, however, that a country is expected to be bailed-out, tax autonomy bears a similar temptation than spending autonomy: the national government has every incentive to spend excessively and to tax very modestly so as to please its people/electorate. If a national government assumes to be able to shift the burden to another national 'payer' in a bailout, it has little incentive to burden its own people/electorate with taxes and to invest much effort into tax enforcement.

---

252 COUNCIL DIRECTIVE 2006/112/EC (28 November 2006).

253 CECILE REMEUR, 'Tax Policy in the EU–Issues and challenges' (2015, February) European Parliamentary Research Service PE 549.001, see especially 4–6 and 10–13. In this light one can also understand the Apple-case, in which the European Commission declared the tax deal between Ireland and Apple to be an illegal state aid. See: EUROPEAN COMISSION, Commission Decision of 30.08.2016 ON STATE AID SA. 38373 (2014/C) (ex2014/NN) (ex2014/CP). Ireland was ordered to recover 13bn euros in illegal financial aid. This decision, however, does not fundamentally question the EU member states' right to choose their own tax base and set their own tax rates, but it only addresses the case of 'special treatment' for a single (powerful) taxpayer; a treatment which would disturb free market competition. If Ireland had set their corporate tax rate for Apple at the same low level for other corporations, it could have done so without intervention from the European Commission.

254 See the discussion in section IV. 2.3.

In principle, tax competition can promote a race towards the best price-product relation for the public good when truly autonomous parties compete with each other. In this case, the tax is charged as a price for the public good. Sovereign or public entities with a superior infrastructure can charge a higher price while their competitors with a less developed infrastructure can attract potential taxpayers with a lower tax rate. Eventually, there is an incentive not to waste tax money and not to overcharge taxpayers. If there is a bailout expectation, however, tax competition can turn into a dangerous spiral of underperformance/indebtness. The incentive is to undercharge taxpayers for the public good so as to outdo other competitors and to finance the public good on debt, which may later be shifted to the 'rescuers.' The incentive to create a cost-effective public good has turned into an incentive to shift the financial burden of the public good from the own taxpayers to the taxpayers of the (potential) rescuers.

3.4 Decisions about Debt

The question of the EMU members' debt autonomy is a tricky one. There is neither a supreme debt authority nor a central debt facility from which the member states can extract their debt share–even though a common pool debt financing facility has (informally) emerged through the back door in a constant bailout and transfer regime.[255] Nevertheless, every member is first and foremost free to make decisions on debt acquisition by itself.

Concerning the question of debt responsibility, the institutional architecture of the EMU is incoherent. Artt. 123 and 125 TFEU say: 'every state on its own.' The no-bailout principle would render any other type of borrowing/deficit restriction obsolete if it were properly enforced. The market would exercise control. However, the EMU was designed with a Stability and Growth Pact (1997)[256], i.e., a component which one should expect in the integration model. Most importantly, the Pact says that (i) no member state shall have a deficit of more than 3% of its GDP, (ii) no member state shall have a debt level of more than 60% of its GDP.

255 See sections V. 3.5.2 and V. 3.5.3.

256 The Pact was reformed later on. See section V. 3.7.

The Stability and Growth Pact operates with a pre-warning and with a penalty system.[257] On paper, it looks like as if the EU member states' debt authority was bound to a pretty strict top-down rule, i.e., as if the EU member states were not fully autonomous in making decisions about debt acquisition/financing. In reality, the story is different. Since its enactment, the violation of the Stability and Growth Pact has turned out to be the norm rather than the exception. The debt level constantly kept rising. A weak rule without predictable and credible enforcement is not worth the ink and paper. It is, therefore, fair to say that the EMU member states generally decide in full autonomy about debt acquisition, albeit the formal restrictions in the Stability and Growth Pact.

3.5 Decisions about Transfers

3.5.1 Explicit Transfers from the EU Budget

The official EU budget is primarily used for re-distributional purposes within the union. About 15% are spent on administration, foreign relations (including development aid), and security and citizenship (e.g. boarder protection). About 85% of the EU budget goes into: (i) subsidies for 'growth and jobs' which fit into a pre-defined cluster (e.g. for research and development, training, SME) (about 15%), (ii) regional cohesion policy to support less developed regions in the EU (about 30%), and (iii) subsidies for natural resources, mostly agriculture (about 40%). The entire budget of the European Union was approximately 158 billions euro in 2017.[258] That is about half the German federal budget and three times the Greek public budget. Considering that the EU budget is primarily spend on re-distribution instead of that public goods accessible to all EU citizens are created, this is a significant amount.[259]

---

257 Artt. 126 (2) a) (for the deficit-to-GDP rule) and b) (for the debt-to-GDP rule) TFEU and Protocol (No 12) Article 1 to the TFEU (Treaty on the Functioning of the European Union. See further section V. 3.7.

258 EUROPEAN COMMISSION (2018) budget info page.

259 The EU budget is re-distributed in favour of the economically/financially weaker member states. The regional support funds primarily go to economically less developed EU members, the same as the natural resource funds disproportionally go to economically less developed countries with typically a strong primary and less competitive secondary sector. The transfers from the EU budget are clearly targeted to close the gap between the less and more developed member

While the re-distributional character of the EU budget fits perfectly in the model of integration, the way budget decisions are made rather fits the description of the autonomy model. The member states have to agree unanimously on a multiannual framework for the budget; [260] a procedure which, in the past, has often been associated with lengthy and cumbersome negotiations, and regularly a deadlock in the innovation of the budget itself, i.e., high decision-making costs.[261]

3.5.2 The EU Bailout Policy

In 2009, the EMU was hit by the most severe debt crisis in its history. Artt. 123 and 125 TFEU, as agreed upon in the design of the common currency union, had established a very clear solution for the event of crisis: No member state (Art. 125) nor the European Central Bank (Art. 123) should bail-out financially distressed member states. Every state on its own! This solution would have required that any member state with an unsustainable debt level would have had to approach its creditors and bargain about a debt restructuring deal for a fresh start. As a concession, the debtor countries would have had to present a plan for governance reform to their creditors so as to signal that they will be able to pay their restructured debts in the future. It was, however, decided to bluntly ignore the no bailout provisions and to start a giant bailout mission instead. This section will describe the most significant components of the bailout programme while the following section will analyse its impact (3.5.3).[262]

---

states. It is, however, questionable in how far the development funds actually achieve the desired cohesion. A dispersion of rents in the application for support funds is the likely and empirically measured effect of the rent-seeking game for the EU subsidies, in particular for the regional cohesion and 'growth and jobs' subsidies. BLANKART and EHMKE (2015) with further references.

260 See Art. 312 TFEU, especially paragraph Art. 312 (2) and (4) TFEU.

261 See CHARLES BLANKART and DAVID EHMKE, 'Alternative Voting Rules for the EU Budget' (typescript); CHARLES BLANKART and CHRISTIAN KIRCHNER, 'The Deadlock of the EU Budget' in Charles Blankart and Dennis Mueller (eds) *A Constitution for the European Union* (MIT Press 2004) 109 and CHARLES BLANKART and GERRIT KOESTER, 'Refocusing the EU Budget–An Institutional View' (2009) Journal of Public Finance and Management, Special Issue on EU finances 536.

262 The IMF has consistently been involved in the debt crisis management in the Eurozone. Since this section will concentrate on the relation between the EMU and its members, there will be no discussion of the IMF's involvement. See for

Greek Loan Facility: The start of the Greek Loan Facility in 2010 precedes the structured bailout programmes EFSF, EFSM, and ESM. The Greek Loan Facility is a tailor-made bailout programme for Greece (and its creditors) to provide up to 110bn euros in rescue loans. The EMU member states contributed a share proportional to their ECB share in bilateral loans, the IMF the remainder. Eventually, 52.9bn euros from the Eurozone member states and 20.1bn euros from the IMF, i.e., 73 bn euros in total were paid out to Greece.[263]

European Financial Stability Facility (EFSF): In operation between 2010 and 2013, the EFSF was an instrument created to raise about 440bn euros in newly issued bonds, jointly and severely guaranteed in the amount of about 780bn euros by all EMU member states. The excess guarantee was necessary in order to secure an AAA rating for the EFSF. The funds raised by the EFSF were available for rescue loans to EMU member states. Greece received 130.9bn euros, Portugal 26bn Euros, and Ireland 17.7bn Euros from the EFSF.[264] The average blended lending rate, for early 2018, is shown as 1.44%.[265]

European Financial Stability Mechanism (EFSM): To accompany the EFSF, the European Commission launched the EFSM as a programme to raise up to 60bn euros guaranteed by the EU budget. The funds raised by the EFSM are available for rescue loans to Eurozone member states. Portugal received 24.3bn euros and Ireland 22.5bn euros from the EFSM.[266]

European Stability Mechanism (ESM): The ESM was established in 2012. Different from the EFSF and EFSM, the ESM is designed as a permanent

---

instance: IMF, 'Ireland: Ex Post Evaluation of Exceptional Access Under the 2010 Extended Arrangement' (2015, February) IMF Country Report No. 15/20 prepared by A. Chailloux, J. Gobat, H. Imamura, J. McHugh, H. Poirson Ward, and T. Krueger; IMF, 'Greece: Ex Post Evaluation of Exceptional Access Under the 2010 Stand-By Arrangement' (2913, June) IMF Country Report No. 13/156 prepared by J. Gordon, I. Karpowicz, S. Lanau, J. Manning, W. McGrew, M. Nozaki, and M. Shamloo.

263 ESM, What is the Greek Loan Facility–information page (2017).

264 With a liquidity buffer of 10 billions Euros, and 144.5 committed to Greece (of which 13.6 bn were not disbursed), 241.8 of the 440 billions Euros lending capacity were not used. The EFSF does not provide rescue loans anymore. In order to manage and finance the existing rescue loan commitments, the EFSF, nonetheless, continues to operate as bond issuer. For this information see: GERMAN FEDERAL MINISTRY OF FINANCE, European Financial Assistance – information page (2017) under the link EFSF and EFSM.

265 ESM, Lending Rates–information page (2018).

266 EUROPEAN COMMISSION, EFSM –information page (2017). (Follow the links to Portugal and Ireland for more specific information.).

bailout facility. The member states are not jointly and severely liable for the entire lending capacity. Each member state is liable only for a share corresponding to its ECB share. A smaller portion of each member state's commitment comes as paid-in-capital and the remainder as callable capital. The ESM capital stock is 704.8bn euros, and the ESM maximum lending capacity 500bn euros. Up until early 2018, the following loans were promised and paid out: 86bn euros to Greece (paid out 46.9bn), 9bn euros to Cyprus (paid out 6.3 bn), 100 bn to Spain (paid out 41.3bn). The financial assistance to Spain was labelled as bank recapitalisation and not as a sovereign debt assistance programme. The average blended lending rate, for early 2018, is shown as 0.99%.[267]

Security Markets Programme (SMP): The SMP programme was in operation from May 2010 until September 2012. Under the SMP programme, the ECB purchased bonds of distressed Eurozone member states on the secondary markets. The total volume of the SMP programme was approx. 210bn euros, of which almost half the capital was invested in Italian bonds, followed by Spanish, Greek, Portuguese, and Irish bonds.[268]

Outright Monetary Transactions (OMT): In 2012, Mario Draghi prominently declared: "Within our mandate, the ECB is ready to do whatever it takes to preserve the euro. And believe me, it will be enough."[269] Under the OMT programme, the ECB has made a public commitment to make unlimited bond purchases on the secondary market so as to prevent a default and so as to bailout a seriously distressed Eurozone member state. The OMT programme has not been used up until early 2018, but the announcement of the bailout guarantee alone was enough to create a bailout subsidy of its own.[270]

Low Interest Rates and Quantitative Easing (QE): The dangers of a constantly low interest rate policy have already been discussed in section II. 2.3. The ECB has used the low interest rate policy as a way to encourage investments and to ease the burden for especially the economically and financially distressed Eurozone member states. Naturally, low interest rates benefit especially countries with a high debt level. In addition to the low

---

267 GERMAN FEDERAL MINISTRY OF FINANCE (2018), ESM, Lending Rates–information page (2018), ESM, Financial assistance–information page (2018) under the link Greece – ongoing programme, Spain, and Cyprus.

268 ECB, 'Details on securities holdings acquired under the Securities Market Programme' (2013, 21 February) Press Release.

269 MARIO DRAGHI, Verbatim of the remarks made by Mario Draghi at the Global Investment Conference in London (26 July 2012).

270 See V. 3.4.3.

interest policy, the ECB has made enormous investments under the Asset Purchase Programmes, comprising the third covered bond purchase programme, the asset-backed securities purchase programme, the public sector purchase programme, and the corporate sector purchase programme, all together known as quantitative easing (QE). The vast majority of debt investments goes into purchases of sovereign bonds. Since its onset in March 2013, the ECB has made investments of about 60bn euros per month, of 80bn euros per month from April 2016 to March 2017, and of 30 bn per month since January 2018. The giant volume of the QE-programme may give an explanation for why the OMT programme has not yet been triggered: the emergency measure of the OMT programme has already turned into a case of normality under the Asset Purchase programme.

The QE-programme makes the ECB the biggest creditor of sovereign debtors in the Eurozone. If the assumption was that the EMU member states repay their debt (without assistance), the QE-programme could be seen as 'only' a stimulus and as a boost of liquidity. If, however, some member states default in the future, the ECB will be the biggest creditor forced to make concessions. These debt concessions, then, will fall on the equity-holders of the ECB, i.e., the (solvent) EMU member states. Assuming that several member states' finances are not rock-solid, the QE-programme is a giant anticipated bailout for distressed debtors. During the ongoing Eurozone sovereign debt crisis, the sustainability of the debt burden of not only of Greece has been questioned, but also of Portugal, Italy, Ireland, and Spain. In early 2018, the ECB held bonds with an accumulated book value of together approximately 620bn Euros from these four countries.[271]

Emergency Liquidity Assistance: The Emergency Liquidity Assistance programme allows the national central banks (NCB) to create central bank money in order to advance the 'freshly printed money' to their national financial institutions considered to be solvent but illiquid. The question of solvency and is answered by the respective national central bank. The money is provided at 100 to 150 basis points on top of the most favourable ECB refinancing rate. The collateral which financial institutions have to provide is of generally lower/questionable quality as if compared to the standard requirements for collateral applicable for ECB financing. The ECB decides about the ceiling for ELA financing for the individual NCBs. At times, the

271 Rounded, for end January 2018: 31.5 billion: Portugal, 25.5 billion: Ireland, 330 billion: Italy, 233 billion: Spain. For a description of the programme and the here presented information see: ECB, Asset purchase programmes–information page (2018) with a spreadsheet for past purchases.

ELA-ceiling for the Bank of Greece reached almost 90bn euros. In other words, in case of a default of Greece, the shareholders of the ECB would have had advanced roughly 90bn euros for collateral of low value to Greek banks, of which some might turn out to be actually bankrupt and not just illiquid.[272]

Target-2-Balances: In 2012, the German economist Hans-Werner Sinn prominently brought the risk of the Target-2 system to public attention. The Target-2[273] system works as follows: A buyer in country G orders a good/service for the price X offered by a seller/provider in country N. The national central bank of G debits the central bank account of the buyer's bank for this transaction and proceeds the transaction through the Target2-clearing system of the ECB. G's central bank now owes X to the ECB. The ECB in turn creates a claim of N's central bank against the ECB. N's central bank credits the account of the commercial bank of the seller/provider. Many of these transactions take place every second.

Ideally, the balances should even out at the end of the day. If, however, the citizens of country G tend to consume more than they produce and the citizens of country N tend to produce more than they consume in their bilateral trade relation, the central bank of country G will build up liabilities towards the ECB clearing system and the central bank of country N will build up claims against the ECB clearing system. The Target2-system allows the central bank in G to 'keep' the money in exchange for a Target2-liability. G's central bank does not actually transfer central bank money. In order to source liquidity, the commercial banks in G refinance their budget with credit from G's central bank. In N, the commercial banks have no need for extra liquidity–their accounts are well credited. There is little risk that the central bank in G will 'dry out' as long as it is not forced to actually transfer book money so as to clear its accumulated Target2 liabilities.

The Target2-system, eventually, results in a capital flow towards the Target2-debtors. As long as the balance is not cleared, N's central bank has paid for goods/services delivered to the buyer in G while G' central bank was still able to 'print money' for G's commercial banks in a refinancing loan arrangement. The Target2-system implies a twofold bailout/transfer.

---

272 ECB, Agreement on emergency liquidity assistance (17 May 2017). For a discussion see: MATTHIAS BRENDEL and SEBASTIAN JOST, 'Jeder druckt für sich allein' (2012, 20 May) Welt; MARTIN GÖTZ, RAINER HASELMANN, JAN PIETER KRAHNEN, and SASCHA STEFFEN, 'Did emergency liquidity assistance (ELA) of the ECB delay the bankruptcy of Greek banks? (2015) Policy Letter No. 46. SAFE–Frankfurt House of Finance.

273 Target=Trans-European Automated Real-Time Gross Settlement Express Transfer.

First, the Target2 claims/liabilities are credited/charged with the ECB's main refinancing rate, which is not risk-adjusted. Since 2016, the ECB's main refinancing rate is 0%, i.e., there is no interest gain on the Target2 claims. Second, in case that the pay day comes and the debtor central banks are unable to pay the bill, the ECB and its shareholders are responsible to clear the default. This will, eventually, affect those countries with a high ECB share and a high Target2 claim significantly.[274] Just to illustrate the gigantic volume of the Target2 claims/liabilities: In January 2018, Germany had outstanding target claims of 882.1 bn euros, Luxemburg of 195.2 bn euros, and the Netherlands of 114.1 bn euros while Italy had outstanding target liabilities of 433.2 bn euros, Spain of 399 bn euros, and Portugal of 83.1 bn euros.[275]

3.5.3 The Threefold Bailout Subsidy

The EU bailout policy provides a threefold subsidy: an ex-ante, a present, and a future subsidy.

Ex-ante: Without that a bailout has taken place, the expectation of the bailout alone affects a transfer from the strong to the weak members of the transfer union. In the autonomy model, the interest rates reflect each individual debtor's distinct default risk. If, however, several debtors are bound together by a mutual bailout commitment/shared responsibility for their debts, the interest rates reflect the pooling risk. Consequently, the individual risk of a weak debtor is reduced by the expectation of a (partial) creditor bailout, which translates into lower credit costs for the weak debtors amongst the 'bailout community'. The strong members have to carry the bailout burden in comparatively high credit costs. The impact, i.e., the de-

274 Hans-Werner Sinn prominently brought to light and discussed the risks of the Target-2-imbalances. For a discussion and description of the Target-2-system see: HANS-WERNER SINN and TIMO WOLLMERSHÄUSER, 'Target loans, current account balances and capital flows: the ECB's rescue facility' (2012) 19 International Tax and Public Finance 468; HANS-WERNER SINN, 'Die Target-Kredite der Deutschen Bank' (2012, 21 March) ifo Schnelldienst Sonderausgabe; HANS-WERNER SINN and TIMO WOLLMERSHÄUSER, 'Target-Kredite, Leistungsbilanzsalden und Kapitalverkehr: Der Rettungsschirm der EZB' (2011, 24 Juni) ifo Schnelldienst.

275 For an overview of Target2-balances see EUROPEAN CENTRAL BANK, 'TARGET balances of participating NCBs: SDW Report Sheet' (2018) ECB Eurosystem – info page.

crease or increase in interest rates, depends on the financial weakness and strength of each member state. The closer the introduction of the euro came, the higher the market's expectations for a bailout regime grew, and the more the interest rates on government bonds were aligned. With the start of the euro currency union in 1999, the interest rates for the financially less sustainable members of the union fell sharply. From around 2000 until the financial crisis of 2008, the yields for 10-year government bonds of Greece, Spain, Ireland, and Italy were (almost) the same as for German and French government bonds. This was not because every debtor from now on would apply a promising and diligent budgetary policy, but because the weak EMU member states benefitted from the market's now rock-solid expectation that they would receive financial assistance from other members in case of distress. The interest rates were determined in a pooling equilibrium and the transfer union was established long before the first official bailout transfers were executed. With the financial crisis and the Ecofin decision in 2008 that the systematically relevant institutions should be bailed-out by their respective home country, the markets were seriously concerned as to whether the bailout expectation would hold and as to whether the financially weak member states would master the financial crisis. The interest rates for financially weak member states sky-rocked for a short period, but fell substantially, once the rescue mission started.[276]

Present: While it is true that bailout recipients have received their funds as a loan and not as a gift, the terms of the loan agreement are extremely favourable and can be considered quite rightly a very generous gift. The bailout has caused a roll-over of credit from the private to the public sector. The vast majority of Greeks debt, for instance, is now held by official bailout-creditors at a long maturity and at low interest rates. These interest rates do not at all reflect Greece' individual default risk. While the nominal value of Greece's government debt to GDP was approximately 175% in 2017, the present value of Greece' debt is likely to be much lower. Nobel laurate Paul Krugman called the Greek debt figures an "accounting fiction"[277] while investor Paul Kazarian argued that if international accounting standards were applied, this would show that the present value of

276 See the discussion of the "euro dividend" by BLANKART and EHMKE (2016) and see especially the graph at 49, displaying the years of the ex-ante bailout subsidy.

277 PAUL KRUGMAN, 'Greece: Think Flows, Not Stocks' (2015, 26 January) New York Times.

Greece's debt massively undercuts the debt's nominal value.[278] This means that a very significant bailout as a present gift from the rescuer nations has already taken place.[279]

Future: It is not yet clear as to whether there will be an additional bailout subsidy in the future in form of an official debt write-down. In one scenario, the distressed debtors take the chance of the present bailout subsidy and implement governance reforms so as to establish a solid financial architecture for the future. In another scenario, the present bailout subsidy stimulates the appetite for more concessions. The people in the debtor countries keep electing politicians who push for more concessions from the already very generous official creditors. At the same time, they delay or reject unpopular but necessary governance reforms. One day the creditors' patience comes to an end. There will be no more concessions. Even though the present value of the distressed debtors' debt is way below its nominal value, the poor implementation of governance reforms makes the debt level still unsustainable. The distressed governments default on their debt, which is by now primarily held by official bailout-creditors. A next round of re-negotiations starts. Additionally to the official bailout funds from the EFSF and ESM, the debtor defaults on its obligations towards the ECB. The concessions exceed the 'loan repayment' by far and the bailout now turns into a gift.

It is not yet clear as to whether the first or the second scenario will apply. But at least for Greece, the credit rating agencies are not that optimistic: In early 2018, Standard&Poor's rated Greece at B, Moody's at B3, and Fitch at B. There is an upward trend, but despite the enormous bailout funds deployed, that is still junk level, non-investment grade, with a high default probability.[280] It might be that the already very generous bailout subsidy will increase substantially in the future.

---

278 PAUL KAZARIN and THEODORE PELAGIDIS, 'Greece's New Agreement with Europe: Is This Time Different?' (2015) 5 Intereconomics 281; PAUL KAZARIAN, 'Strengthening Democracy Through Government Financial Management: Greece and the EU' (2016, 6 October) The Accountant & International Accounting Bulleting Conference and Awards. See also: JULIAN SCHUMACHER and BEATRE WEDER DI MAURO, 'Debt sustainability puzzles: Implications for Greece' (2015, 12 July) VOX CEPR'S Policy Portal, debt-to-GDP ratio, especially slides 6–14.

279 For more details on the post-restructuring credit structure see section V. 3.6.

280 TRADING ECONOMIES, Greece: Credit Ratings (2018, 21 February).

3.6 The Greek Debt Restructuring

While EMU bailout funds have regularly been channelled towards private creditors (amongst these lucky beneficiaries, prominently, French and German banks), the outstanding private sector debt of Greece was eventually restructured in 2012. Up until then, Greece had repaid its private creditors in time and in full with credit advanced to Greece by its official bailout creditors. During and after the 2012 debt restructuring, Greece continued to meet its legal obligations of debt repayment to its creditors, including to the few holdouts remaining after the 2012 debt restructuring. The credit rating agencies, nonetheless, are sceptical as to whether Greece will continue its debt service in the future.

After the Greek debt service had been kept alive with the support of bailout funds for about two years, Greece's debt to GDP level had risen to new heights in 2012. It became more than obvious, as it should have been from the very beginning, that Greece would not be able to meet its debt obligations on its own. The call for a substantial debt restructuring became louder, and also the IMF made a bail-in of private creditors conditional for its continued support. In autumn 2011, debt restructuring negotiations began. Private creditors, primarily banks from France, Germany, and Greece organised in a steering committee of 12 to lead the negotiations and to represent 32 institutional creditors in the creditor committee.

The final restructuring offer was announced in February 2012 and 8 March 2012 was set as the deadline for accepting the offer. Greece was under pressure to complete the deal before 20 March 2012 when a significant tranche of its domestic-law bonds would become due. Negotiations continued until 26 April 2012 to strike a deal with additional creditors. Creditors of 25 different bonds with a face value of together 6.4bn euros held out, i.e., they rejected the proposed amendments. The holdouts are still being repaid in full and on time.

Through the restructuring deal, almost 200bn euro of Greek debts owed to private creditors were reduced by more than half in face value. The offer was designed as package of: short-term EFSF notes, new Greek bonds, and GDP-linked securities.[281] Since the deal would prolong the maturity of a significant part for the newly issued Greek bonds at a low coupon, the

281 EFSF notes with a one-to-two year duration would cover 15% face value of the original debt and 6-month EFSF notes would cover 100% face value of accrued but not yet paid interests. New Greek government bonds would be issued under English-law, including the standard set of protective covenants, and under a co-

present value reduction of the newly issued security package was much more significant than the reduction in face value. If compared to the old securities, the haircut has been estimated to be between 76.9–78.8% by Zettelmeyer, Trebesch, and Gulati, and between 59.6–64.6% if the present value of the old bonds is compared to the newly issued security package at the same discount rate.[282] Interestingly, the losses suffered by creditors were quite unevenly distributed, since all creditors were offered the same security package in exchange for their bonds, no matter as to whether their debt claims would mature in weeks or decades. While bond creditors with a short time until maturity would suffer losses of around 80%, creditors with a long term until maturity would have to accept a haircut of only about 20%.[283]

The question is how could Greece succeed with its debt restructuring offer despite the fact that holdouts could speculate on full debt repayment. Greece and its official creditors endeavoured to avoid a default for several reasons. First, while a default should be avoided, this was not at all costs. If the debt restructuring offer had failed all together, the next bailout tranche was likely to be withhold, making a default inevitable. A debt restructuring without the support of bailout funds would have forced an even more brutal haircut. The debt restructuring offer, thus, must have been accounted for as the value-maximising alternative as compared to a debt restructuring with Greece 'on its own'.[284] Second, the creditor structure was most favourable for Greece. The vast majority of debt held by private creditors was owed to institutional investors, mostly banks with seats in France, Germany and Greece. Despite peer pressure to avoid a free ride, the banks

financing agreement with the EFSF so as to avoid a selective default to the disadvantage of private creditors. The maturity of the new Greek bonds would range from 2023 to 2042 with 31.5% face value and a 2 to 4.3% coupon. The GDP-linked security would add a 1% coupon on the face value of the newly issued Greek bonds in case GDP targets are met. The information on the Greek debt restructuring offer as cited in this section are presented by: JEROMIN ZETTELMEYER, CHRISTOPH TREBESCH, and MITU GULATI, 'The Greek Debt Restructuring: An Autopsy' (2013) CESifo Working Paper No. 4333, 8–14.

282 ZETTELMEYER, TREBESCH, and GULATI (2013) 17–20. The authors calculate with 3 distinct yields measured for in the direct aftermath of the restructuring offer (15.3%, 16.3%, and 18.7%) and curve yield combining different discount rates depending on the respective bond's maturity (table at 18).

283 ZETTELMEYER, TREBESCH, and GULATI (2013) 21–22.

284 ZETTELMEYER, TREBESCH, and GULATI (2013) 26–27.

were reportedly subject to immense pressure from authorities of their respective home countries.[285]

Eventually, the incentive to holdout and free ride could be reduced and the social dilemma of the public good could be (partly) resolved by a voting mechanism. English-law bonds, which accounted for about 10% of the outstanding privately held debt, contained collective action clauses which would allow the required majority of bondholders to modify the terms for all holders of the same issue. Greek-law bonds, accounting for over 85% of the outstanding privately held debt, did not contain such clauses. However, the Greek legislator was able to retrospectively include collective action clauses in all bond contracts subject to Greek law. The Greek Bondholder Act from February 2012 established collective action clauses with a quorum requirement of 50 per cent and a threshold of two-third. Different from the English-law bonds, the vote on the Greek-law bonds would aggregate all Greek-law bondholders to a single voting group. The minimum participation rate for the offer was set at 90 percent of privately held debt by face value. Unsurprisingly, the participation and acceptance rate amongst Greek-law bonds was significantly higher than under the English law bonds, since creditors of a single bond issue could not opt out and free ride without threatening the entire deal to go through and since the Greek-law bonds were vulnerable to future amendments by parliament, which–supposedly–would not have been in the interest of bondholders.[286] In the same year, Greece received funds from the EFSF in order to buy back newly issued exchange bonds (from spring 2012) with a face value of 31.9bn euros for 11.3bn euros on the secondary markets.[287]

The debt exchange and the debt buyback together entirely changed the debt structure for Greece. Since the end of 2012, the vast majority of Greek debt is held by official bailout creditors, primarily by the EFSF, other Eurozone governments (directly), the ESM, and the ECB. Debt owed to private bond investors/treasury bill holders made up for only about 17% in summer 2017.[288] While official creditors have, so far, been spared from a haircut in form of face value reductions, it is fair to say that the official cred-

285 ZETTELMEYER, TREBESCH, and GULATI (2013). At 24, they cite Martin Blessing (Commerzbank CEO) stating that the banks' concessions were "as voluntary as a confession during the Spanish inquisition".

286 ZETTELMEYER, TREBESCH, and GULATI (2013) 26–27.

287 ZETTELMEYER, TREBESCH, and GULATI (2013) 28–35. The secondary market price, thus, was 34 cents per euro.

288 In CHARLES FORELLE, PAT MINCZESKI, and ELLIOT BENTLEY, 'Greece's Debt Due' (2017) The Wall Street Journal, the authors present a constantly up-

itors have gifted Greece with a significant debt relief. The official rescue funds have been advanced to Greece at long maturities for very low interest rates, way below the risk-appropriate rate, so that Greece has, in fact, benefitted from a most generous debt relief in present value.[289]

And not only Greece, but significantly, its private creditors have taken huge advantage from the official bailout programme. From May 2010 until the Greek debt exchange became effective in 2012, official bailout funds were first and foremost used for interest and debt repayments to private creditors.[290] Private creditors were gifted the time until their bail-in to restructure their balance sheet so as to avoid financial distress/contagion as a consequence of a Greek default. And even for the 2012 debt restructuring, the haircut, presumably, would have been much higher if it had not been backed by the next bailout packages. While private creditors had to assume some of the costs of Greece's factual insolvency, the price which has been paid by official rescue creditors and which will be paid by them in the ongoing/future distress is likely to be much higher.[291]

3.7 Bailout and Crisis Management Top-Down: A New Era?

The EMU financial crisis made obvious that full autonomy in matters of spending, taxation, and debt acquisition under the umbrella of a bailout

---

dated overview on the Greek debt structure. As of 22 August 2017, debt held in form of treasury bills and by private investors accounted for about 49 out of 287 billion euros of outstanding debt. By this time, a substantial portion of the debt owed to the IMF was already repaid so that the outstanding debt to the IMF was only about 12 billion euros. The vast portion of outstanding debt, was held by official EU creditors, together 227 billion euros (EFSF: 131 billion, Eurozone governments: 53 billion, ESM: 30 billion, ECB: 13 billion).

289 See section V. 3.5.3.

290 JÖRG ROCHOLL and AXEL STAHMER, 'Where did the Greek bailout money go?' (2016) ESMT No. WP–16–02. Rocholl and Stahmer show that only a small portion (about 5%) of the bailout funds provided in the first and second programme for Greece flowed into the fiscal budget of Greece while about 64% (or 139.2bn euros) were channelled to creditors via the Greek debt service, about 17% (or 37.3bn euros) were used for the recapitalisation of Greek banks, and about 14% (or 29.7bn euros) were used as a direct pay-out to creditors in the 2012 debt restructuring (for the short-term EFSF-notes). Similarly, the third programme is mostly planned for debt repayment; this time for debt repayment to the official creditors, i.e.,. bailout funds advanced in the third programme are used to repay loans as part of previous bailout packages.

291 See the discussion of the present bailout subsidy in section V. 3.5.3.

regime is toxic for the financial stability in Europe. As it was argued throughout this book, there are generally two ways to approach financial stability: reform towards autonomy or reform towards integration. The European leaders put in place reforms which have developed the EMU more into the direction of integration. The reforms have two dimensions: *precaution* and *reaction*.

Precaution: As a response to the excessive European debt crisis, the Stability and Growth Pact was tightened in its design. The Stability and Growth Pact in its current design sets the goal that every member state has to have a balanced budget (with no more than 0.5% of GDP deficit) and a debt level of <60% of GDP. In a 3-yearly updated Medium-Term Budgetary Objectives (MTO) report, it is lined out for every member state how this goal may be achieved. Stability programmes (for Eurozone members) and convergence programmes (for other EU members) concretise the plan for the MTO, i.e., (i) what policies they have to implement, (ii) a forecast for growth/budget/deficit figures, and (iii) an explanation on which economic predictions/assumptions forecast and policies are based. The stability and convergence programmes are evaluated by the Commission.

In case that a member state does not comply with the guidelines for debt and deficit, a multi-step procedure sets in: The Commission issues a warning and makes a proposal for policy recommendations by the Council. If the Council's recommendations are not implemented until a specified deadline, the Commission requests a Council's decision to declare a 'lack of action' and possibly to recommend revised policies. This may be repeated in a second round. If the Commission still recognises a 'lack of action,' it may request a Council decision on an interest-bearing 0.2% of GDP deposit to be made by the country in non-compliance.

Especially for a member state in the Excessive Deficit Procedure, i.e., for a country with a deficit of >3% of GDP or a debt level or >60% of GDP, which is not reduced at a rate of 1/20 per year, the supervision and penalty system is strengthened. In regular intervals, policy measures are assessed and recommended, and progress reports are requested. If the Commission comes to the conclusion that the member state has not taken effective action to reduce the excessive deficit, a multi-step procedure of warnings and Council decision's is initiated. A deposit of 0.2% of GDP may be requested (if not already under the precautionary measures), which may be changed to a non-interest bearing deposit, and eventually to an 'appropriate' fine. Importantly, for the adoption of the sanctions as requested by the Commission, the reverse qualified majority rule applies. The Council has to reject the Commission's request for sanctions with a qualified majority in order to stop them from becoming effective. Continued non-compliance may result in a fine of up to 0.5% of GDP.[292]

Nonetheless, a fining system for deficit-/debtor countries seems odd. The past experience has already put into question its effectiveness. Sanctions which have proven to be an effective deterrent and measure, such as forced administration/regulatory supervision are not yet feasiable in the EMU.[293] Considering the EMU's bailout history, the 'punishment' of a fine or a deposit for the debt/deficit transgressor may be rather seen as a (heavily under-priced) insurance premium for future bailouts than as an effective enforcement mechanism to prevent excessive debts and deficits.

Reaction: Once a member state becomes officially a bailout country, the bailout is tied to conditions which can severely impact the country's autonomy in spending and taxation. The bailout country may be asked to perform tax, public sector, and private sector reforms as part of the 'Economic Adjustment Programme'. The goal of these governance reforms is to foster economic growth and to reduce the deficit of the programme country. The bailout volume is regularly paid out in tranches and a tranche may be held back unless the bailout country proves compliance with the agreed upon terms of the bailout programme. As the recent bailout experience shows, these Adjustment Programmes do not simply define the general parameters for reform, which would still allow the national government to make decisions on its own measures to achieve the goal. They tend to be quite specific, e.g., require the government of the bailout country to take certain agreed upon measures of fiscal, labour market, or financial market reform, and to privatise part of its national assets.[294]

---

292 EUROPEAN COMMISSION, Stability and Growth Pact – information page (2017). See especially the sub-pages 'Legal basics and related stages' for the 'preventive arm' and the 'corrective arm'. In order to avoid confusion, please note: The European Commission describes a 'preventive' and a 'corrective arm' of the Stability and Growth Pact. Both are discussed under the title 'precaution' in this sub-section since none of the available measures can resolve an already existing crisis. For that purpose, measures as described under the title 'reaction' in this sub-section have to be taken. The Stability and Growth pact finds its legal fundament in Artt. 121 ("preventive arm") and 126 ("corrective arm") and 136 (only relevant to EMU members) TFEU and Protocol (12) to the TFEU (Treaty on the Functioning of the European Union).

293 See the Puerto Rico Case Study in section IV. 2.5.2.

294 See for instance the First and Second Economic Adjustment Programme for Greece: EUROPEAN COMMISSION, 'The Economic Adjustment Programme for Greece' (2010, May) Economic and Financial Affairs Occasional Papers No. 61; EUROPEAN COMMISSION, 'The Economic Adjustment Programme for

The economic adjustment programmes have caused great anger and criticism.[295] The most significant problem of the economic adjustment programmes and their greatest vulnerability is probably that they are perceived as the diktat of a foreign power over a sovereign country. The protests and election results in the bailout countries tell a story about the people's dissatisfaction. Even though the conditions tied to the bailout come as a logical consequence of integration, since they are targeted to re-establish the unity between payers and decision-maker, they have the potential to destroy the support for the union in the bailout countries. And this is, by the same token, the greatest vulnerability of the policy measures/ conditions to the bailout. If the support for a 'cooperative' debtor government fades, the people can vote for an anti-reform government which promises to end the austerity policies imposed by the rescuing countries. In the end, the member states remain fully sovereign and retain their power to decide about spending, taxation, and borrowing. The agreements for governance reform are fragile. Threats by the rescuing countries to finally withhold bailout transfers in case of non-compliance are not credible. The politicians in the rescuing countries themselves fear that a default would unmask the real volume of past transfers and of the present value haircut in the highly subsidised rescue loans advanced to high-risk sovereign debtors. Thus, they have an incentive to 'keep on rescuing', so that the rescued country receives at least enough funds to constantly repay the previous rescue loans.[296]

Greece' (2012, March) European Economy Occasional Papers No. 94. See also the Memorandum of Understanding and the privatisation plan for Greece as part of the Third Economic Adjustment Programme: EUROPEAN COMMISSIAN and THE HELLENIC REPUBLIC et al., Memorandum of Understanding Between the European Commission Acting on Behalf of the European Stability Mechanism and The Hellenic Republic and The Bank of Greece (2015, August); and HELLENIC REPUBLIC ASSET DEVELOPMENT FUND, 'Asset Development Plan' (2015, July).

295 The most prominent and vocal economist to criticise the focus on austerity is probably Nobel laureate Joseph Stiglitz. See for instance: JOSEPH STIGLITZ, 'Greece, the Sacrificial Lamb' (2015, July 25) The New York Times.

296 See sections II. 3.2., V. 3.5.3, and V. 3.6.

3.8 Contagion, Systematic Risk and Banking Union

Contagion and Systematic Risk: The bailout programme has regularly been justified with the goal to avoid a crisis spill-over. There are arguably two channels for contagion:

First, the default of one EMU member state, it is said, could raise doubts about the financial sustainability of other EMU member states. This concern lacks reason. The Maastricht Treaty was designed in the spirit that every state would stand on its own and that the markets would be able to distinguish good from bad borrowers – also in times of crisis. The enforcement of this principle should not weaken the creditworthiness of its members solely on the basis that they stand on their own, but it should reinforce the accurate risk calculation for individual member state based on their distinct default risk. The 'contagion' is nothing than the final rejection of common pool financing, which will sort the wheat from the caff in a seperating equilibrium.

Second, the default of a EMU member state can trigger the default of its creditors in case that they hold substantial debt claims against the debtor. With a high volume of non-performing loans, the creditors may lack the assets to balance their own liabilities. The creditors themselves may be forced into bankruptcy. If the creditors of the defaulting sovereign debtor are systematically relevant financial institutions, the national government of their seat may come under pressure to bail them out.[297] The bail-out of the financial institutions considered to be systematically relevant may exceed the abilities of the national government or at least force the national government to acquire additional debt so as to finance the bank bailout.

The concern about the second channel of contagion holds some truth. It is, nonetheless, an odd strategy to rescue the sovereign debtor in order to rescue its systematically relevant financial creditors. Not all of the sovereign creditors will be systematically relevant and not all of them will be at the brink of insolvency in case that they have to account for the (full)

297 On the question of the bailout of systematically relevant financial institutions see: KENNETH AYOTTE and DAVID SKEEL, 'Bankruptcy or Bailouts?' (2010) 35 The Journal of Corporation Law 469; ELIJAH BREWER and JULAPA JAGTIANI, 'How Much Did Banks Pay to Become Too-Big-to-Fail and to Become Systemically Important' (2013) 48 (1) Journal of Financial Services Research 1; WILLEM BUITER, 'Kornai on Soft Budget Constraints, Bail-Outs and the Financial Crisis' (2009, 14 October) Financial Times; ALAN MORRISON, 'Systematic Risk and the 'too-big-to-fail' problem' (2011) 27 (3) Oxford Review of Economic Policy 498.

losses suffered in a default of the sovereign debtor. Instead of bailing out the sovereign debtor G for the loss in default X, the bailout could be made available (i) only for G's systematically relevant creditors and for the portion of debt in default held by such creditors, (ii) only for G's systematically relevant creditors which are unable to write down G's debt without financial assistance, and (iii) only for the portion of their loss which they are unable to shoulder themselves. Assume, for instance, that (i) 0.75X of G's debt is held by systematically relevant creditors, that (ii) only two-thirds of G's systematically relevant debtors hold substantial amounts of G's debt and are of critical financial health and, and that (iii) they could – in average – write down 40% of their individual share in X without being at risk of insolvency. A selective bailout available only to specific creditors for only part of their loss, i.e., with a volume of 0.3X in our example, will naturally be the cost-effective alternative to an ongoing and indirect bailout of all creditors via a bailout of the sovereign debtor.

This way, also the principle of market discipline is re-introduced. Not every sovereign debt capital investor is systematically relevant and not even the systematically relevant investors can predict that they will find themselves in a situation where they will benefit from a bailout to prevent their own insolvency. If they do not operate at the brink of insolvency, they will simply face significant losses suffered by shareholders and mangers with performance-linked compensations. The incentive to price the debtor accurately and to engage in ex-ante debt management remains while it is still reduced for systematically relevant creditors. The problem of moral hazard for systematically relevant creditors expecting a bail-out, nonetheless, is easier to resolve than for sovereign debtors expecting a bail-out. The reason is a workable and enforceable chain of commands. It is a daunting if not often hopeless undertaking to subject a sovereign country to top-down directives by the rescuing nations. The EU/EMU lawmaker has little authority to actually command and enforce a fiscal policy for any of its member states. It is, moreover, a heavy burden for the relationships within the union if payers demand command and control over beneficiaries. It is, despite the challenges to design an effective legal framework for banking regulation, at least in the national lawmakers' and, by delegation, in the EU lawmaker's authority to regulate systematically relevant financial institutions.

Banking Union: The banking union breaks with the principle that monetary policy and banking supervision are regulated by different authorities. Before the banking union came into existence, the national regulatory authorities had to monitor the solvency of their national financial institutions to protect the integrity and stability of the financial system while the ECB was in charge of the monetary policy, which affected the solvency of the financial institutions.[298] As a reaction to the sovereign debt and the financial crisis, the EU/EMU members agreed to establish a so-called 'banking union' and passed several directives with the goal to unify and tighten regulations for financial institutions. The banking union creates a mandatory framework for EMU members. Other EU member states may opt in.

The banking union consists of a 'Single Supervisory Mechanism' (SSM), a 'Single Resolution Mechanism' (SRM), and a harmonised regulatory framework for banking regulation (the 'Single Rulebook'). With the SSM, the ECB has the mandate to monitor financial sustainability and compliance with European law of potentially all banks in the EMU. The main focus of the ECB's supervisory efforts, however, is on banks with assets of 30bn euros and more, banks with assets of more than 20% of their respective home country's GDP, and banks funded by the EFSF or ESM, while other banks remain to be primarily monitored by their national authority.

In case of distress, the ECB as supervisory authority may notify the Board of the Single Resolution Mechanism, which will take action in case that no alternative or private resolution is feasiable and that the operation of the SRM is in the public interests. The SRM may be used for the restructuring or liquidation of a bank. A EMU-wide insurance pool (resolution fund), to which the European banks shall contribute about 1% of their covered deposits (within the next years, about 55bn euros in total), shall be available for the resolution of a banking crisis.[299]

The 'Single Rulebook' comprises the 'CRD IV–Capital Requirements Regulation and Directive' (with the 'CRR–Capital Requirement Regulation'), the 'BRRD–Bank Recovery and Resolution Directive', and the 'DGSD–Deposit Guarantee Scheme Directive', with Binding Technical Standards for their implementation. CRD IV and CRR together set capital and liquidity requirements for financial intermediaries and standards for management compensation.[300] The BRRD lays out the legal framework for

298 The consolidation of both functions, which from now on will be vested in the ECB, may cause an ongoing conflict of interests. On the banking union and the potential conflict of interests see: BLANKART (2017) 464–466.

299 For a discussion of the Single Resolution Mechanism see: DAVID HOWARTH and LUCIA QUAGLIA, 'The Steep Road to European Banking Union: Constructing the Single Resolution Mechanism' (2014) 52 (Annual Review) Journal of Common Market Studies 125.

300 CRD IV Capital Requirement Directive 2013/36/EU and Capital Requirements Regulation (EU) No. 575/2013.

the bank recovery and resolution process, i.e., for the bail-in of bank shareholders and creditors, the resolution fund, and the restructuring, reorganisation, and liquidation of failing banks.[301] The DGSD requires the national authorities to establish a deposit insurance scheme for deposits up to an amount of 100 000 euros per deposit and for pension schemes of SMEs in order to prevent a bank run. Different from the bank resolution fund, the DGSD regulates the establishment of national insurances and not of an EMU-wide insurance pool.[302]

It would go by far beyond the scope of this analysis to provide an in-depth evaluation of the national and EU-wide regulations put in place to manage financial sustainability and to contain moral hazard for systematically relevant institutions. Certainly, one may ask as to whether a 1%-covered deposit pool is sufficient in a financial crisis, as to whether the deposit insurance should or could be organised as an EU-wide pool, possibly with premiums adjusted to the relative risk contribution, or how capital puffers and leverages may be best regulated.[303] But one should also ask the fundamental question as to whether the ECB, in charge of monetary policy and as an important creditor to (distressed) sovereign debtors in the EMU, is fit to exercise good judgement as a banking regulator.[304] Finally, one may ask if the problems of contagion and moral hazard are also home-grown. While banks are generally required to increase their equity with a decreasing quality of their assets, they were allowed or even encouraged to hold sovereign bonds of EMU member state (of questionable quality) without any equity cover. To fight the contagion/moral hazard problem, it would be very important to totally end the accounting privilege for sovereign bonds when it comes to the equity requirements for financial intermedi-

---

301 Bank Recovery and Resolution Directive 2014/59/EU.

302 Deposit Guarantee Schemes Directive 2014/49/EU.

303 In BARRY EICHENGREEN and CHARLES WYPLOSZ, 'Minimal Conditions for the Survival of the Euro' (2016) 1 Intereconomics 24, 27 the authors advocate a strong banking union, e.g. with a credible and union-wide deposit insurance, as a condition "for the survival of the euro". For a discussion of the EU banking union see: DAVID HOWARTH and LUCIA QUAGLIA, 'Banking Union as Holy Grail: Rebuilding the Single Market in Financial Services, Stabilizing Europe's Banks and 'Completing' Economic and Monetary Union' (2013) 51 (Annual Review) Journal of Common Market Studies 103; DANIEL GROS and DIRK SCHOENMAKER, 'European Deposit Insurance and Resolution in the Banking Union' (2014) 52 (3) Journal of Common Market Studies 529; ROLAND VAUBEL, 'Probleme der Bankenunion: Falsche Lehren aus der Krise' (2013) 46 (3) Credit and Capital Markets – Kredit und Kapital 281.

304 BLANKART (2017) 464–466.

aries or maybe even to set a limit for the relative amount of sovereign bonds that banks are allowed to hold.[305]

3.9 Institutional Congruence Review

The pre-bailout time: In the years since the Maastricht Treaty until the first rescue packages, the EMU resembled quite clearly the autonomy model with some smaller deviations from that principle. The member states retained their full sovereignty in matters of spending and taxation. While the Stability and Growth Pact set a limit to deficit-spending and indebtness, Artt. 123 and 125 TFEU established a plain rule against bailouts and unlimited transfers. However, already the pairing of the no-bailout principle with the Stability and Growth Pact was odd. The no bailout-principle is generally established in order to protect the private good of (national) self-responsibility and financial sustainability in the autonomy model while the Stability and Growth Pact would be a sensible top-down institution to protect the public good of common pool financing in the integration model. Albeit this inconsistency, the weak rules of the Stability and Growth Pact and the direct transfers from the official EU budget did not really erode the principle of autonomy until the bailout union finally materialised. Since the market gave little credit to the no bailout principle, the bailout subsidy of interest rates, which were very obviously accounted for in a pooling equilibrium, can be seen as a first sign that the model of autonomy as presented in the treaties was fragile and that the mixed character of the union was soon to be revealed. However, until the bailout programmes were started, the union still had the chance to disappoint the market's expectation of a bailout. If the EMU had actually enforced Artt. 123 and 125 TFEU, the EMU could have established a defensible and credible no-bailout principle, just as the USA did in the 1840s. The story took a different turn.

The bailout time: The bailout policy has changed the character of the EMU fundamentally. The institutional congruence index reveals a mixed model:

---

305 See EWING (2011) on the zero-risk accounting standards for sovereign bonds. EICHENGREEN and WYPLOSZ (2016) argue that banks should be prohibited from holding sovereign debt so as to take away the incentive to bailout states in order to indirectly bailout banks (see page 27).

(Fig. 5) Institutional Congruence Index: European Monetary Union

Autonomy Model ◄	**Mixed Model**	► **Integration Model**
EMU		
Elements of Autonomy		**Elements of Integration**
1A.Aut. No Bailout Principle AND		**1A.Int. Bailout Guarantee AND/OR 1B.**
		EMU
1B.Aut. Borrowing Autonomy AND		**1B.Int. Top-Down Borrowing Constraints AND**
EMU		
2.Aut. Spending Autonomy AND		**2.Int. Top-Down-Controlled Spending Authority AND**
EMU		
3A.Aut. Tax Autonomy AND		**3A.Int. Top-Down Controlled Tax Authority AND**
EMU		
3B.Aut. Tax-Funded Budget		**3B.Int. Transfer-Funded Budget**
	EMU	

Short Explanation:[306]

1A. No-Bailout Principle versus Bailout Guarantee: The past bailouts and the institutions established to permanently bailout distressed member states prove the no bailout principle, as it was originally agreed upon in the Maastricht Treaty, to be worthless. A partial bail-in of private creditors of, so far, only one bailout recipient (Greece) does little to alter the picture of a strong bailout guarantee.

1B. Borrowing Autonomy versus Top-Down Borrowing Constraints: The EMU member states, in principle, have full sovereignty in matters of debt acquisition. The Stability and Growth Pact has proven to be defenceless and it is doubtful as to whether the tightened precautionary measures will be enough to protect the public good of financial stability in a bailout and transfer union.

2. Spending Autonomy versus Top-Down Controlled Spending Authority: Every member state is free to spend its resources without top-down commands. Restrictions apply only as far as the state's spending policy conflicts with the rules of the single market. Once a country, on the other hand, is a programme country under the bailout regime, the spending and debt autonomy may be heavily restricted under the conditions attached to the bailout transfers.

3. Tax Autonomy versus Top-Down Controlled Tax Authority: As long as a country does not receive bailout transfers, it can choose its tax base/rate independently. An exception applies only for the lower and upper limit of the VAT tax. Top-down directives, nonetheless, may be part of the conditions agreed upon for bailout transfers.

4. Tax-Funded versus Transfer-Funded Budget: The transfers from the official EU budget would have relatively little influence on the general rule of a tax-funded budget. The bailout subsidy, however, shifts the EMU towards a transfer-funded budget. Importantly, the bailout subsidy is paid out to the member states in common pool financing already before (!) the bailout itself takes place.

The EMU has arrived at a stage where it is a mess from the perspective of institutional congruence. The analysis of the EMU shows a mixed fiscal regime, with a tendency towards autonomy.

306 For a more detailed analysis with further references, see the previous sections of this chapter.

4. The European Tragedy and the Way Forward

The EMU in its current design is stuck between two stools: autonomy and integration. The fiscal consequences are overindebtness, overspending, misallocation of resources, and an ongoing sovereign debt crisis. The political consequences are a raging dissatisfaction in many parts of Europe and a union at high risk to be torn apart. The incentives to externalise costs remain strong. Instead of effective precautionary measures, reaction is the policy of the time. The puzzle is: Why do the 'rescuing' nations waste their taxpayers money and why do the 'rescued' nations accept bailout funds, which mostly go to their private creditors, if the bailout comes with the diktat of the rescuers?

An answer to this question involves some ambiguity. Public choice theory may give a plausible explanation: The intentions of the political decision-makers in the 'rescuing' nations may be explained with asymmetrically distributed information. Albeit very generous present value haircuts on bailout loans, the official bailout creditors have rejected any face value cuts as they would be hard to sell to the taxpayers and voters in the 'rescuing' country. It appears like as if the direct bailout of systematically relevant financial creditors as well as if the chaos of a default in the EMU in the aftermath of the financial crisis were avoided at a price which has been highly underestimated by taxpayers and voters in the 'rescuing' countries. If the political decision-makers, therefore, have been successful to disguise the real bailout burden, this gives a very reasonable explanation for their actions.

Another explanation may be that it was not even the major concern of the political decision-makers in the 'rescuing' countries to choose the value-maximising option from a financial perspective when comparing the bailout with the insolvency option. Their concern might have been to trade political power in Europe for money. The 'rescuing' nations under the lead of Germany have gained significant say in EU/EMU politics through the bailout programme. Even the fiscal politics of the 'rescued' sovereign countries have themselves become a matter of EU/EMU politics. The austerity and reform programmes in the EMU carry a German handwriting. The bailout funds might have been calculated for as an upfront investment for a diligent budgetary and fiscal architecture: The political decision-makers of the 'rescuers' might have had the rather optimistic idea that they could effectively control the 'rescued' nations in order to reform their economy. If this was the plan, it is not very likely that it will be successful. Another possible motivation of politicians in rescuing countries with a rather strong and export-oriented industry might have been to keep the exchange rate of the euro in relation to other currencies low. This way they could (indirectly) support their own export industry for a short-to-mid-term national gain and on the costs of financial stability in the long-term.

The fact that the 'rescued' nations have accepted the bailout funds for the benefit of their private creditors in exchange for the diktat of the 'rescuers' is baffling at first glance. It, however, makes a lot of sense in the long-run. If the bailout is established as a rule, this will enable common pool financing and a continued bailout subsidy in form of cheap interest rates on capital markets in the future and presently in form of very low interest rates from official creditors. Even if the diktat of the 'rescuers' is unpleasant, the bailout recipients can speculate on lenience once their 'rescuers' are highly committed to and entangled with the bailout recipients via their lending relations. Once the 'rescuing' countries have already advanced large bailout loans to the troubled debtors, their ultimate threat to stop future bailout transfer in case of the debtor's non-compliance with agreements for governance reform loses credibility. A default of the bailout recipients to their official creditors would unveil the actually very high costs for the taxpayers of the 'rescuing nations'. Accounting for this dilemma, the political decision-makers in the 'rescued' nations might hope to secure the continued bailout subsidy for the future and to re-negotiate the terms of governance reform later on or to simply implement them incompletely, if at all.

From the perspective of national political popularity, the EMU crisis management is not even a bad choice for the politicians in the 'rescuing' as well as in the 'rescued' nations. The politicians in the 'rescuing' countries, in particular in Germany, have successfully managed to present themselves as crisis managers in Europe. Any drawbacks on the implementation of reforms are rather accounted for to the disadvantage of the 'rescued' nations in the public opinion in the 'rescuing' countries. For the politicians in the 'rescued' nations, the situation is quite similar. The 'diktat of the rescuers' might be highly unpleasant for the voters. Nonetheless, it provides a very concrete scapegoat for their anger. In the end, the politicians in the 'rescuing' and in the 'rescued' nations might fare well with the bailout policy in terms of national popularity. This is especially true when the dissatisfaction of the taxpayers and voters is targeted at the 'lazy Southerners' or the 'dictatorial paymasters from the North' and not at the own political elite. Nonetheless, the costs of a loss in popularity are still there. In particular the European project suffers a high popularity loss, since the bailout policy antagonises the 'rescuers' against the 'rescued'.

For the long-term benefit of taxpayers and voters and the survival and continued success of the EMU/EU, it would be wise to search for an exit strategy. As it has been argued throughout this book, there are two ways towards financial sustainability: autonomy or integration. The present externalities of fiscal decisions have to be internalised so as to encourage decisions for value-maximisation. The fiscal architecture of the EMU, also after its reform, is not fit to fulfill this requirement. The way towards integration would require a strong fiscal union. Decisions about spending, taxation, and debt acquisition would have to be (partly) centralised. A workable fiscal union may be designed with the following elements: (i) shared taxes from a common tax pool as well as upper and lower limits for own taxes, (ii) the right of a central body to reject a deficit-budget, (iii) the right of a central body to reject future private debt finance as well as strictly enforced and tight rules for borrowing, (iv) an oversight and supervision procedure for overindebted and insolvent members. A fully integrated fiscal union would only be achieved if all members effectively gave up their sovereignty and submitted themselves to top-down rule.

A watered-down but still effective alternative would be an automatic (non-negotiable) exit for sovereign members which do not comply with debt and deficit requirements. The members remain sovereign, since they are free to decide to not comply with top-down orders. However, they would do so in the knowledge that their non-compliance will (possibly after warnings have been issued) cause their automatic exit.

At present, there is no political will feasiable to go that far; neither to have a totally integrated fiscal union nor an automatic exit procedure. Also the gap between rich and poor regions in the EMU/EU is too big to assume that the taxpayers and voters would support a move towards integration, which typically is accompanied by a move towards equalisation.

The alternative way towards financial sustainability goes into the direction of autonomy. The no-bailout principle would have to be enforced strictly and the past bailout operation would have to be explicitly ruled out. The Stability and Growth Pact is an anomaly, which should be abandoned. It serves no purpose in a regime where the fiscal strategy is each member state's responsibility. If, eventually, the contagion of financial intermediaries is seen as a problem because it could pressurize sovereigns to neglect the no-bailout principle, the regulation of financial institutions (possible with a limit to sovereign bond holdings) is the better alternative to a sovereign bailout. Since, despite market discipline, trying implies the possibility of error, i.e., fiscal planning implies the possibility of insolvency, it would be highly recommendable to establish a sovereign insolvency regime (at least for the EMU). The establishment of such a regime itself would be the most credible signal possible for the actual enforcement of the no-bailout principle. For the EMU, a consequent autonomy model would function according to the principle: 'separate funds, good friends'.[307]

---

307 CHARLES BLANKART, "Ich werbe für das Schweizer Modell" Zeit Online, Interview (14 March 2013).

VI. The Challenge of Autonomy: Sovereign Debtors in Insolvency

1. *Challenge and Solution*

The vast majority of countries around the world cannot expect a comprehensive bailout. While they might be able to get limited financial assistance from the IMF, the Worldbank, or other countries, they are first and foremost responsible for their own debts. Creditors cannot and do not calculate with a high bailout probability. The capital costs for sovereign debtors 'outside the Eurozone' are determined by the individual debtor's default risk. Since sovereign debtors 'on their own' cannot externalize the costs of their individual default (risk) and burden other countries, their governments are accountable to the creditors and to their own taxpayers and voters. Room for opportunistic strategies is limited. Sovereign debtors 'on their own' constitute the exhibit A for the fiscal autonomy model.

Nonetheless, the case of autonomous sovereign debtors is more ambiguous than the case of private, corporate, and even subnational public debtors. The law in the books is easy to read: Sovereigns have to repay their debts! There is no orderly insolvency and no excuse for non-repayment. Only a voluntary debt adjustment which requires the unanimous consent of all creditors justifies a lower debt repayment. The reality is more complicated: Sovereign debtors with an 'unsustainable debt burden' cannot repay all their debts in time and in full and a voluntary debt write-down will often fail because of coordination and cooperation problems on the creditors' side. The case of law enforcement, finally, makes the situation even more awkward: While sovereign debtors are legally required to repay their debts, their creditors have little chance to enforce their lawful and due debt claims unless the sovereign debtor is willing to pay. Debt enforcement, in fact, often stops at the borders of the sovereign debtor. Section VI. 2 will deal with the challenges which autonomous sovereign debtors and their creditors face; challenges which develop in the absence of a workable insolvency solution and because of weak law enforcement.

Section VI. 3 eventually discusses the option of an orderly insolvency procedure in public and private ordering designed to overcome the problems identified in section VI. 2; a procedure established in order to close the gap between the law in the books and the law in reality for the benefit of sovereign debtors and their creditors. In section VI. 3.5, the proposal for a sovereign insolvency regime will be briefly transferred to the case of subnational public debtors.

2. *The Challenge*

2.1 Bold Players in a Game With Weak Rules

For 'truly autonomous' debtors, which cannot expect a bailout, and for their creditors, the absence of an orderly debt restructuring/insolvency procedure in public or private ordering creates an awkward situation. On the one hand, collective action problems and perverse incentives to free ride make it hard if not impossible to reach a voluntary debt restructuring agreement; unless the sovereign's creditors are connected to the sovereign and to each other by long-standing borrowing relations. On the other hand, the political agents of sovereign debtors, who so often turn the blame on 'greedy or opportunistic investors,' behave themselves ruthless and aggressive when they blackmail their creditors to accept a 'voluntary' exchange offer.[308]

After briefly exploring the legal framework, i.e., the 'normative' concept of sovereign debt but also the setting for enforcement actions against sovereign debtors in VI. 2.2, the blackmail strategies often played by sovereign debtors in restructuring negotiations will be analysed in VI. 2.3. If creditors reject the sovereign debtor's offer, they regularly have only the choice to either trade their debt claim or to take enforcement actions against the sovereign debtor. Enforcement against sovereigns is practically a tricky business, typically undertaken by sophisticated investors with a substantial debt holding. Enforcement strategies to bypass the enforcement barriers set up by sovereign debtors unwilling to repay their debts will be discussed in sections VI. 2.4. In section VI. 2.5, eventually, the costs which arise when, first, the sovereign's reputation as a debtor, and second, the sovereign's reputation as a reliable 'host country for investments' are compromised, will be analysed.

308 For a review of past sovereign defaults see CARMEN REINHARDT an KENNETH ROGOFF, *This Time is Different* (Princeton University Press 2011).

2.2 The Legal Basics

The principle *pacta sunt servanda* is absolute in the sovereign debt business. A modification of the debt terms always requires the unanimous/individual consent of the debtholder at some point in time. Consent may be given in two ways:

- The debt contract does not contain a majority amendment clause. The debtor asks its creditors to agree to a modification of the original contract or to exchange their old for new debt instruments with different terms. Unanimous/individual consent is required for the modification after the restructuring offer has been presented to the creditors.
- The debt contract contains a majority amendment clause. At the time when the debt contract is concluded, the creditors unanimously/individually agree to a possible modification of the debt contract conditional upon a future event: The debt contract stipulates that the contract shall be modified in case that a proposed modification is approved by a (qualified) majority.

It is important to recognise that majority amendment clauses/collective action clauses do not work without each creditors' individual consent. The modification triggered by a majority vote is legitimized by unanimous consent at an earlier point in time when the debt contract is concluded. An insolvency regime instead would be coercive by its nature, i.e., it would affect legal rights without contractual consent. Presently, there does not exist a sovereign insolvency regime which could affect a binding debt reduction for all creditors without their unanimous/individual consent. The status quo, therefore, is that sovereigns have to fulfill their contractual obligations no matter what.[309]

309 The discussion about odious debts, i.e., debts acquired by a totalitarian regime without the people's approval for the suppression of the very same people, is practically of little relevance; first, because it affects very few debtors; second, because it is far from being an established principle in international law; third, because it is technically hard to prove/trace as to whether debt acquired by a dictator was utilised to fund the secret police or schools and hospitals. Government debt is typically not acquired for/labelled for a specific investment/spending. For an overview on the legal history of the odious debt doctrine see: JEFF KING, 'Odious Debt: The Terms of the Debate' (2007) 32 (4) North Carolina Journal of International Law and Commercial Regulation' 605. For a supportive review see: SEEMA JAYACHANDRAN and MICHAEL KREMER, 'Odious Debt' (2006) 96 (1) The American Economic Review 82. For the contra-perspective see: ALBERT CHOI and ERIC POSNER, 'A Critique of the Odious Debt Doctrine' (2007) 70 (3) Law and Contemporary Problems 33.

While the legal rights of the individual creditors to claim full repayment of their debt, i.e., the outstanding principal plus accrued interests is undoubtly unaffected by whatever agreement the sovereign may reach with other creditors, the situation becomes more complicated when creditors try to actually sue the sovereign and enforce their legal rights. In the past, sovereigns could hide behind the principle of absolute sovereign immunity. This principle was abandoned decades ago by the principle of restricted sovereign immunity in legislation and case law which applies for the jurisdictions of all major trading places for sovereign debt. Today, sovereigns will be held responsible for their actions if their actions constitute a 'commercial activity' (acta iure gestioni versus acta iure imperii), which certainly applies to sovereign debt lending.[310]

It will always be a long and rocky way to go for creditors until they see their debt claim honoured if the debtor is unwilling to repay. The major problem is enforcement. While creditors should win a title in court confirming their legal right to be repaid in full, the debtor may simply ignore the court order. Since litigation and enforcement actions on the sovereign debtor's own soil are regularly pointless, the creditors will have to search for detachable assets of the defaulting debtor abroad. While the sovereign itself is in principle not immune from enforcement orders, many of its assets which are typically held abroad, e.g., central bank deposits, assets for the well-functioning of executive and diplomatic activates, are still placed under special protection from enforcement. Sovereign debtors in default and creditors have long played cat and mouse when it comes to the enforcement of lawful debt claims: Creditors search for assets which may be considered the sovereign debtor's property. Despite the efforts to find such assets, already the question if assets belong to the debtor itself, to a third party, or if the legal owner is not simply the debtor 'in disguise' has to an-

---

310 The vast majority of sovereign debt is traded in New York and England. The principle of restricted sovereign immunity is codified in. In the US, the question of sovereign immunity is regulated by the U.S. Sovereign Immunities Act 1976. In the UK, the question of sovereign immunity is regulated by the State Sovereign Immunity Act 1978. In international public law, the distinction is made between 'acta iure imperii' and 'acta iure gestioni'. The latter comprise commercial activities of a sovereign for which the sovereign may not claim sovereign immunity. Additionally, sovereign debt contracts regularly include a waiver of all possible sovereign immunity defenses. For a good review of the law on sovereign immunity and market practice concerning bond contract design see: MARK WEIDEMEIER and MITU GULATI, 'Market Practice and the Evolution of Foreign Sovereign Immunity' (forthcoming) Law & Social Inquiry.

swered case by case in multiple jurisdictions. The assets may be taken in detention, but the next question to follow is not as to whether the sovereign debtor owes the creditors, which is regularly the case, but as to whether the particular assets are attachable or not, i.e., as to whether not the sovereign but certain of its assets are immune from enforcement. These questions have sometimes been decided in favour of creditors, other times in favour of the debtor.[311]

Presently, the best chance for creditors to enforce their claim is to threaten the debtor with harm. They may block the sovereign debtor's capital market access or they humiliate the debtor as a defaulter.[312] Humiliation translates into a low reputation as a borrower or host country for foreign investments.[313] A good example thereof is the Argentina case: After Argentina had defaulted on its debt in 2001 in the midst of a harsh financial and economic crisis, Argentina approached its bondholders with a restructuring offer in 2005. Bondholders were offered to exchange their original bonds to new bonds with a value of approximately one-third of what was owed to the creditors. While earmarked as a 'voluntary debt restructuring,' this deal was anything but voluntary. Argentina proclaimed that it would pay holdout creditors zero. Especially for small bondholders, this is a highly coercive strategy. There is just but one solution: Accept, or leave with empty pockets! The question as to whether the offer is fair was of little importance.[314] Still, some creditors rejected the offer and even after a second debt restructuring in 2010, more than 8% of the original debt remained outstanding. By then, the debt was mostly held by sophisticated distressed debt investors.[315]

---

311 FAISAL AHMED, LAURA ALFARO and NOEL MAURER, 'Lawsuits and Empire: On the Enforcement of Sovereign Debt in Latin America' (2010) 73 Law and Contemporary Problems 39, 42–44; SEBASTIAN GRUND, 'Enforcing Sovereign Debt in Court – A Comparative Analysis of Litigation and Arbitration Following the Greek Debt Restructuring of 2012' (2017) 1 University of Vienna Law Review 35; JILL FISH and CAROLINE GENTILE, 'Vultures or Vanguards?: The Role of Litigation in Sovereign Debt Restructurings' (2004) 53 Emory Law Journal 1047.

312 For an analysis of the strategies played by a sovereign debtors "on its own" and its creditors and the associated costs, discussed in this section VI. 2., see: DAVID EHMKE, 'Sovereign Debtors in Distress' (2015) 12 (1) University of St. Thomas Law Journal 1, especially 9–11, 14–18, 19–20, 23–24.

313 See VI. 2.4 and 2.5.

314 See therefore VI. 2.3.

315 On the debt restructuring 2005 and 2010 (and also on the enforcement actions by creditors to be discussed in the next paragraph) see: JOHN F HORNBACK,

After several attempts to collect the outstanding debt,[316] finally the holdouts' attack on Argentina's position as a borrower was a major success. Argentina was ordered to comply with the parri passu clause in its original bond contract and to treat its creditors equally, i.e., Argentina was barred from making payments on its new/present bonds unless it would pay the holdout creditors rateably on the outstanding principal plus accrued interests. In order to effectively enforce the equal treatment decisions, third parties (here, Bank of America and Banco de la Nación Argentina) were ordered to provide information for the discovery of Argentina's assets abroad. The former decisions by the Southern District Court of New York were upheld in appeal to the Second Circuit Court[317] and finally the U.S. Supreme Court rejected Argentina's defense of sovereign immunity (regarding the discovery order).[318] Thus, Argentina had just two options: pay no one or pay every one. While Argentina wanted to regain access to the capital markets, Argentina had manoeuvred itself in a trap. In order to make its own blackmail strategy that holdouts would come away empty-handed credible, Argentina had equipped its exchange bonds with a 'rights upon future offer' (RUFO) clause. Would Argentina have bluffed and paid out its holdouts in full, the exchange bonds would re-emerge in full value. In consequence, Argentina defaulted, and 'held out' until the RUFO-clause expired in the end of 2014,[319] before the government of the newly elected President Mauricio Macri reached a settlement with Argentina' holdout cred-

---

'Argentina's Defaulted Sovereign Debt: Dealing with the "Holdouts"'(2013) Congressional Research Service.

316 AGUSTINO FONTEVECCHIA, 'The Real Story Of How A Hedge Fund Detained A Vessel In Ghana And Even Went For Argentina's 'Air Force One' (2012, 5 October).

317 On the equal treatment order see: NML CAPITAL, LTD. v REPUBLIC OF ARGENTINA, 699 F.3d 246 (Second Circuit, 26 October 2012). On the discovery order see: EM LTD. v REPUBLIC OF ARGENTINA, 695 F.3d 201 (Second Circuit, 20 August 2012).

318 REPUBLIC OF ARGENTINA v NML CAPITAL, LTD., 134 S.Ct. 2250 (U.S. Supreme Court, 16 June 2014). For a more detailed review of the Argentina Cases see: ELLEN GINSBURG SIMON and MONTY CRAWFORD, 'The Impact of *Republic of Argentina v. NML Capital, Ltd.*: Why the Supreme Court's Ruling Against Argentina Avoided a Host of Unintended Consequences' (2015) 30 (1) Maryland Journal of International Law 55.

319 BENEDICT MANDER, 'Rufo expiry will test Argentina's willingness to settle debt' (2014, 30 December) Financial Times.

itors. The settlement would award the holdouts a payoff way above the 2005/2010 restructuring offers.[320]

Another, yet still not major, question for creditors is a tendency to curtail the activities of so-called vulture funds. The UK, with English law being one of the two most important laws in governing sovereign debt issuances, set the example in 2010. The Debt Relief (Developing Country) Act 2010 ensures that creditors will be bailed-in for a debt relief if the debtor is part of the Heavily Indebted Poor Countries (HIPC) Initiative of the Worldbank. In this case, the creditors cannot recover the full nominal value of the debt claim. The law, however, applies only to a very limited number of very poor countries, i.e., it would have not applied to Argentina. Belgium went a few steps further. In 2015, an anti-vulture law was enacted according to which the sum a vulture fund (as defined by the law) may recover is limited to the price the fund itself paid on the secondary market when purchasing the distressed debt instrument.[321] The law has the potential to turn the world of sovereign debt restructuring upside down if it were adopted as a model for laws at the world's most significant trading places for sovereign debt. Effectively, it would give the sovereign debtors in distress a gigantic boost in bargaining power–presumably, much to the disadvantage of borrowing costs for sovereign debtors with a less than perfect credit rating.

2.3 Bargain and Blackmail

A sovereign debtor in financial distress finds itself in a thorny situation. Relationship lending has been largely replaced by capital market financing for sovereign debtors. The sovereign debtor's credit structure is, therefore, highly dispersed. A blessing in times of sustainable finances, which comes with the wide availability and marketability of bonds, turns into a curse once the debtor is distressed. If the debtor plays by the rules, i.e., if the debtor honours its obligation under the law to pay each and every creditor in time and in full unless a haircut has been agreed individually, the debtor is very likely to fail with the attempt of a debt restructuring. The reasons for this dilemma are illustrated in the following example:

320 ALEXANDRA STEVENSON, 'How Argentina Settled a Billion-Dollar Debt Dispute With Hedge Funds' (2016, 25 April) NY Times.

321 Loi relative à la lute contre les activités des fonds vauteurs, 12 Juillet 2015.

Example: The Debt Restructuring Public Good Game
Explanation: Assume that the debt claim against the sovereign debtor S is Φ. The sovereign debtor has been advised that at least 90 per cent of its creditors would have to agree to a haircut of ρ (ρ being a multiplier of less than 1) in order to overcome S' financial crisis. If S cannot find an agreement with its creditors, default will be inevitable with disastrous economic consequences. With an expected harsh recession as the consequence of a failed debt restructuring attempt, S will not be able to offer its creditors more than ρ/2 of Φ. S presents an exchange offer to all its creditors to tender their bonds for new bonds of the value sX× ρΦ, with s being the individual share of Φ owed to any creditor (X). The exchange offer only becomes effective conditional upon that 90 per cent tender their bonds. iC=individual creditor (holding less than 10% of the outstanding debt).

payoff iC	If 90% of creditors accept (the offer succeeds)	If less than 90% of creditors accept (the offer fails)
iC accepts	siC×ρΦ	siC×0.5ρΦ
iC rejects	**siC×Φ**	siC×0.5ρΦ

Inference: While a 90 per cent acceptance rate leads to a collectively desirable result of (ρΦ > 0.5ρΦ), individual creditor with a debt holding of significantly less than 10 per cent have an incentive to free ride, i.e., to reject the offer in the expectation that the offer will be accepted by the majority of 90% so that the dissenting creditors can free ride on the majority's concessions and collect siC×Φ.

From the previous example follows, a voluntary debt restructuring agreement is not very likely to reach unanimous consent. So as to bring its debt restructuring offer to success, a sovereign debtor may be tempted to coerce its creditors into an exchange offer. For this purpose, debtors often resort to a blackmail strategy, as shown in the subsequent example. If the debtor's government were a benevolent agent working honestly and relentlessly to secure the creditors an as high as possible payoff, the blackmail strategy would yield a win-win-situation (Constellation A). Since, however, the debtor's government can be assumed to follow its own interests, an effective blackmail is likely to be a rip-off for the creditors, which will ultimately backfire on the debtor (see Constellation B and VI. 2.5).

Example: Sovereign Debtor's Blackmail Strategy

Constellation A: The same constellation as in The Debt Restructuring Public Good Game. However, S knows that it is each individual creditor's incentive to reject the exchange offer. In the best interest of all creditors to reach a collectively desired outcome, S commits itself not to pay out the holdout creditors more than sX×ρΦ (1. Var.) or 0 (2. Var.). The exchange offer is executed conditional upon that at least 90 per cent of the creditors tender their bonds.

payoff iC	If 90% of creditors accept (the offer succeeds)	If less than 90% of creditors accept (the offer fails)
iC accepts	siC×ρΦ	siC×0.5ρΦ
iC rejects	siC×ρΦ (1. Var.) or 0 (2. Var.)	siC×0.5ρΦ

Inference: iC should be at least indifferent (1. Var.) and it should most likely be iC's (weakly) dominant strategy to accept the exchange offer (2. Var.), since siC×ρΦ > siC×0.5ρΦ. The 2. Var. is a typical blackmail strategy chosen by sovereign debtors to promote a certain restructuring outcome. It is a coercive, i.e., a blackmail strategy, because it leaves iC without no choice conditional upon that iC wants to increase its individual payoff in any given constellation.

Constellation B: The same constellation as in The Debt Restructuring Public Good Game. However, this time the sovereign debtor S is not only aware of its power to influence the creditor's decision-making by changing the rules of the game. This time, S wants to increase its own payoff by forcing its creditors to accept an exchange offer way below what S could reasonably afford (sX×ρΦ). S offers sX×0.5ρΦ, i.e., the worst case simulation, and threatens its creditors that holdouts will not be paid at all if the offer succeeds. The exchange offer requires an approval rate of at least 90 per cent to become effective.

payoff iC	If 90% of creditors accept (the offer succeeds)	If less than 90% of creditors accept (the offer fails)
iC accepts	siC×ρ0.5Φ	siC×0.5ρΦ
iC rejects	0	siC×0.5ρΦ

Inference: There is no gain for the creditors from cooperation. S collects the entire surplus. However, while the creditors should be indifferent when deciding upon the offer if viewed as a collective, the individual creditor is still better off when s/he accepts the offer ($siC \times \rho 0.5\Phi > 0$).

2.4 The Enforcement Game

As pointed out in VI. 2.2, creditors will sue successfully for a title against the debtor in default in most developed countries. The chance, however, to enforce the debt claim against the sovereign debtor in default within its own boarders tends to zero. Abroad, the chance to enforce the debt claim is theoretically high, since foreign courts, especially located in countries with reputational bond trading places, can be expected to enforce the debt contracts as they were concluded. Practically, however, enforcement often fails due to the lack of the sovereign debtor's attachable assets abroad.[322] The best chance for the creditor is, therefore, to beat the sovereign in default at its own game and turn the blackmail strategy around. This strategy works twofold: First, the creditor may force the debtor to default on its future debt repayments for newly issued debt instruments and block the debtor's access to the capital markets. Second, the creditor may hunt the debtor in default and thereby establish a constant reminder to the markets that the sovereign debtor is a ruthless and remorseless defaulter, i.e., that the debtor is not to be trusted in (debt) business. The principle is humiliation. The underlying idea is that the costs of evading the creditor's lawful claim exceed the costs of full repayment (on the holdouts' claims).[323]

Example: The Enforcement Game

Setting: The same as in the previous section in the Sovereign Debtor's Blackmail Strategy, Constellation B. The exchange offer has been successful. 90 per cent of the sovereign debtor's creditors have tendered their bonds and accepted new bonds worth $sX \times \rho 0.5\Phi$ in exchange for old bonds worth $sX \times \Phi$. Creditors holding together 10 per cent of the

322 The exception that their legal rights might have been altered by way of a majority vote legitimised by a collective action clause, to which every creditor agreed individually at the time the contract was concluded, will not be discussed as part of this chapter. See therefore: VII. 2 and 4.

323 For an early theoretical and empirical discussion of the 'punishment strategy' see: JONATHAN EATON and MARK GERSOVITZ, 'Debt with Potential Repudiation: Theoretical and Empirical Analysis' (1981) 48 (2) The Review of Economic Studies 289.

outstanding bond debt have resisted the blackmail. S has declared that the holdouts will receive zero. S holds no attachable assets abroad. 'Holdout' creditors have, therefore, traded their debt claims on the secondary debt market and specialist investors have taken one the challenge to combine efforts to collect the outstanding 0.1Φ. S has the financial resources to pay 0.1Φ after the exchange offer has succeeded. Paying out the holdouts, however, will take away most of the surplus of cooperation which S has collected all for itself.

The holdout creditors' blackmail strategy looks as follows: By blocking S' access to international debt capital markets, they can inflict costs upon S of 0.02Φ each year until the debt is repayed. Additionally, the holdout creditors try to enforce against any kind of government's property temporarily abroad (the President's plane, military equipment etc.) so that S is constantly in the headlines as a defaulter country. The negative popularity erodes the credibility of S as a reliable partner for trade worldwide. The constant humiliation of S as defaulter is assumed to have an impact on S' economy of 0.01Φ every year. The applicable discount rate in each case is 8 per cent.

Ex Post: Will S pay?

Yes, because (0.1Φ) < (0.375Φ). Assuming that the punishment will create costs of 0.03Φ each year until the debt is repaid, the costs of never paying can be calculated as a perpetuity (0.03Φ ÷0.08). The costs of 'not paying' and continued punishment, thus, exceed the costs of 'paying' the holdouts.

The creditors' enforcement strategy has an immediate and visible effect ex post. The ex-ante reflection is rather opaque. In some cases, it is clear that the threat of a penalty enforced by holdouts will (significantly) exceed the sovereign debtor's potential to 'safe' from not paying the holdouts. In other rare cases, e.g., where the sovereign debtor is not (anymore) dependent on future capital market financing, the creditors will have a hard time to turn the scale and enforce their claim by way of punishing. In many other cases, the result is entirely uncertain.

Example: The Fine Line in the Dark

After the debt restructuring will have taken place, S will pay out the holdouts if

$s(\text{Holdout}) \times \Phi < E$

while S will not pay out the holdouts if

$s(\text{Holdout}) \times \Phi > E$

with s(Holdout) being the share of the original debt claim (Φ) not tendered, and E being the penalty, which the holdouts can enforce upon S for not paying.

The individual creditor (iC) will try to make up the following calculation:

payoff iC	If Majority: Exchange	If Majority: Does Not Exchange
iC: Exchange	$siC \times \rho\Phi$	$siC \times \Psi\Phi$
iC: Holdout	$P[s(Holdout) \times \Phi < E] \times siC \times \Phi$	$siC \times \Psi\Phi$

with $\Psi\Phi$ being the no-cooperation payoff, i.e., the worst case, ρ being the multiplier of less than 1 which determines the proposed haircut, so that ρ ⌑ Ψ (threat point), and $P[s(Holdout) \times \Phi < E]$ being the probability that $s(Holdout) \times \Phi < E$ will happen, so that S will pay out iC's share of Φ.

The problem is that $\rho\Phi$ is known while $P[s(Holdout) \times \Phi < E]\Phi$ is uncertain. The question as to whether $s(Holdout) \times \Phi < E$ or $s(Holdout) \times \Phi > E$ will be true, i.e., the probability of $s(Holdout) \times \Phi < E$, depends on many different factors. Amongst other factors, the amount of the outstanding holdouts' claims after the exchange offer has taken place plays a crucial role. Paradoxically, if S offers a lower $\rho\Phi$ this can swing into various different directions: first, fewer creditors may accept $\rho\Phi$ and speculate on $P[s(Holdout) \times \Phi < E]\Phi$ with the result that the outcome is actually $s(Holdout) \times \Phi > E$ because of such an high amount of still outstanding holdout debt, i.e., if the possible punishment is relatively minor as compared to the still outstanding debt burden. However, if more holdout debt is outstanding, this will increase the incentive for specialised distressed debt investors to sue the debtor and thus to contribute towards a high penalty. Absent the possibility to coordinate and commit, too many creditors may 'holdout,' as a result of a low $\rho\Phi$, which may turn the scale to $\Psi\Phi$, a collective undesirable outcome.

While S may fashion its offer calculating with the respective probabilities that iC will decide to vote 'Exchange' or 'Holdout,' accounting for the possible penalty (E), which iC may inflict on S, it is hard if not often impossible to look through the actual strategy of iC. The solution has to be found in the design of a mechanism which allows S and its creditors to coordinate and to commit.

The Belgian approach: While the situation of the sovereign debtor's blackmail strategy followed by the creditors' reverse blackmail/enforcement strategy is unsatisfying, the situation would be most upsetting if the 'Belgian approach' became widely applied. The enforcement game would end right away. The vulture fund's business is based on the assumption that there is an upside to the purchase price in exchange for the high risk that the enforcement game is not crowned with success. Absent the threat of being targeted by sophisticated distressed debt investors, the sovereign debtor can fashion the offer more aggressively to its own advantage. Since it would be pointless to buy debt on the secondary market with no upside potential but a substantial risk of not being repaid at all, the secondary market price would crash. If now the sovereign debtor approaches its creditors with a debt restructuring offer, the blackmail will be perfect and credible: the creditors accept the offer or they receive nothing. Certainly, the original bondholders who did not buy their bonds on the secondary market could reject the exchange offer and sue the debtor on their own without being barred by the anti-vulture law. The problem, however, is that the enforcement game requires significant sophistication and investment. The creditors must be willing to assume a high risk of failure and they must be ready to put forward large sums for legal proceedings. The threat of 0 in Constellation B of The Sovereign Debtor's Blackmail Strategy in the previous section becomes more realistic, which fundamentally strengthens the sovereigns and weakens the creditors bargaining position in debt restructuring. The bill will have to be paid for by all sovereign debtors at a recognizable default risk.

2.5 The Ex-ante Costs of Unrestricted Opportunism Ex Post

2.5.1 Capital Costs

When sovereign/public debtors can opportunistically default and extract a discount from their debt obligations by playing a coercive strategy ex post, this will have a reflection in the sovereign debtor's debt capital costs ex-ante.[324] The creditors try to anticipate the risk of default times their individual loss in default so as to make an informed decision about the price and conditions they are willing to accept. The creditors will have to account, first, for the sovereign debtor's ability to pay its debts (financial obligations in relation to financial capacity) and, second, for the sovereign debtor's willingness to pay its debt. As the analysis in VI. 2.2 and 2.3 has shown, the sovereign debtor finds itself in an extraordinarily strong bar-

324 For a short version of this analysis see EHMKE (2015) 14–15.

gaining position when it comes to the renegotiation of its debt obligations. The creditors have little prospect to satisfy their claim by enforcement directly while they have a realistic chance to incentivize the debtor to pay them by threatening to inflict harm upon the debtor (see VI. 2.4). The willingness of the debtor to pay is, therefore, as important as its ability to pay.

In order to evaluate the probability of default times the creditor's individual loss in default, creditors will have to calculate: (i) the debtor's financial obligations in relation to its financial capacity, (ii) the debtor's 'emergency plan', i.e., its contractual regime to deal with the challenges of financial distress by early and effective debt restructuring measures,[325] and (iii) the debtor's past behaviour in debt service and crisis management. Possibly, the (ii) point – the debtor's plan for distress – can be substituted with a statutory regime in the future, as it will be discussed in section VI. 3. In particular, the past behaviour of the debtor can give a clue about its future strategies in case of distress. This is not primarily because the debtor can be expected to depend on a certain path. It is because the debtor has less to lose from future misbehaviour once its 'good name' is already ruined. This follows from the same logic as in the case of the capital credence good of a consequently applied no-bailout-principle. Good debt service and a fair and equitable treatment of creditors in case of distress contribute towards the reputation of the debtor. Even in distress, a debtor can distinguish itself by showing its firmest commitment to act in the best interest of its creditors. Thereby, the debtor can convince its creditors and the markets of its willingness to repay its debt. This willingness has a value in lower debt capital costs.[326] If a debtor, however, has cheated on and has blackmailed its creditors before, the debtor will have already lost its reputation: there is no more gain in form of lower interest rates to be defended. Sometimes, theoretical and empirical papers talk about the 'punishment' effect in this regard. The term is misleading. It is rather irrational to assume that creditors and even new creditors without prior business contact would coordinate to

325 See therefore the discussion in section VI. 3.

326 Sovereign debt lending compares to a repeated trust game. The creditor decide to cooperate and to provide credit to the sovereign debtor. The sovereign debtor may honour its commitment or try to exploit the creditors. The credit markets will observe and learn. For an experimental analysis of repeated trust games and reputation building see: VITAL ANDERHUB, DIRK ENGELMANN, and WERNER GÜTH, 'An experimental study of the repeated trust game with incomplete information' (2002) 48 (2) Journal of Economic Behaviour & Organization 197.

punish the debtor (unless they follow a strategy to enforce their 'old claim'). It is, however, rational to assume that creditors would base their predictions about the risk of their investment on the debtor's past behaviour.

Empirical research has largely confirmed the assumption that the debtor's opportunistic actions of the past will negatively affect the debtor's ability and costs to borrow. Two consequences are commonly observed. The debtor is excluded from the debt capital markets (understood as a period where the debtor is not willing or able to pay the entry price required for newly issued debt), and the debtor is charged higher interest rates once the debtor (re-)enters the debt capital markets. In a quite extensive study evaluating the impact of all sovereign debt restructurings between 1970 to 2010, Juan Cruces and Christoph Trebesch find that the size of the haircut correlates with the time that a sovereign debtor is excluded from the debt markets and with the costs of debt capital after its re-entry. According to Cruces and Trebesch, the average haircut in sovereign debt restructurings is 37 per cent. A standard deviation of 1 in the increase of the haircut is associated with >120 basis points higher bond-spread in years 4-7 after the crisis as well as a 50 per cent lower chance to re-enter the debt capital markets in any given year after the restructuring deal has been sealed.[327] The research of Cruces and Trebesch confirms the assumption that especially the sovereign debtor's behaviour and crisis management and the gravity of the haircut for its creditors each have a significant impact on the sovereign debtor's access to and the cost of capital; i.e., those factors which cast light on the sovereign debtor's willingness to pay. In this line, also Christine Richmond and Daniel Dias have presented an interesting study. One of their findings is that debtors which have defaulted because of a natural catastrophe will re-gain market access within a significantly shorter time than other sovereign debtors in default. Obviously, a default out of the debtor's control says nothing about the debtor's willingness to pay, i.e., it should not damage the debtor's reputation and it should not lead to higher debt capital costs as a consequence thereof. The findings of Richmond and Dias are clearly in line with the assumption that creditors do not only price the (expected) ability but also the (expected) willingness of the debtor to repay its debt.[328]

327 JUAN CRUCES & CHRISTOPH TREBESCH, 'Sovereign Defaults: The Price of Haircuts' (2013) 5 (3) American Economic Journal: Macroeconomics 85.

328 CHRISTINE RICHMOND and DANIEL DIAS, 'Duration of Capital Market Exclusion: An Empirical Investigation' (2009) SSRN Manuscript.

An early study by Susan Özler about bank lending confirms the previous assumption that the debtor's reputation and identity is key for debt capital costs and conditions. Özler finds that commercial banks in the 1970s accounted for defaults dating back up until the 1930s and that countries which just recently acquired sovereignty were charged higher interest rates, which suggests that a new debtor identity disconnects the country from a previously 'good behaviour'/reputation as a reliable debtor.[329]

2.5.2 Spill-Over Costs

There is another dimension to the reputational damage caused by the debtor's misbehaviour. While it is quite obvious that a 'bad reputation' as debtor must have a negative impact on the debtor's cost of debt capital and its borrowing conditions, it is only one more step to conclude that the opportunistic sovereign defaulter must face consequences as a trade partner or as a 'host country' for investments as well.[330] The negative impact of previously 'bad behaviour' as a debtor has two potential sources:

First, if a sovereign neglects the rule of law as the governing principle of its debtor-to-creditor relation so as to increase its own payoffs on the costs of its creditors, outside investors will have to assume that the sovereign will act opportunistically not only as a debtor but also as a trade partner or 'host country' for foreign investments. Once a sovereign defaulter has ruined its 'good name' as a debtor and has ignored the terms of its debt agreement, outside investors can reasonably expect that the sovereign will disregard the terms of trade and investor protection agreements as well if it suits the sovereign's short term interests. Patriotic, protectionist, and short-sighted populist law-making are more likely to come from an opportunistic defaulter than from a sovereign which has built up a reputation as a reliable debtor, trade partner, and 'host country' for foreign investments. In this perspective, trade and foreign investments do not decline because creditors want to punish the debtor for past misbehaviour but because they adjust their risk calculation and form their expectation about the debtor's future opportunism.[331]

---

329 SULE ÖZLER, 'Have Commercial Banks Ignored History' (1993) 83 (3) The American Economic Review 608.

330 For a another version of this analysis see EHMKE (2015) 15–18.

331 For the theoretical account of this argument see: HAROLD COLE and PATRICK KEHOE, 'Models of Sovereign Debt: Partial Versus General Reputa-

Second, a decline in foreign investments might also be seen as a direct punishment; typically executed and coordinated by creditor countries. The reason, however, is unlikely to be retaliation. A creditor country may want to enforce its debt claim against the (potential) defaulter and apply a reverse-blackmail strategy. Otherwise, a creditor country might want to send out a signal, i.e., build up its own reputation as a tough creditor so that other sovereign debtors are threatened to pay their debts. The strategy is deterrence. The same strategies might be applied by a country which is not itself a creditor but by a country which is home to private creditors which were harmfully affected by the sovereign debtor's default. The 'punishment' is then executed by the country as agent for private creditors.

Empirical research has widely confirmed that opportunistic defaulters will suffer from a decline in trade and foreign investments. Carlos Arteta and Galina Hale find a significant decline of foreign investments in form of debt financing for emerging market firms after a default, i.e., of 20% during debt restructuring negotiations, between 30% to 40% for about 2 years after the debt restructuring, and still a decline of 20% after a recovery in year 3.[332] Ubaibir Das, Michael Papaioannou, and Christoph Trebesch find that private debtors' access to external debt capital is highly negatively affected by their sovereign home country's default in the past. They estimate a decline of about 40%. Interestingly, they can show that delays in debt renegotiations which are associated with the sovereign debtor's misbehaviour intensify the negative impact for private debtors seated in the sovereign debtor's territory while delays which are related to the actions of the sovereign debtor's creditors, i.e., holdout strategies, do not further affect the private debtor firms within the sovereign debtor's territory negatively.[333] Similarly, Trebesch concludes from his empirical investigations that the more coercive a debt renegotiation is, the harsher is the negative impact on credit to the private sector in less volume and higher costs.[334]

tions' (1998) 39 International Economic Review 55; GUIDO SANDLERIS, 'Sovereign defaults: Information, investment and credit' (1998) 76 (2) Journal of International Economics 267; GUIDO SANDLERIS, 'The Costs of Sovereign Default: Theory and Empirical Evidence' (2016) 16 (2) Economia 1.

332 CARLOS ARTETA and GALINA HALE, 'Sovereign Debt Crisis and Credit to the Private Sector' (2008) 74 (1) Journal of International Economics 53.

333 UDAIBIR DAS, MICHAEL PAPAIOANNOU, and CHRISTOPH TREBESCH, 'Sovereign Default Risk and Private Sector Access to Capital in Emerging Markets' (2010) IMF Working Paper WP/10/10.

334 CHRISTOPH TREBESCH, 'Inexcusable Sovereign Default' (2010) Working Paper.

These findings are in line with the expectation that a sovereign, who has opportunistically defaulted on its debt obligations, is unlikely to hold the protection of foreign investments in high regard. Thus, the 'bad reputation' of a sovereign as debtor reflects on its reputation as a trade partner and 'host country' for foreign investments.

In another set of empirical evaluations, Andrew Rose measures a decline of about 8 per cent for a period of 15 years in the bilateral trade of the debtor country with its creditor countries.[335] Miguel Fuentes and Diego Saravia show that the decline of bilateral foreign direct investments (FDI) from creditor countries amounts to 0.4% less GDP-growth for the defaulting debtor country, a figure which is doubled if there has been a previous default by the same debtor.[336] These findings are in line with the assumptions about the sovereign debtor's 'bad reputation' while they may also prove that sovereign creditors punish the default of their debtor countries.

The theoretical and empirical evidence presented in this section highlight the benefit of a rule-based and predictable sovereign debt restructuring/insolvency mechanism. The costs of a default reflected in higher debt capital costs and spill-over effects for trade and foreign investments constitute a substantial burden for autonomous sovereign debtors.

2.6 Conclusion

The situation of a sovereign debtor's financial distress in the absence of an orderly insolvency procedure is most upsetting for the debtor and its creditors. Debtor and creditors basically play a very costly ping-pong game. The debtor is unable to repay all its debt in full and in time. A truly voluntary debt restructuring is condemned to fail in a public good dilemma with strong incentives to holdout and to free ride. The sovereign debtor, which is unable and/or unwilling to repay its debt, forces its creditors into a debt restructuring agreement by a dubious blackmail. Some creditors resist, trade their debt claims, and those capable to turn the tables try to inflict harm on the debtor or threaten to do so in order to enforce their lawful

---

335 ANDREW ROSE, 'One Reason Countries Pay their Debts: Renegotiation and International Trade' (2005) 77 (1) Journal of Development Economics 189.

336 MIGUEL FUENTES and DIEGO SARAVIA, 'Sovereign defaulters: Do international capital markets punish them?' (2010) 91 Journal of Development Economics 336.

debt claims. Much value is lost in this game. In the following sections, an exit strategy from this situation will be presented.

3. *The Solution*

3.1 Chaos versus Orderly Sovereign Insolvency

Presently, there does not exist a sovereign insolvency regime in public ordering. In this sub-chapter VI. 3, a comprehensive proposal will be presented for how such an orderly insolvency regime for sovereign debtors in distress could be designed. A sovereign insolvency regime should provide a solution to the challenges faced by autonomous sovereign debtors and their creditors. A bailout will not be discussed as an alternative, as it would clearly wreck the fundament of an otherwise autonomous fiscal design.[337] In section VI. 3.5 the findings of this sub-chapter VI. 3.4 will be transferred to the case of subnational public debtors.

When it comes to the discussion about the best possible insolvency regime, the insolvency scholarship and practice, especially in corporate insolvency, are traditionally concerned with questions of 'restructuring' and 'reorganisation'. For the case of sovereign debtors, the debate rather circles around the question of restructuring and acute debt relief. The questions of how to resolve the underlying problems of financial and economic mismanagement, i.e., of how to implement appropriate governance reforms, are generally left to the sovereign debtor's discretion. Moreover, while the traditional insolvency scholarship in corporate and personal insolvency deals with questions of how to prevent the debtor and its creditors from opportunistic actions, and how to incentivize them to take value-maximising decisions, the sovereign insolvency debate regularly turns a blind eye on the debtor's misbehaviour and almost exclusively focuses on the creditors' opportunistic actions.

---

337 A bail-out is the perfectly appropriate solution for debtors and their creditors in the integration model. While a bail-out can, admittedly, relief the debtor and possibly even a third party from the chaos, unpredictable blackmail strategies, and the threat of a crisis spillover, the ex-ante reflections of a (confirmed) bailout expectation are disastrous for the fiscal performance of autonomous debtors. For the distortion caused by a bailout see Chapter III., and the practical analysis in Chapters IV. (Subnational Debt Experiments) and V. (The Eurozone). For the costs of chaos and blackmail strategies see Chapter V.

This focus is quite understandable from a political perspective. Politicians have often treated the crisis as if it were an act of God or an attack by outside investors, and as if the only threat to a successful crisis resolution were 'greedy' holdout investors.[338] Such a bias is terribly dishonest and dangerous at the same time. A successful crisis resolution scheme has to be designed to cure the underlying problem of financial and economic mismanagement and not only to treat the acute symptoms of financial distress. Therefore, the discussion about what are the causes of the current crisis and how the debtor can re-approach financial sustainability in the long run has to include questions about 'What went wrong in the past?' (analysis of past governance) and 'How can it be done better?' (governance reform).[339] Crucially, a successful insolvency regime has to set the right incentives for the debtor and its creditors to work towards value-maximisation in distress and, similarly important, before distress, so that the crisis resolution strategy becomes an effective crisis prevention strategy. Opportunistic actions, which devalue the pool of assets, have to be avoided.

The analysis in sub-chapter VI. 3 is not intended to provide a complete review of the discussion on instruments which have been proposed for a sovereign/public debt restructuring and insolvency mechanism so far.[340] The goal is to present a framework which is suitable to increase the payoff for creditors and debtors, i.e., their taxpayers and voters, accounting for the ex-ante reflections of the crisis resolution scheme and the incentives/potential misbehaviour on both the debtor's and the creditors' side. An efficient insolvency regime for sovereign debtors cannot only focus on acute debt

338 As an example thereof see: CHRISTINA KIRCHNER, 'Speech at the 69th U.N. General Assembly' (2014, 24 September).

339 The first question asks the government to deal with its own mistakes while the second question puts the government under pressure to commit to a future path of budgetary discipline.

340 For the most prominently discussed proposal of the SDRM by the IMF see: ANNE KRUEGER, 'A New Approach to Sovereign Debt Restructuring' (International Monetary Fund 2002); FRANCOIS GIANVITI and TIMOTHY GEITHNER, 'The Design of the Sovereign Debt Restructuring Mechanism–Further Considerations' (International Monetary Fund 2002); FRANCOIS GIANVITI and TIMOTHY GEITHNER, 'Proposed Features of a Sovereign Debt Restructuring Mechanism' (International Monetary Fund 2003). For a good overview on different early proposals for sovereign insolvency see: KENNETH ROGOFF and JEROMIN ZETTELMEYER, 'Bankruptcy Procedures for Sovereigns: A History of Ideas, 1976–2001' (2002) IMF Working Paper 02-133. For a proposal presented by the author in (co-authored) papers see: KIRCHNER and EHMKE (2012) and EHMKE (2015).

relief. A sovereign insolvency regime has to be the cornerstone of a sustainable financial architecture.

3.2 Lessons from Corporate and Personal Insolvency

While there exists no sovereign insolvency regime, there are plenty of different versions for corporate and personal insolvency in practice. So, it makes sense to draw on the treasures of experience from corporate and personal insolvency in order to establish the fundament for the design of a sovereign insolvency regime. In this section VI. 3.2, the economic rational of corporate and personal insolvency will be explored before a proposal for the concrete design of a sovereign insolvency regime shall be presented in section VI. 3.3.

Credit Conditions as a Mirror Image of Insolvency: Talking about insolvency bears the temptation of a pathological perspective on the debt business: A debtor has run out of resources and will break the promise to repay all creditors in time and in full. Expectations are disappointed. A chaotic situation is looming ahead and a crisis resolution is sought following the logic 'Once the house is burning, you call for the fire brigade and not for the fire prevention officer.' It is, however, important to recall that insolvency does not only serve the purpose to overcome the acute crisis, but that the design of the insolvency regime has a mirror image in the credit conditions ex-ante. The debt capital investors calculate to the best of their abilities and information the probability of the debtor's distress and their individual payoff in such a situation. Uncertainties, as the consequence of a weak institutional design, should be accounted for to the disadvantage of the debtor. In the debtor-creditor relation, it will be in the best interest of the debtor ex ante if debt capital investors are offered a transparent and predictable plan for the worst case; and this is true for personal, corporate, and sovereign debtors. An efficient insolvency regime has to set the right incentives for the debtor to walk a path of budgetary discipline in the creditors' interest.

If the debtor, instead, can play opportunistically ex post, the debtor will have to pay for the own anticipated opportunism ex ante in higher debt capital costs and a restricted access to debt capital. The discussion of how to set the right incentives for the 'captain on board' plays a prominent part in corporate insolvency.[341] There is certainly a need to think about how institutions of a debt crisis resolution mechanism influence the sovereign debtor's behaviour as well; precisely, about institutions which set incentives to invest effort into avoiding financial distress but at the same time about institutions which encourage the debtor to preserve and increase value in distress.

The Fundamental Problem–An Insufficient Common Pool: The fundamental problem in corporate, personal, and sovereign insolvency alike is a pool of assets insufficient to fulfill all debt claims in full and in time. This raises especially three connected questions to be answered in this section:

- How can the pool of assets be protected from depletion?
- How can the value of the pool of assets be increased?
- How shall the assets be distributed?

Collective Debt Collection: In order to protect the pool of assets from depletion, most modern insolvency laws in corporate and personal insolvency provide (i) for a stay on enforcement to avoid certain creditors to jump the line and to seek preferred satisfaction, and (ii) for recovery rights so as to prevent the debtor from diverting assets for preferred, undervalue, and fraudulent transactions, and for creditors/third parties to pressurize the debtor for special treatment, respectively. Especially in corporate insolvency, holding the debtor's assets together is often also a core prerequisite for value-maximisation, as the business can hardly function with (production) assets being ripped apart. In personal and corporate insolvency, a stay and recovery rights are the cornerstone for a fair and predictable distribution of assets according to the ranking of claims and the pari passu principle.[342]

Liquidation versus Reorganisation/Restructuring: When it comes to the question of how to increase the value of the pool of assets and of how to ensure the best value for creditors, there are several options on the table in corporate insolvency and naturally less options in personal insolvency. In corporate insolvency, the value of the firm is assessed in three different scenarios: (i) the firm is run by the debtor, (ii) the firm is run by an outside administrator, or (iii) the firm is liquidated. In personal insolvency, the as-

341 For a profound analysis of ex-ante versus ex-post oriented corporate bankruptcy regimes see: DAVID SKEEL, 'An Evolutionary Theory of Corporate Law and Corporate Bankruptcy' (1998) 51 Vanderbilt Law Review 1325.

342 Recovery rights do not only complement the protection of the pool of assets from individual creditor's demands in sovereign insolvency, but they can also discourage the sovereign debtor from destructive behaviour, since they force the debtor to enter a collective procedure instead of picking whom to pay and whom not to pay. See section VI. 3.3.3.

sets owned by the debtor are generally available for liquidation[343] while the debtor him- or herself is not subject to administration. The creditors cannot demand a qualified work performance from the debtor so that the debtor's earning go towards debt repayment. Assuming that the debtor's previous credit history is related to the debtor's past earnings and future earnings potential (job qualification etc.), i.e., that the debtor's main stream of income for debt repayment comes from his or her own work, it is essential to incentive the debtor to earn as much as possible for debt repayment. The same is true in corporate insolvency for a debtor-run firm. Insolvency has to set the right incentives for the debtor to make value-maximising decisions. If, however, the debt burden is overwhelming, i.e., if all profits only go to the creditors, the debtor will have little incentive to run the business and to make value-maximising decisions.

The situation for a sovereign debtor is quite similar to the situation of a debtor-run firm in corporate insolvency and even more to the situation of a private individual in personal bankruptcy. The assets of the sovereign debtor may be liquidated to serve its debt obligations (often only upon its voluntary participation), but many assets essential for the well-functioning of the country are not available for liquidation.[344] The country will not be dissolved as well as not the entire government property will be sold for the creditors' satisfaction. The major stream of income for debt repayment has

343 Regularly, assets for basic maintenance are unseizeable. Otherwise, the government would have to 'bail-out' the debtor with social benefits up to the amount of basic maintenance costs.

344 Proposals for a sovereign or public debt crisis resolution mechanism are often introduced by the statement that the sovereign or public debtor may not be liquidated under any circumstances. The problem might be that 'liquidation' is by its term associated with the liquidation of a corporate debtor, i.e., the dissolution of the firm and the sale of all its assets. In contrast, for a sovereign or public debtor, the question must be 'What assets are available for liquidation?' and not 'Is the country or public entity to be dissolved and are all its resources to be sold?'. Asking the question about which assets are available for distribution means drawing the line between what assets are essential for the well-functioning of the country and which assets may be turned into cash for the debt investors. Take the following example: Is every piece of valuable art in the sovereign debtor's museum indispensable? Does it really constitute a national treasury–even if it was acquired just recently with the funds made available from excessive indebtedness? Are not the pensions and incomes of civil servants better spared from radical budgetary cuts when art can be sold instead? While it is certainly hard to find a one-size-fits-all solution to this problem, the question of what assets should be available for distribution is a question which should be on the negotiation table in a winning debt restructuring bargain.

to come from the 'going-concern' and the debt write-down serves the purpose to free the debtor from desperate overindebtness where there is no realistic purpose to repay all debts despite best efforts to increase tax revenue and to cut spending. In a collective debt agreement, the debt has to be adjusted to a level where the debtor has every incentive to make value-maximising decisions in the best interests of its creditors. Similar to personal bankruptcy, the sovereign debtor cannot be forced to a specific performance (e.g. ordered to set a specific tax rate), so that it becomes pivotal to set the right incentives for value-maximising decisions.[345] When making decisions about lending and monitoring, the creditors have to calculate for the limited availability of the debtor's assets for liquidation and for their limited power to influence the debtor's decision-making ex post.[346]

Cooperation for Value-Maximisation and the Need for Early Action: While the debtor is threatened by liquidation and external administration in corporate insolvency, and while the creditors can take over control and opt for the value maximising strategy in corporate insolvency themselves, a cooperative agreement between the debtor and its creditors is the only 'value-maximising' option in personal and sovereign insolvency. The creditors offer a debt write-down and the debtor promises to do the best possible in order to repay the outstanding debt in exchange. In personal insolvency, the debtor may promise to work hard to repay a reduced sum of the outstanding debt according to a repayment plan. In sovereign insolvency, the debtor may promise to execute governance reforms, to raise taxes, and to cut spending in order to secure an as high as possible satisfaction quota for its creditors. Since, however, the alternative is neither liquidation nor external administration, the debtor has a quite strong bargaining position in personal and in sovereign insolvency, which makes it even more important for the creditors to constantly monitor the debtor, to price the debt accurately, and to take early action. The options to correct a wrong direction ex post are significantly limited if compared to corporate insolvency.

David Skeel has trenchantly pointed out the similarity of personal and sovereign insolvency on the forenamed grounds, especially if compared to corporate insolvency.[347] According to Skeel, also the rather short-sighted

345 This may be different for sub-ordinate public debtors which may be subject to external administration by the next higher level of government. E.g. 'Beiratschaft' in Switzerland or a Municipal Oversight Board in the USA.

346 SKEEL (2013) 1071–1074; SKEEL (2014) 2225–2230, 2234–2235.

347 Summarized: the 'privileged position' of the debtor, the focus on cooperation as the value-maximising option, and the creditors' role in monitoring, debt pricing, and risk management.

perspective of personal debtors and political agents (acting for sovereign debtors) create a need for constant monitoring and early action by creditors. While corporations, ideally, are run on a net present value calculation,[348] personal insolvency has its roots often in short-sighted investments for personal consumption, the same as sovereign insolvency is often caused by overspending for short-term political benefit.[349]

Collective Debt Adjustment: Once a debtor gets into serious financial distress, it is clear that the common pool is insufficient to pay all creditors in full and in time. A debt restructuring has to take place which is not an act of kindness but the most effective strategy to encourage high debt repayment. In case that liquidity is essential for the 'going-concern' of the debtor, a debt write-down combined with super-priority rights for new debts can encourage a liquidity inflow. As shown in VI. 2.3., a value-maximising debt restructuring deal, however, may not take place because creditors are caught up in a prisoner's dilemma. In case of a concentrated creditor structure, the inter-creditor relationship can remove otherwise insurmountable dilemmas. Concentrated creditor structures are typical for personal insolvency, less so in corporate insolvency. In sovereign debt lending, a rather concentrated creditor structure was the norm decades ago, e.g., during the Latin America crisis in the 1980s.[350] In case of a dispersed credit structure, as this is regularly the case for corporate debtors and nowadays also for sovereign debtors, only the option of a binding majority vote, possibly subject to court appeal/review and cram-down, allows the debtor and its creditors to approach a win-win-situation while an unanimous, open, and free vote is likely to fail. The option of a binding majority vote, presently, does only exist where the bond contract contains a collective action clause for the modification of payment terms.

Reorganisation/Governance Reform: As mentioned before, financial distress is in almost all cases the consequence of failed financial and economic management of the past. Certainly, external factors out of the debtor's control contribute towards the situation of distress or they might even give the

348 Certainly, here is an intensive debate on how to set the right incentives (by compensation) for the management as well: ALCHIAN and DEMSETZ (1972); OLIVER HART, 'An Economist's Perspective on the Theory of the Firm (1989) 89 (7) Columbia Law Review 1757; JENSEN and MECKLING (1976); CHRISTIAN KIRCHNER and DAVID EHMKE, 'Economics of Legal Concepts for Management Compensation Schemes in the Credit Sector and Their Regulation' (2013) 2 Oxford University Comparative Law Forum.

349 SKEEL (2013) 1071–1074; SKEEL (2014) 2227–2228.

350 FISH and GENTILE (2004) 1058–1073, especially 1063–1067.

debtor the death blow. In any case, something has gone wrong in the past. And it is precisely the job of an efficient insolvency regime to ask the hard questions about what exactly did go wrong in the past so that it can be done better in the future. In case of personal insolvency, this will mostly include questions of financial management. In case of corporate and sovereign insolvency, this will have to include questions of financial and economic management; the difference between corporate and sovereign insolvency being that reorganisation/governance reform can only be the result of a bargain in sovereign insolvency while the creditors or an external administrator may take over control in corporate insolvency. If, in case of sovereign insolvency, the debtor's politicians refuse any such analysis of past mistakes and guidelines for future governance with the argument that this would unduly interfere with the country's sovereignty, this most significantly harms the debtor country's own citizens. They are derived of a chance that past mistakes are investigated and governance reform is executed for the better financial/economic development of the country.

Curtailing the Debtor's Misbehaviour: The question of how to curtail the debtor's misbehaviour is a pillar of the design in private and corporate insolvency. It is the question of how to punish the debtor for (wilfully) destructive actions, about how to revoke the debtor's transactions which deplete the pool of assets available for the creditors' satisfaction, and about how to void legal actions, e.g., a vote on the debt restructuring plan in case that the debtor has unduly influenced the procedure. Instruments to curtail the sovereign debtor's misbehaviour are especially necessary, since, in a setting of weak law enforcement, the sovereign debtor has even more options to play false than personal and corporate debtors. The sovereign debtor can prefer to pay selected creditors, blackmail and coerce creditors into an exchange offer, and frankly break the law. In fact, the sovereign debtor has the potential to be the most 'naughty' amongst all other debtors. It is especially in the creditors' ex post interest of 'fair and equal treatment' that institutions are in place to curtail the debtor's misbehaviour ex post and it is in the debtors ex-ante interest of favourable credit conditions to be held accountable for its actions ex post.

Ranking: The distribution of assets and the ranking of claims is the main interest of creditors. It has also an influence on the debt overhang, because the creditors will adjust their lending decision on where they expect to stand in line. In case of corporate and personal insolvency, there is typically a well-defined and predictable ranking according to which creditor claims are satisfied. In principle, there are secured and unsecured creditors, but in practice, there are many layers within these categories.[351] This ranking may be determined by the law with effect to every third party, e.g., in case of a security interests, or it may only bind certain creditors contractually and refer one party to a subordinate ranking. In case of insolvency, the ranking and seniority may be modified in so far as new debts are granted (super-)priority to secure liquidity inflow. For a debtor, it would otherwise be impossible to acquire debt in financial distress. If the liquidity inflow from new debt capital is believed to increase the value of the assets, it will also benefit the existing creditors. The ranking, by law or by contract, performs a pivotal role in private lending. Most importantly, a transparent ranking is an highly effective instrument to prevent claim dilution, i.e., the (disproportional) growth of debt claims beyond the value of the assets available for their satisfaction. Moreover, it allows the debtor to borrow at low costs as long as the claims can be secured while the costs increase once new creditors have to line behind more senior creditors.

In case of a sovereign debtor, however, a sophisticated and transparent ranking does typically not exist or it is not enforced with the same level of predictability as in corporate insolvency. Some authors, and prominently Patrick Bolton and David Skeel, have called for a transparent ranking and seniority order for sovereign debt lending according to the 'first-in-time' principle. The first-in-time principle says: In insolvency, creditors who have lent first in time will have a right to receive full satisfaction before other creditors next in time will have a right to claim satisfaction.[352] This proposal would create a transparent and predictable ranking which could replace the presently arbitrary practice as well as it would help to mitigate the claim dilution problem.[353]

351 There are, e.g., fixed and, possibly, floating securities, first and second liens, senior unsecured, unsecured, and mezzanine claims to the debtor's assets.

352 See section VI. 3.3.5.

353 See section VI. 3.2.4.

3.3 The Design of a Sovereign Insolvency Regime

3.3.1 Private v Public Ordering

There are four ways by which a sovereign or public debt restructuring mechanism may be implemented:

(1.) *Ad Hoc in Private Ordering:* Many sovereign debt restructuring negotiations of the past did not work within a formal (contractual or statutory) framework. The financial situation of the debtor became precarious. The sovereign approached its creditors in negotiations about a debt restructuring. The inter-creditor relations were, depending on the case, more or less established. The closer the inter-creditor relations were, the easier it was to find a common ground, a common strategy, and a common position of the creditors. The looser the inter-creditor relations were, the higher was the probability that opportunistic actions of debtors and creditors and coordination problems would hinder an otherwise efficient outcome.[354] While ad hoc solutions of negotiations in private ordering can work smoothly within a setting of informally established relations between creditors, they are highly vulnerable to exploitations from both the creditors' and the debtor's side in a diffuse situation of loose debtor-creditor and creditor-creditor relations.

(2.) *By Contract in Private Ordering:* The negotiations in private ordering may also be structured by contract. The rules for the negotiation process can be formalised in a contract ex ante. The negotiation agreement as approved by a qualified majority may be made binding for all creditors connected by contract ex ante. In practice, collective action clauses which allow for such a collective procedure are present in–by now–the majority of newly issued sovereign bond contracts. This was different in a time when especially contracts under US law required unanimous consent for a binding modification of the contractual document. This dramatically changed in the early 2000s. Today, collective action clauses in many sovereign debt contracts help to resolve collective action problems and to omit costs of strategic play on the creditors' side. Problems of the debtor's misbehaviour, however, are generally not effectively mitigated by the typical sovereign bond contract.

(3.) *By National Law in Public Ordering:* Conditional upon that the sovereign debtor has issued its debt under its own national law, the sovereign debtor may enact a law which alters the debt contracts or which

354 See section VI. 3.3.3. FISH and GENTILE (2004) 1073–1091.

creates a binding restructuring procedure for debt contracts retrospectively. There is a possibility that a property guarantee in the constitution of the sovereign prevents the government from such action. To put it differently, a sovereign with high regard for property rights and an established reputation for fair procedure and the rule of law may not have this option while a sovereign with a weak protection level and a presumably patriotic judiciary may unilaterally change the rules of the game without the creditors' consent. The Greek case exemplifies the latter case.[355] For good reason, bonds traded under Greek law were traded at a discount if compared with bonds traded under English law.[356]

(4.) *By International Agreement in Public Ordering:* A sovereign insolvency regime may be established by international law agreement, requiring all signature states to comply with the rules to which they have signed up. The challenge of this approach is to reach an agreement about the design of this mechanism. The advantage would clearly be the comprehensive and uniform character of such a regime, and therefore, its predictability in credit cost calculations. Once the sovereign debtor commits to a sovereign insolvency regime, the sovereign cannot easily divert from this mechanism, since the sovereign is bound and held accountable by international law. The sovereign would risk a very serious reputational damage if the sovereign disregarded its commitment fortified by international law contract.

3.3.2 Acceleration

A key question to be asked in context of any insolvency/restructuring procedure is under which conditions the procedure may be initiated. If only one party were given the right to initiate the procedure, this could open the door for strategic and exploitative behaviour. If only the debtor had the right to initiate the procedure[357] without that further conditions were to

355 See section V. 3.5.3 and V. 3.6.

356 STEPHAN CHOI, MITU GULATI, and ERIC POSNER, 'Pricing terms in sovereign debt contracts: a Greek case study with implications for the European crisis resolution mechanism' (2011) 6 (2) Capital Markets Law Journal 163, especially 172–185; SEBASTIAN GRUND, 'Restructuring government debt under local law: the Greek case and implications for investor protection in Europe' (2017) 12 (2) Capital Markets Law Journal 253.

357 The IMF, represented by Krueger, Gianviti, and Geithner argued in favour of a SDRM-procedure to be accelerated unilaterally by the debtor (possibly condi-

be fulfilled, the debtor could try to get an easy debt relief, especially if the opening of the procedure had automatic consequences such as a stay. Greece has sometimes tried to present inflated debt levels so as to initiate a next round of debt relief negotiations with its creditors,[358] which gives a good example for the sovereign debtor's strategy to bargain for an opportunistically high debt relief. If, on the other hand, creditors were given the right to initiate a procedure without that further conditions had to be fulfilled, individual creditors would have the power to mark the sovereign debtor with the stigma of insolvency; the creditors were given a powerful tool to blackmail the debtor.

Since the acceleration of the procedure on the unconditional request of the debtor as well as the unconditional request of creditors poses a significant risk and possibly comes with a substantial destruction of value, the best solution would be to demand some provable test for the opening of the procedure. This seems to be especially sensible in case that automatic consequences such as a stay follow the opening of the procedure. A requirement for the acceleration often proposed in context of sovereign insolvency is the 'unsustainable debt burden' test. The question when a sovereign's debt level becomes unsustainable is not an easy one. It is not sufficient to compare the time-value of the outstanding debt claims against the sovereign's GDP. First, the type of debt – held by domestic or foreign investors – has to be analysed. Second, the necessary state expenses, which may vary substantially, e.g., depending on the development standard, the sovereign's geographical, political, and demographic structure, have to be considered, the same as a prognosis about the sovereign's future development has to be conducted. While it is no easy task to assess the financial sustainability of a sovereign debtor, it is a job regularly performed by rating agencies.[359] A dispute about the question as to whether a sovereign carries an 'unsustainable debt burden' should be evaluated by an independent institution.

Proposals for a sovereign debt restructuring mechanism, often, limit the right to open the procedure to the sovereign debtor, as a concession to the debtor's sovereignty. This makes sense if opportunistic behaviour is mostly seen to be a problem on the creditors' side. Since, however, opportunistic strategies are similarly likely to be played by the debtor and since a well-

---

tional upon a third party's approval): GIANVITI and GEITHNER (2002) 25–27; GIANVITI and GEITHNER (2003) 4; KRUEGER (2002) 11.

358 See section V. 3.5.3.

359 See sections II. 2.2 and III. 3.3.5.

designed sovereign insolvency mechanism should aim to curtail the debtor's misbehaviour as well, it is necessary that creditors – similarly as the debtor – should be entitled to request the opening of the procedure.

A workable solution to this conflict may be: The debtor OR the creditors can request the opening of the procedure.

- *Multi-lateral acceleration:* If the debtor and a qualified minority of creditors holding at least 25% of the outstanding financial debt request the acceleration, the procedure may be accelerated without further review.
- *Unilateral acceleration:* If only the debtor or if creditors request the acceleration of the procedure, an independent institution (see VII. 3.3.8) shall determine as to whether the debtor's debt level is unsustainable and if an acceleration of the procedure is in the best interest of the creditors.[360]

This way, it can be ensured that a procedure will be initiated if it is requested by the debtor and its creditors or if a neutral institution finds after diligent investigation of the sovereign debtor's financial sustainability that an acceleration of the procedure would protect (the debtor's and) the creditors' best interests.[361]

3.3.3 Collective v Individual Action and Decision-Making

Key instruments – probably the most thoroughly discussed instruments in case of sovereign insolvency – are instruments established to transfer individual debt relations into a collective procedure. In case of concentrated and well established inter-creditor relations, a common ground is found in a bargain between the creditors and enforced by informal rules and sanc-

360 To rule out requests by creditors with only an insignificant debt portion, the request may be conditioned on an initiative by creditors holding a qualified debt portion, e.g. more than 5% of the outstanding financial debt.

361 In PATRICK BOLTON and DAVID SKEEL, 'Inside the Black Box: How Should a Sovereign Bankruptcy Framework Be Structured?' (2004) 53 Emory Law Journal 763, 786–787 and in CHRISTIAN KIRCHNER and DAVID EHMKE, 'Private Ordering in Sovereign Debt Restructuring: Reforming the London Club' (2012) 3 Oxford University Comparative Law Forum in section 3.7.1, the authors argue for a debt restructuring mechanism (in private ordering) to be accelerated upon the debtor as well as upon (qualified) creditors' request.

tions. In case of a concentrated creditor structure, the process can take place ad hoc in private ordering'.[362]

Example "Concentrated creditor structure": Several banks regularly lend to sovereign debtors worldwide in a syndicate. Their debtor D is in serious distress and proposes to reduce the debt Φ by the factor ρ ($\rho<0.9$).

1. Variation: The bank syndicate is convinced that the offer is 'fair' and that a rejection of this offer would force D into an even harsher financial and economic crisis so that in the long run only a payoff of significantly less than ρΦ would be feasiable. If, however, all banks agreed but one bank (O=opportunistic bank), O would keep its full claim while the risk for all claims would increase and devalue all claims by 0.9.
2. Variation: The bank syndicate is convinced that the offer is 'too low' and that an offer of 1.5ρΦ is feasiable. According to their prognosis, they will be able to claim and enforce the fair offer in the second round of negotiations if they reject the restructuring offer of ρΦ all together. If, however, one bank (O) accepts the offer, because O wants to establish a special business relation with D of the value 0.25ρΦ (which is more than any individual bank's share in Φ is worth), the syndicate will not be able to establish its reputation for the second round and the syndicate will be forced to accept the offer of ρΦ.

In order to achieve unity and strengthen their reputation as lenders worldwide, the banks have agreed informally, that they will exclude any free rider bank from future lending business in the syndicate. The long-term costs of this punishment (lost business opportunities) at present value are estimated to be Ω. Ω by far exceeds the value of sO× (1–ρ)Φ and 0.25Φ.

362 See therefore the following model example 'Concentrated creditor structure'. See also DIRK ENGELMANN and NIKOS NIKIFORAKIS, 'In the long-run we are all dead: on the benefits of peer punishment in rich environments' (2015) 45 (3) Social Choice and Welfare 561 for an experimental investigation of peer punishment strategies and the conditions of their success. See also FISH and GENTILE (2004) 1058–1073, especially 1063–1067 for a historical example of bank lending strategies in sovereign debt restructurings.

	Syndicate B (minus bank O)		
Bank O	payoff O/B	Accept (1. Var.)	Reject (2. Var.)
	1. Var. Accept	sO×ρΦ / sB×ρΦ	-
	1. Var. Reject	sO×0.9Φ – Ω / sB×0.9ρΦ	-
	2. Var. Accept	-	0.25Φ+sO×ρΦ – Ω / sB×ρΦ
	2. Var. Reject	-	sO×1.5ρΦ / sB×1.5ρΦ

Inference: O could win from an individual free ride (i.e., 1. Var. sO× 0.9Φ>sO×ρΦ, 2. Var. 0.25Φ+sO×ρΦ> sO×1.5ρΦ) on the costs of the syndicate (i.e., 1. Var. sB×0.9ρΦ<sB×ρΦ, 2. Var. sB×ρΦ<sB×1.5ρΦ). However, with the punishment Ω inflicted upon the defecting party, O will make an individually and collectively value-maximising decision (i.e., for each O and B: 1. Var. [sO×ρΦ / sB×ρΦ] > [sO×0.9Φ – Ω / sB× 0.9ρΦ], 2. Var. [sO×1.5ρΦ / sB×1.5ρΦ] > [0.25Φ+sO×ρΦ – Ω / sB×ρΦ]. Informal institutions support value-maximisation.

If, however, the body of creditors is dispersed, only formal solutions via a contractual workout in private ordering or via international agreements in public ordering promise to maximise value, as the following model example of a dispersed creditor structure shows.

Model example "Dispersed creditor structure": Recall the model example 'The Debt Restructuring Prisoner's Dilemma' discussed in section VI. 2.3.

1. Variation: The sovereign debtor makes the offer to exchange bonds of the value Φ into new bonds devalued by the factor ρ. If the debt restructuring fails, the sovereign debtor will enter a very serious and long financial and economic crisis. The prognosis is that the debt, in this case, will only be repaid by the factor 0.5ρ.
2. Variation: The sovereign debtor makes the offer to exchange bonds of the value Φ into new bonds devalued by the factor ρ. The creditors' prognosis is that this is an opportunistically low offer, that the sovereign debtor can reasonably offer the discount factor 1.5ρ instead, and that the sovereign debtor will be forced to offer 1.5ρ to prevent further damages to its own country if the first offer is rejected.

The voting rule of a public/private debt restructuring mechanism says: If at least 75% approve a restructuring offer, the offer will become binding for all creditors.

	MajC (≥ 75%)				
iC (≤ 25%)	payoff iC/ MajC	1.Var. Accept	1.Var.Reject	2. Var. Accept	2.Var. Reject
	1.Var. Accept	siC×ρΦ / sMajC×ρΦ	siC×0.5ρΦ / sMajC×0.5ρΦ	-	-
	1.Var. Reject	siC×ρΦ / sMajC×ρΦ	siC×0.5ρΦ / sMajC×0.5ρΦ	-	-
	2.Var. Accept	-	-	siC×ρΦ / sMajC×ρΦ	siC×1.5ρΦ / sMajC×1.5ρΦ
	2.Var. Reject	-	-	siC×ρΦ / sMajC×ρΦ	siC×1.5ρΦ / sMajC×1.5ρΦ

Inference: There is no gain from free riding. Whatever the majority decides becomes binding for the dissenting minority. Individually value-maximising option=collectively value-maximising option.

In practice, a binding super-majority amendment rule has become a common term in most newly issued bond contracts. It is, moreover, a standard in all modern corporate insolvency laws and it would clearly be a good solution for a sovereign debt insolvency regime. In order to avoid that one group of creditors free rides on the concessions of other creditors, it would be, furthermore, essential to group creditors of different rights in different classes and to count a (qualified) majority for each group. A cram-down mechanism of entire classes, in which a (qualified) majority was not achieved, may be made available conditional upon a thorough evaluation of the 'fair treatment' and 'the best interests' of dissenting creditors by a neutral institution.[363] If the first-in-time principle were to be established, the different 'priority groups' offer a good orientation for group-building. In this case, a cross-class-cram-down should only be approved if the restructuring plan respects the first-in-time priority order.[364]

Another institution to turn the debt collection into a collective undertaking is the institution of a stay or a hotchpot rule.[365] While any limitation on individual enforcement actions is key to most modern corporate

363 On a binding (super-) majority vote and group-formation see: KIRCHNER and EHMKE (2012) section 3.7.3., 3.7.7.1, 3.7.7.3, 3.8.1, 3.8.3; KRUEGER (2002) 14–15; GIANVITI and GEITHNER (2002) 44–45; GIANVITI and GEITHNER (2003) 8–13.

364 BOLTON and SKEEL (2004) 788–801.

365 A stay would halt and invalidate any legal enforcement action and possibly any legal procedure against the sovereign debtor brought forward by an individual creditor. A hotchpot rule would exclude creditors from satisfaction in the collective procedure up to the amount of their recovery outside the procedure by way

insolvency laws, it is of less importance in the design of a sovereign debt insolvency regime. Certainly, creditors can inflict harm on the debtor, but practically they can so only when the debtor tries to re-enter the capital markets.[366] Provided that the debt re-negotiations have been a success, the debt renegotiations will have been completed and the dissenting creditors' claims will have been modified/reduced at the time of the sovereign debtor's market re-entry. The risk that the debtor's assets are being ripped apart during negotiations by individual creditors' enforcement actions is negligible. A more interesting and practicaly relevant question is how the debtor can be prevented from diverting its assets from the pool available for equal distribution to its creditors, i.e., how the debtor can be bound to a 'fair procedure'.[367]

3.3.4 Debtor's Commitment to a 'Fair Procedure'

Much time has been spent to discuss how a sovereign insolvency regime can be designed to fight the creditors' misbehaviour. More time needs to be spent to answer the question: How can a sovereign insolvency regime be designed to curtail the debtor's misbehaviour? The most perilous misbehaviours of sovereign debtors may be grouped in four categories:

(1.)Misinformation/delays: The same as the director of a corporate debtor, the government of a sovereign debtor has a perverse incentive to present false information about the debtor's financial sustainability and to either delay the time of default to a date after re-election or to present the situation worse so as to bargain for a higher debt cut. The latter case will be discussed in (3). Undue influence on negotiations/voting. Depending on the particular design of the corporate insolvency law, directors who present misinformation or delay the insolvency procedure may be punished with liability or even criminal prosecution. Both is not feasiable (and hardly appropriate) for the case of a sovereign insolvency regime. The best protec-

---

of individual action. In its version presented by KRUEGER (2002) 15–16, the SDRM was proposed to incorporate a stay. In modified versions, a stay was still discussed (possibly with a qualified support by creditors) but a hotchpot rule was supported as a more agreeable solution. See: GIANVITI and GEITHNER (2002) 33–39; GIANVITI and GEITHNER (2003) 8–13. For a detailed discussion of the pro- and cons- of a stay in context of sovereign debt restructuring see: BOLTON and SKEEL (2004) 780–786.

366 See section VI. 2.2, 2.3, and 2.4.

367 See section VI. 3.3.4.

tion against misinformation/delays is creditor action and market discipline enforced by a strict no-bailout regime. If the markets have an interest to assess the sovereign debtor's distinct risk correctly, misinformation is likely to be unveiled. The presence of a workable sovereign insolvency regime sends out a strong signal that the no-bailout principle will be upheld.

(2.)Preference transaction/discriminatory treatment: The risk that the sovereign debtor arbitrarily discriminates against selected creditors is real and practically rather relevant than the risk that creditors themselves circumvent the collective procedure and collect assets from the common pool. The assets may have to be protected from the debtor's transactions which violate the principle of equal treatment. Moreover, the risk that the debtor discriminates in favour of creditors, who are able to put pressure on the debtor, is higher than the risk that the creditors' themselves can get a hold on the debtor's assets. A promising instrument against the deployment of resources from the common pool is to create a right against creditors which have been paid after the commencement of the procedure (and arguable for a specific time, e.g., 90 days/one year, before the procedure's initiation). These creditors may be obliged to transfer whatever they have collected to a trust from which all creditors will be paid according to a predefined ranking. The major advantage of recovery rights is that the incentives of the debtor to discriminate as well as the incentive of creditors to push for favourable treatment are reduced if not eliminated in the first place. Importantly, recovery rights should not depend on the debtor's initiative. If recovery rights are available to the creditor committee without the sovereign debtor's approval, the sovereign debt insolvency mechanism may evolve to a creditor-friendly regime in the ex-ante interest of the debtor itself.

(3.)Undue influence on negotiations/voting: Many sovereign debtors have tried, often successfully, to unduly influence the debt restructuring negotiations by establishing the threat to (unlawfully) neglect their debt obligation in order to coerce creditors into accepting an exchange offer.[368] The risk would persists even under a voting regime. The experience from corporate bond debt restructuring shows that debtors coerce creditors or provide them with false information so as to achieve a higher haircut.[369] If undue influence of some gravity has been detected, the only effective deter-

368 See sections VI. 3 and 5.

369 For the example of an extremely coercive debt restructuring case see: ASSÉNAGON ASSET MANAGEMENT SA v IRISH BANK RESOLUTION CO-OPERATION LIMITED [2012] EWHC 2090 (Ch).

rent is to allow for an orderly process to invalidate the debt restructuring bargain, so that the sovereign is threatened by the sanction to see itself confronted with the original debt claims re-emerged in full value.[370]

(4.)Plan execution/performance: The debt restructuring deal is built on an estimation of what kind of assets are currently available for distribution and what resources can be made available for distribution to satisfy the creditors' (reduced) debt claims in the future. The future perspective includes a calculation of the estimated tax potential minus the estimated government expenses. In order to increase the payoff for creditors, a plan will not only comprise the creditors' concessions but also the sovereign debtor's commitment for governance reform.[371] As a consequence of violations of the sovereign debtor's debt service obligations or its obligations to execute agreed upon governance reforms, the creditors' concessions may be (partly) revoked and in an extreme case, the debt restructuring deal may be terminated and the debt claims may re-emerge in their full original (i.e. pre-restructuring) nominal value.

3.3.5 Inter-Creditor Relations: Who gets paid how much?

A question of major importance in the inter-creditor relation in personal, corporate, and sovereign insolvency is: Who gets paid how much? If the debtor could, in the absence of insolvency regulation, arbitrarily choose whom to pay from the limited pool of available resources, the result would be most inefficient: The debtor would pay primarily selected creditors such as allies, trade partners, financial investors with long-established relations, and creditors who successfully threaten the debtor, i.e., sophisticated creditors with the ability to harm the debtor. The sovereign debtor, moreover, has an incentive to discriminate between domestic and foreign creditors. The debtor's bias in the ex post satisfaction of debt claims back-fires on the debtor in the ex-ante perspective.[372]

In order to create predictable rules for the distribution of assets in insolvency, it is essential to, first, have a clear rule of 'par conditio creditorum'/ 'pari passu,' i.e., of the strictly equal treatment of creditors of the same right. Second, a priority order has to be established ex-ante: firmly and

370 See 'Renewal of Original Claims,' KIRCHNER and EHMKE (2012) section 3.7.7.2.

371 See section VI. 3.3.6.

372 See section VI. 2.5.

transparently. This way, the rule of law replaces the arbitraribiliy of the sovereign's discretion. As suggested in section VI. 3.2., it would be of advantage for the debtor to apply the 'first-in-time' principle for the ranking of its debt claims, as it was proposed by David Skeel and Patrick Bolton; the benefits being: The 'first-in-time' principle is very transparent. So, it allows the creditors to easily assess their position in line. It makes debt cheap for countries with a low level of debt and with a diligent budgetary policy. The higher the debt level rises, the higher also the costs of newly acquired debt capital will be. The acquisition of new debt does not dilute the value of debt claims first-in-time. Newly issued debt is just increasingly risky for creditors who will demand a risk-appropriate compensation. A natural barrier for over-indebtedness is easily achieved and if the sovereign debtor cannot anymore afford to buy new debt capital, the debtor will be forced to reorganise and possibly to restructure. The first-in-time concept is, in any case, superior to an arbitrary and unilateral ranking of claims within the debtor's (factual) discretion. In order to avoid a too high fragmentation of different priority ranks and classes (in the voting procedure), it can be a simple and clear solution to rank all claims issued within one fiscal year at the same level of priority.[373]

One can reasonable argue that it is not advisable for the debtor to submit all possible debt claims to the 'first in time'-principle, since this could harshly affect the debtor's ability to trade in times of crisis and to maintain the scope of action necessary in such situations. [374] To allow for some flexibility, the sovereign may – by transparent contractual provision or by international agreement – maintain the right to exempt certain claims from the

373 BOLTON and SKEEL (2004) 788–801. For the first-in-time principle as a seniority arrangement for sovereign debt lending see also: SATYAJIT CHATTERJEE and BURCU EYIGUNGOR, 'A Seniority Arrangement for Sovereign Debt' (2015) 105 (12) American Economic Review 3740.

374 It would, however, undermine the concept of the first-in-time principle if the debtor were given the right to agree upon a higher ranking, a floating security, or a general tax obligation unilaterally. Especially a general tax obligation bond which is a bond typically issued by municipal, i.e., non-sovereign governments would contradict the first-in-time principle. In a (general) tax obligation bond, the government commits to levy taxes, or a specific tax, typically the property tax (up to a certain level) to fulfill ist bond debt commitment. Such a (general) security by a sovereign government would contradict the idea of the first-in-time principle as the guiding and transparent principle to rank claims. A sovereign government has access to all tax bases and can set the tax rates independently within the self-chosen limits of its constitution, i.e., all unsecured claims may be satisfied with tax revenues.

first-in-time principle and to agree on a higher ranking for such claims. These exceptions must be firmly and transparently defined by type and/or amount. Most sensible is a basket limited by the amount from which the sovereign debtor can choose to award super-priority. Another exception may be made for trade debt, possibly secured by specified fixed securities. Apart from these exceptions, the first-in-time principle can only function conditional upon that it is applied to the vast majority of debt claims. To ensure liquidity inflow in the interest of value-maximisation, the sovereign debt insolvency mechanism has to allow for (a limited amount of) super-priority financing after the initiation of the procedure (conditional upon the creditors' qualified approval, and/or an neutral institution's confirmation of super-priority financing).[375]

3.3.6 Governance Reform

Financial distress is rarely caused by a coincidence of external effects. Regularly, the cause of financial distress is failed governance in the past. While a debt reduction/modification may be necessary for a fresh start, it is not sufficient for the re-establishment of a solid financial architecture. Debt restructuring without governance reform is like treating symptoms while ignoring the underlying disease. Governance reform as integral part of a comprehensive debt restructuring may be subject to criticism as it may be seen to limited the sovereign debtor's scope of action and therewith its sovereignty. This concern, however, is not well justified. The sovereign debtor is not made subject to governance reform by a top-down decision of its creditors or a court. A commitment to governance reform instead will be the debtor's side of the bargain, to which the debtor commits in full sovereignty. In order to pay its creditors as much as reasonably possible and in order to serve their debt claims with an as high as possible probability, the debtor has to commit (i) to an investigation of governance failures of the past and (ii) to governance reform for the future, since the question of what the debtor can pay with which probability depends on the debtor's future performance. It is not only in the creditors' interests that debt restructuring negotiations deal with questions of governance, it is in the best

375 For exemptions from the first-in-time principle see BOLTON and SKEEL (2004) 801–809. For super-priority financing so as to secure liquidity inflow during the debt restructuring process see also: GIANVITI and GEITHNER (2002) 45–47; GIANVITI and GEITHNER (2003) 13–14; KRUEGER (2002) 16.

interests of taxpayers/voters that the moment of 'default' is taken as a trigger for a truly fresh-start. Without appropriate governance reform, the problem solution might just be delayed by a debt restructuring.

Governance investigation and reform have to address four questions: (1.) expenses, (2.) revenues, (3.) the framework for economic development, and (4.) decision-making.

(1.) Expenses: Financial distress comes either from too much spending or from too little income. A thorough investigation must analyse the debtor's spending behaviour of the past and its past commitments from which present and future obligations may arise, e.g., guarantees, social security and pension obligations (i.e., it must cover the implicit debt level).[376] The investigation must translate into governance reform when answering the question what kind of obligations can be restructured, e.g., by a reform of the welfare/pension-system, and what kind of future expenses are beneficial for the sovereign debtor's development, e.g., infrastructure investments, so that the debtor can achieve a sustainable debt level while fulfilling its duty to provide proper public services. A long-term fiscal plan, therefore, may provide a forecast of expenditures and of legislative and administrative actions to be undertaken so as to achieve the goals set forth in the plan. A yearly fiscal plan may concretise the long-term fiscal plan and allow for adjustments to present developments.

(2.) Revenues: The major sources of revenue for most sovereign debtors are taxes (and tariffs), natural resources, and possibly the profits collected from state-owned business activities. Each of these revenue streams may be made subject to review and reform. Taxes may be too low to cover the sovereign debtor's obligations. They may be structured in a way that they harm the economic development. Most importantly, they may be not be effectively enforced. The question of how to fight tax evasion can be as least as important as the question of what are the tax bases and tax rates. Insufficient tax enforcement creates a dangerous imbalance, since it rewards the 'dishonourable' and punishes the 'honourable' taxpayers, giving the 'dishonourable' taxpayers an unfair competition advantage. Increasing taxes for the benefit of covering debt obligations albeit an inefficient tax

376 In both the Detroit debt crisis and the Puerto Rico debt crisis, unfunded pension obligations, i.e., the implicit debt obligations, had a great share in the eventually unsustainable burden for Detroit (see section IV. 2.5.1.) and Puerto Rico (see section IV. 2.5.2).

enforcement is, therefore, a desperate undertaking.[377] A plan for the economically efficient tax level should be accompanied by a plan for tax enforcement. For revenues from natural resources and state-owned businesses, an investigation may show as to whether natural resources are deployed efficiently and as to whether state-owned businesses are run at a competitive level with comparative private businesses.[378]

(3.) Economic development: A sovereign debtor can only absorb a percentage of the GDP for its debt service. It is, therewith, in the best interest of creditors to reform the sovereign debtor's framework for economic activity so as to facilitate GDP growth, e.g., by demanding reforms of the labour market, the regulations for finance, businesses, and trade. Especially in case that the creditors' obligations are to be repaid over a longer time frame, the creditors have an interest in the sovereign debtor's ability to grow and to constantly generate resources for its debt service.

(4.) Decision-making: The question of how the process of decision-making is shaped has a fundamental impact on revenue-collection and spending. Institutional congruence forces decision-makers to make value-maximising decisions. The externalisation of benefits causes underinvestment while the externalisation of costs causes over-spending; both lead to a misallocation of resources. A comprehensive analysis for governance reform does not only have to cover the question of case-by-case revenue and expenditure decisions but structural questions of how the decision-making process can be re-shaped so as to provide for a decision making process which aligns the interests of decision-makers with the goal of budgetary discipline.

---

377 MATTHEW KARNITSCHNIG and NEKTARIA STAMOULI, 'Greece Struggles to Get Citizens to Pay Their Taxes' (2015, 25 February) The Wall Street Journal; ANASTASIA LITINA and THEODORE PALIVOS, 'Corruption and Tax Evasion: Reflections on Greek Tragedy' (2015, June) Bank of Greece Working Paper No. 193.

378 KERIN HOPE, 'Greece open for business, head of privatisation programme says' (2015, 19 October) Financial Times; NIKI KITSANTONIS, '14 Airports in Greece to Be Privatized in $1.3 Billion Deal' (2015, 14 December) The New York Times; JENNIFER RANKIN and HELENA SMITH, 'The great Greece fire sale' (2015, 24 July) The Guardian.

3.3.7 Plan and Plan Enforcement

The final result of the negotiations between the debtor and its creditors is a plan. This plan may include:

(1.)*The creditors' concessions*: debt reduction in principal and/or interest, prolongation of the repayment period, modification of the debt terms, exchange of original debt claims for new debt instruments/cash, priority for fresh capital.

(2.)*The debtor's concessions*: commitment to the newly agreed debt terms, to governance reform as specified, to audit by an independent board, to compliance with publication requirements, regularly submission of financial information, performance reports, and fiscal plans to an independent board, and possibly to compliance with directions by an independent board (if so specified in the plan).[379]

The question is how to enforce the plan on both sides. The creditors' concessions are easily enforced. With a binding debt restructuring agreement, the original claim is cancelled.

The enforcement of the debtor's concessions is more complicated. A problem emerges when the debtor applies a piecemeal strategy of re-negotiations or when a government committed to governance reform and budgetary discipline is voted out of office and replaced by a government which violates the debtor's concessions agreed upon in the plan. Since the debtor is sovereign and there is no tool such as forced administration, the creditors' options are limited. The same problems as with the lawful enforcement of a legal debt title against the sovereign exist.

The first, and most obvious response, is to investigate the debtor's misbehaviour, to declare a violation, and to act by the principle 'name and shame'. In order to establish a credible and visible statement, this must be performed by an independent board or by a court empowered to deal with this case. If the violation is grave, i.e., seriously threatens the plan, or if the debtor relentlessly ignores the directions of the board/court to comply with the concessions made in the plan, the creditors must be given the right to request that their concessions are re-evaluated up to a full reinstallment to their original position (as a last resort). While the debtor may not honour its debt obligations after the creditors' claims have been adjusted in their favour, the court's ruling in this matter would entitle the creditors to pursue their (original/re-adjusted) debt claims in courts worldwide, blocking the debtor's access to fresh debt capital. While such a punishment

379 See also VI. 3.2.8.

has the potential to destroy value ex post (especially for the debtor), it is utterly necessary to enforce compliance with the plan ex ante.[380]

3.3.8 Coordination and Supervision

Collective action requires coordination and supervision. To allow for a successful bargain, the creditors must organise in a creditor committee to voice their interests.[381] For the design of a sovereign insolvency mechanism, it would be advisable to institute, first, an independent board for the specific case to monitor the negotiations, the compliance with regulations, and the plan implementation, and second, to have a permanent court to resolve disputes arising in context of the debt restructuring and plan implementation.

Independent board: Similar to the Financial Oversight and Management Board in the Puerto Rican debt restructuring case, and different to the troika in the Greek debt restructuring, an independent board which is not a sole representation of creditors should be installed to advise on debt restructuring and governance reform, to monitor rule compliance, and to control the implementation and execution of the plan. The independent board may be staffed with insolvency/economic/legal experts. While it should not be the responsibility of the board to investigate any potential breach on its own initiative, and while it should be able to rely on certificates issued by the debtor about its performance of the plan, the board may take appropriate measures for a thorough investigation in case that creditors request such an investigation with a qualified minority or in case that they present evidence which shows that a violation of the debtor's commitments is likely. In case of a violation, the independent board may declare such a violation and give directions for further action, or sanction the debtor in a re-adjustments of the creditors' concessions.[382]

---

380 KIRCHNER and EHMKE (2012) section 3.7.7.2.

381 GIANVITI and GEITHNER (2002) 42–44; GIANVITI and GEITHNER (2003) 13; KIRCHNER and EHMKE (2012) section 3.7.2. In a private ordering debt restructuring, a bond trustee may protect against individual creditors' enforcement actions and enforce the bond terms in case of a violation (on the creditor's request). See KIRCHNER and EHMKE (2012) section 3.7.4.

382 An independent board as an institutional solution to the Puerto Rico debt crisis management was suggested by GILETTE and SKEEL (2016) 3–10. No independent board but an interest-group representation of (official) creditors are the troika in the Greek debt crisis management and the IMF in the SDRM-proposal

Permanent court: Disputes arising about the procedure should be dealt with by a permanent court. The independence of such a court is indispensable for its successful operation, especially for its credibility and therewith its beneficial effect on a predictable and smooth debt restructuring. Therefore, the court should not be associated to an institution like the IMF, which itself acts as a creditor with special interests. The court may decide upon disputes arising about the violation of rules, as they were described in the previous sections. The institution of one permanent court allows the court to establish profound expertise and a predictable history of precedent cases in the long-run. Should the sovereign debtor disregard the court's orders, the reputational damage for the sovereign will be substantial as if compared to the case that the sovereign debtor disregards a national court order, which may be justified/presented as a case of conflicting national interests.[383]

3.4 Summary: Proposal for a Sovereign Insolvency Mechanism

This section shall provide a short summary of the core instruments recommended for a sovereign insolvency mechanism:
Acceleration (3.3.2):
- Multi-lateral acceleration on request by debtor and creditors (holding at least 25% of outstanding debt).
- Unilateral acceleration: acceleration conditional upon court review.

---

as presented by KRUEGER (2002) 21–28. In later versions, after considerable criticism, Gianviti and Geithner scaled back from the very powerful role of the IMF in the SDRM-procedure: GIANVITI and GEITHNER (2002); GIANVITI and GEITHNER (2003).

383 GIANVITI and GEITHNER (2002) 56–70; GIANVITI and GEITHNER (2003) 15–17; CHRISTOPH PAULUS, 'A Standing Arbitral Tribunal as a Procedural Solution for Sovereign Debt Restructurings', in Braga, Primo, and Vincelette, Galli (eds), *Sovereign Debt and the Financial Crisis - Will This Time be Different?* (Worldbank 2010) 317; CHRISTOPH PAULUS, 'Staatsinsolvenzen: Gläubiger oder neutral Instanz – wer soll das schlingernde Schiff steuern?' (2012) 10 (1) Zeitschrift für Staats- und Europawissenschaften 30; KIRCHNER and EHMKE (2012) 3.7.6. In BOLTON and SKEEL (2004) 812–818, the authors argue that national courts, most likely of the major trading places for sovereign bonds, should judge on matters of sovereign debt restructuring if a case is filled by the sovereign/the creditors.

Collective v Individual Action and Decision-Making (3.3.3):
- (Super-) majority amendment clause for each class of creditors.
- Cram-down only upon the court's confirmation of the dissenting creditor's 'fair treatment' and 'best interest'.
- (Stay on legal action/enforcement).

Debtor's Commitment to a 'Fair Procedure' (3.3.4):
- No-bailout principle.
- Recovery rights.
- Validity of the vote depends on independency.

Inter-Creditor Relations (3.3.5):
- First-in-time principle.
- Basket for fixed securities, trade debt, and a basket for the debtor's discretion. Limited super-priority for fresh debt capital.

Governance Reform (3.3.6):
- Investigation and reform for (i) expenditures, (ii) revenues, (iii) economic development, and (iv) decision-making.

Plan and Plan Enforcement (3.3.7):
- Plan including creditors' concessions and debtor's concessions. Plan execution to be monitored by an independent board. Re-adjustment of creditors' concessions in case that debtor violates its commitments.

Coordination and Supervision (3.3.8):
- Independent board.
- Permanent court.

3.5 Transfer: Insolvency for Sub-National Public Debtors

The challenges faced by subnational public debtors and their creditors can differ quite significantly from the challenges faced by a sovereign debtor. In how far they differ depends on the fiscal architecture in the respective country.

David Skeel has developed a handy framework to evaluate "when bankruptcy be an option (for people, places, or things)".[384] Skeel presents five criteria: "unsustainable debt", "reshaping decision-making", "preventing premature liquidation", "dignity of the debtor", "spillover effects". Applying his 'five-factor framework' to (US) subnational public debtors, Skeel finds support especially for (US) state bankruptcy. Unsustainable debt is an issue for states and while they do not face the threat of liquidation, a debt

384 See the title of SKEEL (2004).

relief as part of an orderly insolvency procedure could provide a fresh start for the troubled state. The state would be given an incentive to make value-maximising decisions as well as the prospect of insolvency would encourage the state's creditors to monitor the debtor diligently. A fresh start would allow the debtor (in particular, the debtor in default) to preserve and to regain its dignity as well as it would avoid spillover effects to future generations. Provided efficient capital markets able to distinguish between good and bad debtors exist, spillover effects on the bond markets should not be serious problem.[385] The strength of the argument against or for municipal insolvency depends on the autonomy of the respective municipality in relation to the next higher level of government in matters of budget decisions (spending, taxation, debt acquisition).[386]

With his 'five-factor framework', Skeel provides a valuable toolkit not only to answer the question as to whether insolvency should be an option for subnational public debtors. His 'five-factor framework' can also explain how an insolvency regime for subnational public debtors should be designed. The key to work out the differences in the design of a sovereign insolvency regime if compared to the design of an insolvency regime for subnational debtors is *control*. The sovereign government can tax, borrow, and spend its funds in full autonomy and it is only restricted by practical needs. The subnational public debtor, in contrast, has control over taxation, borrowing, and spending only within institutional limits–directed and enforced by the next higher level of government. If a subnational unit has full autonomy about taxation, borrowing, and spending, quite the same considerations as for a sovereign debtors apply. However, the more control the superior government of the first or second tier assumes, the more the insolvency regime should differ from the framework as presented for sovereign debtors in section VI. 3.3. The following paragraphs of this section will briefly describe some possible modifications to the sovereign insolvency regime if transferred to the case of subnational public debtors. Where no explanation of differences is provided, the same considerations apply for subnational public debtors as for sovereign debtors.

(1.) Acceleration: The extent to which the superior government has control over the subnational public debtor should affect the question of acceleration. If the superior government has significant control rights to influ-

385 SKEEL (2004) 2031–2033 (unsustainable debt), 2034–2035 (reshaping decision-making), 2035–2036 (preventing premature liquidation), 2036–2039 (dignity of the debtor), 2039–2043 (spillover effects), respectively.

386 SKEEL (2014) 2243–2245.

ence the fiscal policy of the sub-ordinate public debtor, it makes a lot of sense to require the approval of the superior government to the multi-lateral and/or unilateral acceleration of the procedure. In case the superior government has a dominant control position, it would even be coherent to give the superior government the right to start the procedure unilaterally.

(2.) Collective v Individual Action and Decision: In principle, the same arguments for collective decision making as for a sovereign debtor apply. Different from a sovereign debtor, however, a stay on enforcement might be essential to prevent a depletion of the pool of assets available if creditors were otherwise able to successfully get their debt claims enforced by court order. A stay (such as in corporate insolvency), therefore, should be a key institution in the design of an insolvency regime for subnational public debtors.

(3.) Inter-Creditor Relations: For subnational public debtors, the inter-creditor ranking of claims is less problematic. Subnational public debtors may issue debt in the forms and according to the ranking as provided by their respective national law. There is generally no need for a radical reform, such as with the first-in-time principle. Different from a private or corporate debtor, subnational public debtors can issue (general) tax obligations. In such an obligation, the debtor commits to use tax revenues, typically from property taxes, to satisfy the creditors' debt claim and to raise taxes (up to a specified level) if necessary in order to be able to repay its creditors. Since property in land and real estate is per definition immobile, the creditors' claim is quite secure. The assumption is that the national courts will enforce the creditors' debt claim by ordering the subnational public debtor to levy the promised tax.

(4.) Debtor's Commitment to a 'Fair Procedure': In principle, the same considerations as for sovereign debtors apply. Misinformation/delays are best prevented by the strict application of the no-bailout principle, i.e., market discipline. Preference transaction/discriminatory treatment are best avoided and revoked by recovery rights. Undue influence on negotiations/voting is prevented by a threat to invalidate the vote. Different from a sovereign debtor, however, the debtor's misbehaviour can already be curtailed by the command of a national court or by the respective superior territorial authority. The more control powers the superior territorial authority has and the more effectively and reliably these control powers are exercised, the less important are special insolvency rights for the creditors' protection.

(5.) Governance Reform: Governance reform is key to a successful reorganisation. If, however, the superior territorial authority has significant control rights, the superior unit may be part of the problem as well as of the

solution. A review of what went wrong in the past has to include a review of the relation between the superior and its sub-ordinate units. A plan for what should be done better in the future (i.e. plan for governance reform) may also include the relation between the superior and the sub-ordinate unit.

(6.) *Plan and Plan Enforcement*: Different from a sovereign debtor, the plan could be enforced by the command of a national court or by the command of the superior territorial authority if these institutions are equipped with the appropriate control rights. The option of a re-adjustment of the creditors' claims remains as a last resort.

(7.) *Coordination and Supervision*: Different from a sovereign debtor, the role of an independent board can, alternatively, be performed by the authority of a higher level of government. Nonetheless, an independent board, such as in the Puerto Rico debt restructuring case, is strongly recommended. A national court, and possibly a specialised court for the purpose of subnational public debt restructuring, may act as a dispute resolution forum.

VII. Conclusion: Leviathan, Hydra, or Institutional Congruence

What is the state's identity from a fiscal point of view? James Buchanan and Jeffrey Brennan re-discovered Thomas Hobbes' famous description of the omnipotent and gluttonous beast of Leviathan. If the government is not constrained, the government will raise and extend its taxes and collect revenues from its citizens excessively. A solution to keep Leviathan at bay, according to Buchanan and Brennan, is fiscal decentralisation. If only the power to decide on taxes and expenditures was decentralized, competition would sort it out. But is decentralisation really the key to financial sustainability? Empirical research has provided mixed results on the issue of centralisation versus decentralisation. For some countries, decentralisation seems to have worked out very well while other unions, which are undoubtly decentralized to a very high extent, are characterized by overspending and exploding debt levels.

From time to time, decentralisation may call the many-headed monster Hydra to the scene. The competition between the decentralised governments does not necessarily lead to financial sustainability in a well-managed tax budget. The decentralized governments may actually compete for the largest share from common pool funding. In this case, the decentralized governments spend and borrow excessively and try to shift the burden to other outside taxpayers. To put it differently, the many heads of Hydra compete with each other for the largest share of the prey. The goal of this book was to contribute towards a solution to the riddle how the fiscal architecture in centralisation and decentralisation shall be designed so as to withstand Leviathan and Hydra.

Fundament: Good intentions are of little help while good institutions can pave the way towards financial sustainability. The methodologic fundament of public choice theory was introduced and related to the question of taxation, spending, and debt in Chapter II. In Chapter III. 2., a summary of the academic discussion of decentralisation and centralisation in fiscal federalism was provided, based on which the idea of institutional congruence could be developed in Chapter III. 3. Two institutionally congruent models were presented: integration and autonomy.[387]

Centralised Model Integration: In the centralised integration model, the group of decision-makers, payers, and beneficiaries of a budget decision is typically larger than in the decentralised autonomy model. Even though different public and sovereign entities might be identified, they are all connected by one central authority which assumes responsibility for financial sustainability and which eventually has to pay the bill. The union or the centre may give its sub-ordinate parts a transfer and bailout guarantee or enforce strict deficit and borrowing constraints. Eventually, all sovereign or subnational entities cling and swing together in a multi-tier union. In the integration model, it is rational for creditors to treat all members of the union as one and calculate the capital price based on the default risk of the entire union. Weaker members in such a transfer union benefit from direct and indirect subsidies in transfers and low interest rates, so that they can use transfer payments and cheaply acquired debt capital towards the development of their economy. The integration model requires effective control measures. The main challenge for the union of integrated sovereign or public entities is to establish efficient information and control mechanisms and a working chain of commands top-down so as to avoid overspending and overindebtness.

Decentralised Model Autonomy: The relevant political agents of an autonomous sovereign or public debtor make financing and spending decisions of which their principal taxpayers will enjoy the benefits and for which they will pay the bill. Autonomous debtors compete against each other in making an offer for public services which shall attract individual taxpayers and beneficiaries, who see their preferences realised in this offer and who are willing and able to pay the price. Essentially, autonomous sovereign and public debtors compete for scarce capital, so that they have an interest to signal a diligent budgetary policy to the markets. But they can also gamble and take a risk while they are not constrained by deficit and/or borrowing rules imposed upon them top-down. In distress, however, public and sovereign entities in a decentralised autonomy model cannot expect that transfers from other parties will ease their financial burden.

387 For a brief summary of the potential benefits and costs of the autonomy and the integration model and mixed systems see section III. 3.5 and for a summary of the elements constituting the autonomy and the integration model see section III. 3.6.

They have to face their creditors and negotiate about a debt restructuring deal. Ex ante and ex post, the financial markets will exert control.

The First Road-Test–Subnational Debt Experiments: Chapter IV. was the first road-test for the theory of institutional congruence in this book. Five quite different countries were analysed. The intention was not to present a broad cross-country study. The approach of Chapter IV. was to provide a close institutional analysis of different informal and formal institutions constituting different fiscal regimes from the perspective of institutional congruence theory. On an autonomy-to-integration spectrum, the fiscal architecture of the USA, Switzerland, Canada, Germany, and France were analysed and proposals for reform/further improvements presented.[388] Chapter IV. can serve as a template for further institutional analysis of different fiscal regimes.

The Second Road-Test–The Challenge of Integration: The EMU started as a currency union. Autonomy was the promise but the markets knew better. Weak member states were already cashing in the bailout subsidy of common pool financing long before the bailout eventually took place. The institutional measures to prevent the risks of integration proved to be defenceless. It is questionable where the EMU is heading. With the establishment of permanent bailout funds and a tightened stability and growth pact, everything points into the direction of integration. However, there is a lack of political will to take bold action and to create a strong fiscal union with an effective chain of commands top-down. The move towards integration will manoeuvre the EMU more likely into the direction of a mixed system with a common bond pool and weak institutions to curtail overfishing. The best chance for the EMU to return to the path of financial sustainability is to abandon the anyhow meaningless Stability and Growth Pact and to strictly enforce the principle of self-responsibility and autonomy in a no-bailout regime. Contrary to the belief of those who claim that solidarity demands bailout, the most prosperous and 'long-lived' union worldwide is the USA where each subnational debtor stands 'on its own'.[389]

The Third Road-Test–The Challenge of Autonomy: Once sovereign debtors are 'on their own' with no bailout to expect, they face a special challenge of autonomy and sovereignty. Creditors will have a hard time to enforce their debt claim against a sovereign unwilling to pay its debt. The power of a sovereign to block debt enforcement increases its bargaining power signifi-

388 For a brief summary of the country-specific studies see the comparative review in section IV. 3.

389 For a brief summary of the EMU-analysis see section V. 3.9.

cantly in debt workouts. This has a price ex ante which is to be paid by all sovereign debtors, especially by those with a low credit rating. Disorderly distress can extend to long periods of cheating, blackmail, and cat-and-mouse games. It would be in the best interest of the creditors and the sovereign debtor if a predictable and workable sovereign debt insolvency mechanism were established. Based on an analysis of the challenges in case of a sovereign debtor's financial distress, a proposal about how such a sovereign debt insolvency mechanism shall be designed was presented in Chapter VI.[390]

Outlook: There will always be politicians, taxpayers, voters, and beneficiaries of public goods who will strongly dislike the idea of fiscal decentralisation. They will argue that decentralisation creates differences between rich and poor and between strong and weak regions. They have a point. While the proponents of decentralisation will say that decentralisation, in the end, creates a surplus for (almost) everyone, that the poor regions might be better off than they would be in a centrally managed fiscal regime, the proponents of autonomy and decentralization have to admit that the surplus they hope for evolves through competition–in competition, some (temporarily) lose and others win.

This book did not try to answer the question as to whether autonomy or integration will yield the better outcome for taxpayers and voters. It shall be acknowledged that for good (political) reasons, some people will favour a centralized regime. The message of this book, therefore, is: However you choose, follow through on your plan! If you opt for integration so that the funding burden via tax and debt shall be shared, be sure to have a workable chain of commands top-down. If you choose autonomy instead, each unit must have sufficient tax authority to finance its spending decisions. If a unit has gambled too high, let the debtor and its creditors sort it out. The worst possible decision would be to go for a mixed fiscal regime. Decentralized spending and borrowing authority combined with centralized tax-funding and transfers will be no good for anyone in the long run.

The strong focus on decentralisation or centralisation has all too often let to the wrong impression that financial performance will be improved if (only certain institutions of) spending, taxation, or borrowing responsibility and authority are decentralised or centralised. The theory of institutional congruence opens an opportunity: Whatever a multi-tier union agrees upon as their solution (decentralisation or centralisation), financial perfor-

390 The problem analysis is conducted in section VI. 2. The proposal is presented in section VI. 3. For a brief summary of the proposal, see section VI. 3.4.

mance will be improved if the choice for autonomy or integration is implemented consequentially, so that eventually the circles of decisions-makers, payers, and beneficiaries overlap to the highest possible degree.

BIBLIOGRAPHY

The URL of internet resources is only referenced in the bibliography, not in the footnotes.

Bibliographic sources with author reference

AFONSO, ANTÓNIO, 'Understanding the Determinants of Government Debt Ratings: Evidence for the Two Leading Agencies' (2003) 27 (1) Journal of Economics and Finance 56.

AKERLOF, GEORGE, 'The Market for "Lemons": Quality Uncertainty and the Market Mechanism' (1970) 84 (3) The Quarterly Journal of Economics 488.

ALCHIAN, ARMEN and DEMSETZ, HAROLD, 'Production, Information Costs, and Economic Organization' (1972) 62 (5) The American Economic Review 777.

ALESINA, ALBERTO and TABELLINI, GUIDO, 'A Positive Theory of Fiscal Deficits and Government Debts' (1990) 57 Review of Economic Studies 403.

ALLEN, MARK and LEIPZIGER, DANNY, 'Operational Framework for Debt Sustainability Assessment in Low-Income Countries–Further Considerations' (International Monetary Fund and International Development Association 2005).

ALLEN, MARK and LEIPZIGER, DANNY, 'Applying the Debt Sustainability Framework for Low-Income Countries Post Debt Relief (International Monetary Fund and International Development Association 2006).

ANDERHUB, VITAL and ENGELMANN, DIRK and GÜTH, WERNER, 'An experimental study of the repeated trust game with incomplete information' (2002) 48 (2) Journal of Economic Behaviour & Organization 197.

ARROW KENNETH and DEBREU, GERARD, 'Existence of an Equilibrium for a Competitive Economy' (1954) 22 (3) Econometrica 265.

ARTETA, CARLOS and HALE, GALINA, 'Sovereign Debt Crisis and Credit to the Private Sector' (2008) 74 (1) Journal of International Economics 53.

AYOTTE, KENNETH and SKEEL, DAVID, 'Bankruptcy or Bailouts?' (2010) 35 The Journal of Corporation Law 469.

BARETTI, CHRISTIAN, 'Wird gute Standortpolitik bestraft? Die Anreizeffekte des kommunalen Finanzsystems' (2002) 7 ifo Schnelldienst 10.

BARRO, ROBERT 'Are government bonds net wealth?' (1974) 82 (6) Journal of Political Economy 1095.

BARRO, ROBERT, 'On the Determination of the Public Debt' (1979) 87 (5) Journal of Political Economy 940.

BAYOUMI, TAMIM and GOLDSTEIN, MORRIS and WOGLOM, GEOFFREY, 'Do Capital Markets Discipline Sovereign Borrowers? Evidence from the U.S. States' (1995) 27 (4) Journal of Money, Credit and Banking 1046.

BERNANKE, BEN, 'The Global Saving Glut and the U.S. Current Account Deficit' (March 10, 2005) Remarks by Governor Ben S. Bernanke, At the Sandridge Lecture, Virginia Association of Economists, Richmond, Virginia.

BESLEY, TIMOTHY and CASE, ANNE, 'Incumbent Behaviour: Vote-Seeking, Tax-Setting, and Yardstick Competition' (1995) 85 (1) The American Economic Review 25.

BESLEY, TIM and HENNESSY, PETER, Letter to Her Majesty the Queen (British Academy, 22 July 2009).

BEETSMA, ROEL and POPLAWSKI RIBEIRO, MARCOS and SCHABERT, ANDREAS, 'A Comparison of Debt and Primary-Deficit Constraints' CEPR Discussion Paper No. DP6897.

BIRD, RICHARD and TASSONYI, ALMOS, 'Constraints on provincial and municipal borrowing in Canada: markets, rules, and norms' (2001) 44 (1) Canadian Public Administration 84.

BLAIS, ANDRÉ and DION, STÉPHANE, 'Are Bureaucrats Budget Maximizers? The Niskanen Model & Its Critics' (1990) 22 (4) Polity 655.

BLANCHARD, OLIVER and CHOURAQUI, JEAN-CLAUDE and HAGEMANN, ROBERT and SARTOR, NICOLA 'The Sustainability of Fiscal Policy: New Answers to an Old Question' (1990) 15 OECD Economic Studies 8.

BLANKART, CHARLES, 'An Economic Theory of Switzerland' (2011) 3 CESifo DICE Report 74.

BLANKART, CHARLES, *Föderalismus in Deutschland und Europa* (Nomos 2007).

CHARLES BLANKART, "Ich werbe für das Schweizer Modell" Zeit Online, Interview (14 March 2013) <https://www.zeit.de/2013/12/Interview-Charles-Blankart-Schweiz>.

BLANKART, CHARLES, *Öffentliche Finanzen in der Demokratie* (Vahlen 2017).

BLANKART, CHARLES, 'Oil and Vinegar: A Positive Fiscal Theory of the Euro Crisis' (2013) 66 (4) Kyklos, International Review for Social Sciences' 497.

BLANKART, CHARLES, 'Swiss Role–What the Eurozone Could Learn from Switzerland' (2015) 2 CESifo Forum 39.

BLANKART, CHARLES, 'The Process of Government Centralisation: A Constitutional View' (2000) 11 (1) Constitutional Political Economy 27.

BLANKART, CHARLES, 'Wie finanzieren sich Völkergemeinschaften? Vom Kaiserreich zur Eurokrise–Drei Modelle im Vergleich' (2012) 61 (3) Zeitschrift für Wirtschaftspolitik 241.

BLANKART, CHARLES, 'What the eurozone could learn from Switzerland' (2015, 18 May) Institute of Economic Affairs <https://iea.org.uk/blog/what-the-euro-zone-could-learn-from-switzerland>.

BLANKART, CHARLES and EHMKE, DAVID, 'Alternative Voting Rules for the EU Budget' (typescript).

BLANKART, CHARLES and EHMKE, DAVID, 'Are euro and transfer union the price for German reunification?' in Wulf Kaal, Matthias Schmidt, and Andreas Schwartze (Mohr Siebeck 2014) *Festschrift in Honour of Christian Kirchner* 665.

BLANKART, CHARLES and EHMKE, DAVID, 'Collective Decisions on Public Debts' (2016) 3 CESifo DICE report 3.

BLANKART, CHARLES and EHMKE, DAVID, 'Kommunaler Bail-Out oder beschränkter Insolvenzfähigkeit–Zum Umgang mit überschuldeten Kommunen' (2014) 63 (2) Zeitschrift für Wirtschaftspolitik 173.

BLANKART, CHARLES and EHMKE, DAVID, 'Overcoming the Rent-Seeking Defect in Regional Policy: Time to Re-think the Institutional Design' (2015) 3 CESifo DICE Report 44.

BLANKART, CHARLES and FASTEN, ERIK, 'Schuldengrenzen im Föderalismus: Ein Optionsmodell für Vielfalt in Einheit' (2017, 3 March) 53 Frankfurter Allgemeine Zeitung.

BLANKART, CHARLES and KIRCHNER, CHRISTIAN, 'The Deadlock of the EU Budget' in Charles Blankart and Dennis Mueller (eds) *A Constitution for the European Union* (MIT Press 2004) 109.

BLANKART, CHARLES and KLAIBER, ACHIM, 'Subnational Government Organisation and Public Debt Crisis' (2006) Economic Affairs 48.

BLANKART, CHARLES and KOESTER, GERRIT, 'Refocusing the EU Budget–An Institutional View' (2009) Journal of Public Finance and Management, Special Issue on EU finances 536.

BOADWAY, ROBIN and WATTS, RONALD, 'Fiscal Federalism in Canada, the USA, and Germany' (2004) 6 IIGR Working Paper, Queen's University.

BOHN, HENNING and INMAN, ROBERT, 'Balanced Budget Rules and Public Deficits: Evidence From U.S. States' (1996) NBER Working Paper 5533.

BOLTON, PATRICK and SKEEL, DAVID, 'Inside the Black Box: How Should a Sovereign Bankruptcy Framework Be Structured?' (2004) 53 Emory Law Journal 763.

BOLTON, PATRICK and FREIXAS, XAVIER and SHAPIRO, JOEL, 'The Credit Ratings Game' (2012) 67 (1) The Journal of Finance 85.

BOLTON, PATRICK and ROLAND, GERARD, 'The Breakup of Nations: A Political Economy Analysis' (1997) 112 (4) The Quarterly Journal of Economics 1057.

BOLTON, PATRICK and SKEEL, DAVID, 'Inside the Black Box: How Should a Sovereign Bankruptcy Framework Be Structured?' (2004) 53 Emory Law Journal 763.

BORDIGNON, MASSIMO and CEMIGLIA, FLORINA and REVELLI, FEDERICO, 'In Search for Yardstick Competition: Property Tax Rates and Electoral Behaviour in Italian Cities' (2002) CESifo Working Paper No. 644.

BORDIGNON, MASSIMO and MANESSE, PAOLO and TABELLINI, GUIDO, 'Optimal Regional Redistribution Under Asymmetric Information' (2001) 91 (3) The American Economic Review 709.

BORDO, MICHAEL, 'The Bretton Woods International Monetary System: A Historical Overview' in Michael Bordo and Barry Eichengreen (eds) *A Retrospective on the Bretton Woods System: Lessons for International Monetary Reform* (University of Chicago Press 1993) 3.

BOUND, JOHN and GROEN, JEFFREY and KEZDI, GABOR and TURNER, SARAH, 'Trade in university training: cross-state variation in the production and stick of college-educated labor' (2009) 112 Journal of Econometrics 143.

BOVENBERG, LANS and KREMERS, JERON and MASSON, PAUL, 'Economic and Monetary Union in Europe and Constraints on National Budgetary Policies' (1991) 38 (2) IMF Staff Papers 374.

BREDFORD, DAVID and OATES, WALLACE, 'Towards a Predictive Theory of Intergovernmental Grants' (1971) 61 (2) The American Economic Review 440.

BREMMER, IAN, 'Managing Risk in an Unstable World' (2005) June Issue, Harvard Business Review 2.

BRENDEL, MATTHIAS and JOST, SEBASTIAN, 'Jeder druckt für sich allein' (2012, 20 May) Welt <https://www.welt.de/print/wams/wirtschaft/article106344100/Jeder-druckt-fuer-sich-allein.html>

BRENNAN, GEOFFREY and BUCHANAN, JAMES, *The Power to Tax: Analytical Foundations of a Fiscal Constitution* (Liberty Fund 1980).

BREWER, ELIJAH and JAGTIANI, JULAPA, 'How Much Did Banks Pay to Become Too-Big-to-Fail and to Become Systemically Important' (2013) 48 (1) Journal of Financial Services Research 1.

BRUECKNER, JAN, 'Fiscal Decentralisation with Distortionary Taxation: Tiebout vs. Tax Competition' (2004) 11 International Tax and Public Finance 133.

BUCHANAN, JAMES and FAITH, ROGER, 'Secession and the Limits of Taxation: Towards a Theory of Internal Exit' (1987) 77 (5) The American Economic Review 1023.

BUCHANAN, JAMES and TULLOCK, GORDEN, *The Calculus of Consent* (University of Michigan Press 1962).

BUCHANAN, JAMES and WAGNER, RICHARD, *Democracy in deficit: The political legacy of Lord Keynes* (Academic Press 1977).

BUITER, WILLEM, 'Kornai on Soft Budget Constraints, Bail-Outs and the Financial Crisis' (2009, 14 October) Financial Times <http://blogs.ft.com/maverecon/2009/10/kornai-on-soft-budget-constraints-bail-outs-and-the-financial-crisis/#axzz48n7wBrlF>.

CARLSEN, FREDERICK, 'Rational Partisan Theory: Empirical Evidence for the United States' (1998) 65 (1) Southern Economic Journal 64.

CHATTERJEE, SATYAJIT and EYIGUNGOR, BURCU, 'A Seniority Arrangement for Sovereign Debt' (2015) 105 (12) American Economic Review 3740.

CHOI, ALBERT and POSNER, ERIC, 'A Critique of the Odious Debt Doctrine' (2007) 70 (3) Law and Contemporary Problems 33.

CHOI, STEPHAN and GULATI, MITU and POSNER, ERIC, 'Pricing terms in sovereign debt contracts: a Greek case study with implications for the European crisis resolution mechanism' (2011) 6 (2) Capital Markets Law Journal 163.

COATE, STEPHEN and MORRIS, STEPHEN, 'On the Form of Transfers to Special Interests' (1995) 103 (6) The Journal of Political Economy 1210.

COLE, HAROLD and KEHOE, PATRICK, 'Models of Sovereign Debt: Partial Versus General Reputations' (1998) 39 International Economic Review 55.

CORKERY, MICHAEL and WALSH, MARY WILLIAMS, 'Message of Puerto Rico Debt Crisis: Easy Bets Sometimes Lose' (2017, 7 May) The New York Times <https://www.nytimes.com/2017/05/04/business/dealbook/puerto-rico-creditors-hedge-funds.html>.

COTTARELLI, CARLO and MOGHADAM, REZA, 'Modernizing the Framework for Fiscal Policy and Public Debt Sustainability Analysis' (International Monetary Fund 2011).

CRUCES, JUAN and TREBESCH, CHRISTOPH, 'Sovereign Defaults: The Price of Haircuts' (2013) 5 (3) American Economic Journal: Macroeconomics 85.

DAS, UDAIBIR and PAPAIOANNOU, MICHAEL and TREBESCH, CHRISTOPH, 'Sovereign Default Risk and Private Sector Access to Capital in Emerging Markets' (2010) IMF Working Paper WP/10/10.

DÖRING, THOMAS and VOIGT, STEFAN, 'Reforming Federalism German Style: A First Step in the Right Direction' (2006) July/August, Intereconomics 201.

DRAGHI, MARIO Verbatim of the remarks made by Mario Draghi at the Global Investment Conference in London (26 July 2012) <https://www.ecb.europa.eu/press/key/date/2012/html/sp120726.en.html>.

EATON, JONATHAN and GERSOVITZ, MARK, 'Debt with Potential Repudiation: Theoretical and Empirical Analysis' (1981) 48 (2) The Review of Economic Studies 289.

EHMKE, DAVID, 'Sovereign Debtors in Distress' (2015) 12 (1) University of St. Thomas Law Journal 1.

EICHENGREEN, BARRY and WYPLOSZ, CHARLES, 'Minimal Conditions for the Survival of the Euro' (2016) 1 Intereconomics 24.

ENGELMANN, DIRK and NIKIFORAKIS, NIKOS, 'In the long-run we are all dead: on the benefits of peer punishment in rich environments' (2015) 45 (3) Social Choice and Welfare 561.

EWING, JACK, 'Is Greek Debt Risk-Free? European Banking Officials Think So' (2011, 21 July) The New York Times <http://www.nytimes.com/2011/07/22/business/global/europes-new-bank-rules-still-favor-government-debt.html>.

FAIRCHILD, LISA and KOCH, TIMOTHY, 'The Impact of State Disclosure Requirements on Municipal Yields' (1998) 51 (4) National Tax Journal 733.

FASTEN, ERIK, 'Sudden Death or Glorious Convalescence: Risk Transfers, Cross-Country Spillovers and Sovereign Defaults' in *Financial Markets and Public Finance* (Nomos 2012) 19.

FASTEN, ERIK, 'Two-Sided Certification: The market for Rating Agencies' in *Financial Markets and Public Finance* (Nomos 2012) 86.

FELD, LARS, *Braucht die Schweiz eine materielle Steuerharmonisierung?* (economiesuisse 2009).

FELD, LARS and FUERST, CLEMENS and HAUCAP, JUSTUS and SCHWEIZER, HEIKE and WIELAND, VOLKER and WIGGER, BERTHOLD, 'Für eine echte Reform der Bund-Länder-Finanzbeziehung' (2016) 62 Kronberger Kreis, Stiftung Marktwirtschaft.

FELD, LARS and KALB, ALEXANDER and MOESSINGER, MARC-DANIEL and OSTERLOH, STEFFEN, 'Sovereign bond market reactions to fiscal rules and no-bailout clauses: The Swiss experience' (2013) ZEW Discussion Papers, No. 13-034.

FELD, LARS and KIRCHGÄSSNER, GEBHARD, 'On the Effectiveness of Debt Brakes: The Swiss Experience' in Reinhard Neck and Jan-Egbert Sturm (eds) *Sustainability of Public Debts* (MIT Press 2008) 223.

FELD, LARS and KIRCHGÄSSNER, GEBHARD and SCHALTEGGER, CHRISTOPH, 'Decentralized Taxation and the Size of Government: Evidence from Swiss State and Local Governments' (2010) 77 (1) Southern Economic Journal 27.

FINOCCHIARO, CHARLES and ROHDE, DAVID, 'War for the Floor: Partisan Theory and Agenda Control In the U.S. House of Representatives' (2008) 33 Legislative Studies Quarterly 35.

FONTEVECCHIA, AGUSTINO, 'The Real Story Of How A Hedge Fund Detained A Vessel In Ghana And Even Went For Argentina's 'Air Force One' (2012, 5 October) <https://www.forbes.com/sites/afontevecchia/2012/10/05/the-real-story-behind-the-argentine-vessel-in-ghana-and-how-hedge-funds-tried-to-seize-the-presidential-plane/#3df9238b25aa>.

FORELLE, CHARLES and MINCZESKI, PAT, and BENTLEY, ELLIOT, 'Greece's Debt Due' (2017) The Wall Street Journal <https://graphics.wsj.com/greece-debt-timeline/>.

FUENTES, MIGUEL and SARAVIA, DIEGO, 'Sovereign defaulters: Do international capital markets punish them?' (2010) 91 Journal of Development Economics 336.

FUEST, CLEMENS and THÖNE, MICHAEL, *Reform des Finanzföderalismus in Deutschland* (Stiftung Marktwirtschaft 2009).

GARRETT, THOMAS, 'State Balanced-Budget and Debt Rules' (2011) 33 Economic Synopses, Federal Reserve Bank of St. Louis.

GEITHNER, TIMOTHY, 'Assessing Sustainability' (International Monetary Fund 2002).

GEITHNER, TIMOTHY, 'Assessing Sustainability–Review of Application and Methodological Refinements' (International Monetary Fund 2003).

GEY, PETER and SCHREIBER, BENJAMIN, 'Frankreich: Wird der Staat jetzt umgebaut?' (2014) Working Paper Friedrich Ebert Stiftung.

GIANVITI, FRANCOIS and GEITHNER, TIMOTHY, 'The Design of the Sovereign Debt Restructuring Mechanism – Further Considerations' (International Monetary Fund 2002).

GIANVITI, FRANCOIS and GEITHNER, TIMOTHY, 'Proposed Features of a Sovereign Debt Restructuring Mechanism' (International Monetary Fund 2003).

GILETTE, CLAYTON, 'In Partial Praise of Dillon's Rule, or, Can Public Choice Theory Justify Local Government Law' (1991) 67 Chicago-Kent Law Review 959.

GILETTE, CLAYTON and SKEEL, DAVID, 'A Two-Step Plan for Puerto Rico' (2016) Research-Paper No. 16–3.

GILETTE, CLAYTON and SKEEL, DAVID, 'Governance Reform and the Judicial Role in Municipal Bankruptcy' (2016) 125 The Yale Law Journal 1150.

GÖTZ, MARTIN and HASELMANN, RAINER and KRAHNEN, JAN PIETER and STEFFEN, SASCHA, 'Did emergency liquidity assistance (ELA) of the ECB delay the bankruptcy of Greek banks? (2015) Policy Letter No. 46. SAFE–Frankfurt House of Finance.

GNEEZY, URI and HARUVY, ERNAN and YAFE, HADAS, 'The Inefficiency of Splitting the Bill' (2004) 114 The Economic Journal 265–280.

GREENBERG, SCOTT and EKINS, GAVIN, 'Tax Policy Helped Create Puerto Rico's Fiscal Crisis' (2015, 30 June) Tax Foundation <https://taxfoundation.org/tax-policy-helped-create-puerto-rico-s-fiscal-crisis/>.

GRIFFIN, JOHN and NICKERSON, JORDAN and TANG, DRAGON YONGJUN, 'Rating Shopping or Catering An Examination of the Response to Competitive Pressure for CDO Ratings' (2013) 26 (9) The Review of Financial Studies 2270.

GROS, DANIEL and SCHOENMAKER, DIRK, 'European Deposit Insurance and Resolution in the Banking Union' (2014) 52 (3) Journal of Common Market Studies 529.

GROSSMAN, GENE and HELPMAN, ELHANAN, 'Electoral Competition and Special Interest Politics' (1996) 63 (2) The Review of Economic Studies 265.

GRUND, SEBASTIAN, 'Enforcing Sovereign Debt in Court – A Comparative Analysis of Litigation and Arbitration Following the Greek Debt Restructuring of 2012' (2017) 1 University of Vienna Law Review 35.

GRUND, SEBASTIAN, 'Restructuring government debt under local law: the Greek case and implications for investor protection in Europe' (2017) 12 (2) Capital Markets Law Journal 253.

GUZMAN, ANDREW, 'Against Consent' (2012) 52 (4) Virgina Journal of International Law 747.

HAMILTON, BRUCE, 'The Flypaper Effect and Other Anomalies' (1983) 22 Journal of Public Economics 347.

HANNIMAN, KYLE, 'Provinces in the Credit Market: Market Discipline and the New Classic Federalism' in Bruce Doern and Christopher Stoney (eds) *How Ottawa Spends* (Queens-McGill University Press 2013).

HARDIN, GARRET, 'The Tragedy of the Commons' (1968) 162 (3859) Science 1243.

HART, OLIVER, 'An Economist's Perspective on the Theory of the Firm (1989) 89 (7) Columbia Law Review 1757.

HEPP, RALF and VON HAGEN, JÜRGEN, 'Fiscal Federalism in Germany: Stabilisation and Redistribution Before and After Unification' (2010) ZEI Working Paper B 02.

HIBBS, DOUGLAS, 'Partisan theory after fifteen years' (1992) 8 European Journal of Political Economy 361.

HIBBS, DOUGLAS, 'Political Parties and Macroeconomic Policy' (1977) 71 (4) The American Political Science Review 1467.

HIBBS, DOUGLAS, 'The Partisan Model of Macroeconomic Cycles: More Theory and Evidence for the United States' (1994) 6 (1) Economic and Politics 1.

HILL, NOBMAN, 'Unanimous Consent in International Organization' (1928) 22 (2) The American Journal of International Law 319.

HINES, JAMES and THALER, RICHARD, 'Anomalies: The Flypaper Effect' (1995) 9 (4) Journal of Economic Perspectives 217.

HOBBES, THOMAS, *Leviathan or the Matter, Forme, and Power of a Common Wealth Ecclesiasticall and Civil* (1651) PART I On Man, and PART II On Commonwealth.

HOPE, KERIN, 'Greece open for business, head of privatization programme says' (2015, 19 October) Financial Times <https://www.ft.com/content/562c85d8-75b8-11e5-933d-efcdc3c11c89?mhq5j=e5Y>.

HORNBACK, JOHN F, 'Argentina's Defaulted Sovereign Debt: Dealing with the "Holdouts"'(2013) Congressional Research Service <https://fas.org/sgp/crs/row/R41029.pdf>.

HOWARTH, DAVID and QUAGLIA, LUCIA, 'Banking Union as Holy Grail: Rebuilding the Single Market in Financial Services, Stabilizing Europe's Banks and 'Completing' Economic and Monetary Union' (2013) 51 (Annual Review) Journal of Common Market Studies 103.

INMAN, ROBERT, 'Federal Assistance and Local Services in the United States: The Evolution of a New Federalist Fiscal Order' in Harvey Rosen (ed) *Fiscal Federalism: Quantitative Studies* (University of Chicago Press 1988) 33.

INMAN, ROBERT, 'Transfers and Bailouts: Enforcing Local Fiscal Discipline with Lessons from U.S. Federalism' in Jonathan Rodden, Gunnar Eskeland, and Jennie Litvack (eds) *Fiscal Decentralisation and the Challenge of Hard Budget Constraints* (Massachusetts Institute of Technology 2013) 35.

JAYACHANDRAN, SEEMA and KREMER, MICHAEL, 'Odious Debt' (2006) 96 (1) The American Economic Review 82.

JENSEN, MICHAEL and MECKLING, WILLIAM, 'Theory of the Firm: Managerial Behaviour, Agency Costs and Ownership Structure' (1976) 3 Journal of Financial Economics 305.

JEVONS, WILLIAM STANLEY, Theory of Political Economy (Macmillan and Co. 1871).

JOFFE, MARC, *Provincial Solvency and Federal Obligations* (Macdonald-Laurier Institute 2012).

JOHNSON, CRAIG and KRIZ, KENNETH, 'Fiscal Institutions, Credit Ratings, and Borrowing Costs' (2005) Public Budgeting & Finance 84.

JONES, MARK and MELONI, OSVALDO and TOMMASI, MARIANO, 'Voters as Fiscal Liberals: Incentives and Accountability in Federal Systems' (2012) 24 (2) Economics & Politics 135.

JULIEN, VIOLA, 'Französische Gebietskörperschaften' (2012, 5 October) Helaba Volkswirtschaft/Research.

KALT, JOSEPH and ZUPAN, MARK, 'The Apparent Ideological Behaviour of Legislators: Testing For Principal-Agent Slack in Political Institutions' (1990) 33 Journal of Law and Economics 103.

KARNITSCHNIG, MATTHEW and STAMOULI, NEKTARIA, 'Greece Struggles to Get Citizens to Pay Their Taxes' (2015, 25 February) The Wall Street Journal <https://www.wsj.com/articles/greece-struggles-to-get-citizens-to-pay-their-taxes-1424867495>.

KAZARIAN, PAUL, 'Strengthening Democracy Through Government Financial Management: Greece and the EU' (2016, 6 October) The Accountant & International Accounting Bulleting Conference and Awards <http://www.theaccountant-online.com/Uploads/Event/218/Resources/Paul_Kazarian_Japonica.pdf>.

KAZARIN, PAUL and PELAGIDIS, THEODORE, 'Greece's New Agreement with Europe: Is This Time Different?' (2015) 5 Intereconomics 281.

KELSEN, HANS, *Vom Wesen und Wert der Demokratie* (J.C.B. Mohr 1920).

KING, JEFF, 'Odious Debt: The Terms of the Debate' (2007) 32 (4) North Carolina Journal of International Law and Commercial Regulation' 605.

KIRCHNER, CHRISTIAN and EHMKE, DAVID, 'Economics of Legal Concepts for Management Compensation Schemes in the Credit Sector and Their Regulation' (2013) 2 Oxford University Comparative Law Forum.

KIRCHNER, CHRISTIAN, 'Ökonomik: Eigennutz, Fairness und Empathie' (manuscript) Chapter 2.3.1.

KIRCHNER, CHRISTIAN and EHMKE, DAVID, 'Private Ordering in Sovereign Debt Restructuring: Reforming the London Club' (2012) 3 Oxford University Comparative Law Forum.

KIRCHNER, CHRISTIAN and EHMKE, DAVID, 'Staat und Recht' in Rainer Kollmorgen, Wolfgang Merkel, and Hans-Jürgen Wagener (eds) *Handbuch für Transformationsforschung* (Springer VS 2015) 455.

KIRCHNER, CHRISTINA, 'Speech at the 69th U.N. General Assembly' (2014, 24 September) <https://www.youtube.com/watch?v=EyShGogzIn4#t=1267> (video with English subtitles).

KIRCHGÄSSNER, GEBHARD, 'Fiscal Institutions at the Cantonal Level in Switzerland' (2013) 149 (2) Swiss Journal of Economics and Statistics 139.

KITSANTONIS, NIKI, '14 Airports in Greece to Be Privatized in $1.3 Billion Deal' (2015, 14 December) The New York Times <https://www.nytimes.com/2015/12/15/business/international/14-airports-in-greece-to-be-privatized-in-1-3-billion-deal.html?mcubz=1>.

KORNAI, JANOS, 'Resource-Constrained versus Demand-Constraint Systems' (1979) 47 (7) Econometrica 801.

KNÖPFEL, CARLO, 'Sozialstaatliche Rahmenbedingungen in der Schweiz' in B Wütherich et al. (eds) *Soziale Versorgung zukunftsfähig gestalten* (Springer 2015).

KRUEGER, ANNE, A New Approach to Sovereign Debt Restructuring (2001) Address by Anne O Krueger, First Deputy Managing Director, IMF, Given at the National Economists' Club Annual Members' Dinner, November 26.

KRUEGER, ANNE, 'A New Approach to Sovereign Debt Restructuring' (International Monetary Fund 2002).

KRUEGER, ANNE, 'The Political Economy of the Rent-Seeking Society' (1974) 64 (3) The American Economic Review 291.

KRUGMAN, PAUL, 'Greece: Think Flows, Not Stocks' (2015, 26 January) New York Times <https://krugman.blogs.nytimes.com/2015/01/26/greece-think-flows-not-stocks/?mcubz=0> .

LANCASTER, THOMAS, 'Electoral Structures and Pork Barrel Politics' (1986) 7 (1) International Political Science Review 67.

LANDON, STUART and SMITH, CONSTANCE, 'Government debt spillovers and creditworthiness in a federation' (2000) 33 (3) Canadian Journal of Economics 634.

LECOURS, ANDRE and BELAND, DANIEL, 'Federalism and Fiscal Policy: The Politics of Equalisation in Canada' (2010) 40 (4) Publius 569.

LITINA, ANASTASIA and PALIVOS, THEODORE, 'Corruption and Tax Evasion: Reflections on Greek Tragedy' (2015, June) Bank of Greece Working Paper No. 193 <http://www.bankofgreece.gr/BogEkdoseis/Paper2015193.pdf>.

LIU, LILI and GAILLARD, NORBERT and WEIBEL, MICHAEL, 'France's Subnational Insolvency Framework' in Otaviano Canuto and Lili Liu (eds) *Until Debt Do Us Part* (The World Bank 2013).

LLOYD, WILLIAM, *Two Lectures on the Checks To Population* (Oxford University Press 1833).

LUECHINGER, SIMON and MEIER, STEPHAN and STUTZER, ALOIS, 'Bureaucratic Rents and Life Satisfaction' (2008) 24 (2) Journal of Law, Economics & Organization 476.

LUTZ, BYRON and FOLETTE, GLENN, 'Fiscal Rules, What Does the American Experience Tell Us? (2012) Finance and Economics Discussion Series, Working Paper 2012-38, Federal Reserve Board, Washington D.C.

MANDER, BENEDICT, 'Rufo expiry will test Argentina's willingness to settle debt' (2014, 30 December) Financial Times. <https://www.ft.com/content/e554502e-8fa4-11e4-9ea4-00144feabdc0>.

MARLOW, MICHAEL, 'Fiscal decentralisation and government size' (1988) 56 Public Choice 259.

MASSON, PAUL, 'The Dangers of an Extended Period of Low Interest Rates: Why the Bank of Canada Should Start Raising Them Now' (2013) C.D. Howe Institute Commentary 381.

MENGER, CARL, *Principles of Economics* (original: Grundsätze der Volkswirtschaftslehre 1871, tr James Dingwall and Bert Hoselitz, Ludwig von Mises Institute 2007).

MEYERS, HARRY, 'Displacement Effects of Federal Highway Grants' (1987) 40 (2) National Tax Journal 221.

MILLER, EDWARD, 'The Economics of Matching Grants: The ABC Highway Program' (1974) 27 (2) National Tax Journal 221.

MILLER, MERTON and MODIGLIANI, FRANCO, 'Dividend Policy, Growth, and the Valuation of Shares' (1961) 34 (4) The Journal of Business 411.

MODIGLIANI, FRANCO and MILLER, MERTON, 'The Cost of Capital, Corporation Finance and th Theory of Finance' (1958) 48 (3) The American Economic Review 261.

MONTINOLA, GABRIELLA and QIAN, YINGYI and WEINGAST, BARRY, 'Federalism, Chinese Style: The Political Basis for Economic Success' (1996) 1 World Politics 50.

MORRISON, ALAN, 'Systematic Risk and the 'too-big-to-fail' problem' (2011) 27 (3) Oxford Review of Economic Policy 498.

NISKANEN, WILLIAM, *Bureaucracy and Representative Government* (Aldine Transaction 1971).

NISKANEN, WILLIAM, 'Comment on Tax Policy from 1990 to 2001' in Jeffrey Frankel and Peter Orszag (eds) *American Economic Policy in the 1990s* (MIT Press 2002) 184.

NISKANEN, WILLIAM, 'Limiting Government: The Failure of "Starve the Beast"' (2006) 26 (3) Cato Journal 553.

NORDHAUS, WILLIAM, 'The Political Business Cycle' (1975) Review of Economic Studies 169.

NORDHAUS, WILLIAM and ALESINA, ALBERTO and SCHULTZE, CHARLES, 'Alternative Approaches to the Political Business Cycle' (1989) 2 Brookings Papers on Economic Activity 1.

OATES, WALLACE, *Fiscal Federalism* (Harcourt, Brace, Jovanovich 1972).

OATES, WALLACE, 'Searching for Leviathan: An Empirical Study' (1985) 75 (4) The American Economic Review 748.

OATES, WALLACE, 'Searching for Leviathan: A Reply and Some Further Reflections' (1989) 79 (3) The American Economic Review 578.

OATES, WALLACE and SCHWAB, ROBERT, 'Economic Competition Among Jurisdictions: Efficiency Enhancing or Distortion Inducing?' (1988) 35 Journal of Public Economics 333.

OLSEN, MANCUR, *The Logic of Collective Action* (Harvard University Press 1965).

OLSEN, MANCUR, 'The principle of "fiscal equivalence": The Devision of Responsibilities among Different Levels of Government' (1969) 59 (2) The American Economic Review 479.

OLSEN, MANCUR, *The Rise and Decline of Nations: Economic Growth, Stagflation, and Social Rigidities* (Yale University Press 1982).

ÖZLER, SULE, 'Have Commercial Banks Ignored History' (1993) 83 (3) The American Economic Review 608.

PAULUS, CHRISTOPH, 'A Resolving Proceeding for Defaulting Sovereigns' (2012) International Insolvency Law Review 1.

PAULUS, CHRISTOPH, 'A Standing Arbitral Tribunal as a Procedural Solution for Sovereign Debt Restructurings' in Braga, Primo, and Vincelette, Galli (eds), *Sovereign Debt and the Financial Crisis - Will This Time be Different?'* (Worldbank 2010) 317.

PAULUS, CHRISTOPH, 'Staatsinsolvenzen: Gläubiger oder neutral Instanz – wer soll das schlingernde Schiff steuern?' (2012) 10 (1) Zeitschrift für Staats- und Europawissenschaften 30.

POTERBA, JAMES, 'Balanced Budget Rules and Fiscal Policy: Evidence from the States' (1995) 48 (3) National Tax Journal 329.

QIAN, YINGYI and WEINGAST, BARRY, 'China's Transition to Markets: Market-Preserving Federalism, Chinese Style' (1996) 1 Journal of Policy Reform 149.

RANKIN, JENNIFER and SMITH, HELENA, 'The great Greece fire sale' (2015, 24 July) The Guardian <https://www.theguardian.com/business/2015/jul/24/greek-debt-crisis-great-greece-fire-sale>.

REINHART, CARMEN, 'Default, Currency Crises, and Sovereign Debt Ratings' (2002) 16 (2) The World Bank Economic Review 151.

REINHARDT, CARMEN an ROGOFF, KENNETH, *This Time is Different* (Princeton University Press 2011).

RICARDO, DAVID, 'Essay on the Funding System' (1820) in John Ramsay McCulloch (ed.) *The Works of David Ricardo* (Morrison and Gibb 1888) 516.

RICHARDSON, JESSE, 'Dillon's Rule is from Mars, Home Rule is From Venus: Local Government Autonomy and the Rules of Statutory Construction' (2011) 41 (4) Publius: The Journal of Federalism 662.

RICHMOND, CHRISTINE and DIAS, DANIEL, 'Duration of Capital Market Exclusion: An Empirical Investigation' (2009) SSRN Manuscript <https://papers.ssrn.com/sol3/papers.cfm?abstract_id=1027844>.

RIZZO, MICHAEL and EHRENBERG, RONALD, 'Resident and Nonresident Tuition and Enrollment at Flagship State Universities' in Caroline Hoxby (ed) *College Choices: The Economics of Where to Go, When to Go, and How to Pay For It* (University of Chicago Press 2004) 303.

ROCHOLL, JÖRG and STAHMER, AXEL, 'Where did the Greek bailout money go?' (2016) ESMT No. WP–16–02.

RODDEN, JONATHAN, 'Reviving Leviathan: Fiscal Federalism and the Growth of Government' (2003) 57 International Organization 695.

RODDEN, JONATHAN, 'Sovereignty and Orderly Defaults' (12 July 2016 Library of Law and Liberty) <http://www.libertylawsite.org/liberty-forum/sovereignty-and-orderly-defaults/>.

RODDEN, JONATHAN, 'Soft Budget Constraints and German Federalism' in Jonathan Rodden, Gunnar Eskeland, and Jennie Litvack (eds) *Fiscal Decentralisation and the Challenge of Hard Budget Constraints* (Massachusetts Institute of Technology 2013) 161.

RODDEN, JONATHAN, 'Strengths in Numbers? Representation and Redistribution in the European Union' (2002a) 3 (2) European Union Politics 151.

RODDEN, JONATHAN 'The Dilemma of Fiscal Federalism: Grants and Fiscal Performance Around the World' (2002) 46 (3) American Journal of Political Science 670.

RODDEN, JONATHAN and ROSE-ACKERMAN, SUSAN, 'Does Federalism Preserve Markets?' (1997) 83 (7) Virginia Law Review 1521.

RODDEN, JONATHAN and WIBBELS, ERIK, 'Beyond the Fiction of Federalism: Macroeconomic Management in Multitiered Systems' (2002) 54 World Politics 494.

ROHTER, LARRY, 'Puerto Rico Fighting to Keep Its Tax Breaks for Businesses' (1993, 10 May) The New York Times <http://www.nytimes.com/1993/05/10/business/puerto-rico-fighting-to-keep-its-tax-breaks-for-businesses.html?pagewanted=all>.

ROGOFF, KENNETH and ZETTELMEYER, JEROMIN, 'Bankruptcy Procedures for Sovereigns: A History of Ideas, 1976 – 2001' (2002) IMF Working Paper WP/02/133.

RUSSELL, JON and BOSTROM, AARON, 'Federalism, Dillon Rule and Home Rule' (2016) January, White Paper, American City County Exchange 1.

ROSE, ANDREW, 'One Reason Countries Pay their Debts: Renegotiation and International Trade' (2005) 77 (1) Journal of Development Economics 189.

ROY-CÉSAR, ÉDISON, 'In Brief: Canada's Equalization Formula' (2013) Library of Parliament, Publication No. 2008-20-E, 10 November 2008, Revised 4 September 2013.

SANDLERIS, GUIDO, 'Sovereign defaults: Information, investment and credit' (1998) 76 (2) Journal of International Economics 267.

SANDLERIS, GUIDO, 'The Costs of Sovereign Default: Theory and Empirical Evidence' (2016) 16 (2) Economia 1.

SCHUKNECHT, LUDGER, 'Political Business Cycles and Fiscal Policies in Developing Countries' (1996) 49 Kyklos 155.

SCHUMACHER, JULIAN and WEDER DI MAURO, BEATRE, 'Debt sustainability puzzles: Implications for Greece' (2015, 12 July) VOX CEPR'S Policy Portal <http://voxeu.org/article/debt-sustainability-puzzles-implications-greece>.

SHLEIFER, ANDREI, 'A theory of yardstick competition' (1985) 16 (3) Rand Journal of Economics 319.

SHIELDS, YVETTE and WEBSTER, KEELEY, 'Why Pensions Beat Bonds in Bankruptcy Court' *The Bond Buyer.* (2016) <http://www.bondbuyer.com/news/markets-buy-side/why-pensions-beat-bonds-in-bankruptcy-court-1111233-1.html>.

SIMON, ELLEN GINSBURG and CRAWFORD, MONTY, 'The Impact of *Republic of Argentina v. NML Capital, Ltd.*: Why the Supreme Court's Ruling Against Argentina Avoided a Host of Unintended Consequences' (2015) 30 (1) Maryland Journal of International Law 55.

SINN, HANS-WERNER, 'Die Target-Kredite der Deutschen Bank' (2012, 21 March) ifo Schnelldienst Sonderausgabe.

SINN, HANS-WERNER and WOLLMERSHÄUSER, TIMO, 'Target loans, current account balances and capital flows: the ECB's rescue facility' (2012) 19 International Tax and Public Finance 468.

SINN, HANS-WERNER and WOLLMERSHÄUSER, TIMO, 'Target-Kredite, Leistungsbilanzsalden und Kapitalverkehr: Der Rettungsschirm der EZB' (2011, 24 Juni) ifo Schnelldienst.

SKEEL, DAVID, 'An Evolutionary Theory of Corporate Law and Corporate Bankruptcy' (1998) 51 Vanderbilt Law Review 1325.

SKEEL, DAVID, 'Can Pensions be Restructured in (Detroit's) Municipal Bankruptcy? (2013) ILE Research Paper No. 13-33.

SKEEL, DAVID, 'From Chrysler and General Motors to Detroit' (2015) 24 Widener Law Journal 121, 136–148.

SKEEL, DAVID, 'Is Bankruptcy the Answer for Troubled Cities and States?' (2013) 50 (4) Houston Law Review 1063.

SKEEL, DAVID, 'States of Bankruptcy' (2012) 79 (2) The University of Chicago Law Review 677.

SKEEL, DAVID, 'When Should Bankruptcy be an Option (for People, Places, or Things)? (2014) 55 William & Mary Law Review 2217, 2232–2233.

SKRETA, VASILIKO and VELDKAMP, LAURA, 'Ratings shopping and asset complexity: A theory of ratings inflation' (2009) 56 (5) Journal of Monetary Economics 678.

SMITH, ADAM, *An Inquiry into the Nature and Causes of the Wealth of Nations* (original 1776, MetaLibri 2007) Book IV, 349 <http://www.ibiblio.org/ml/libri/s/SmithA_WealthNations_p.pdf>.

STEIN, ERNESTO, 'Fiscal Decentralisation and Government Size in Latin America' (1999) 2 (2) Journal of Applied Economics 357.

STEVENSON, ALEXANDRA, 'How Argentina Settled a Billion-Dollar Debt Dispute With Hedge Funds' (2016, 25 April) NY Times. <https://www.nytimes.com/2016/04/25/business/dealbook/how-argentina-settled-a-billion-dollar-debt-dispute-with-hedge-funds.html?mcubz=0>.

STIGLER, GEORGE, 'The Process of Economic Regulation' (1972) The Antitrust Bulletin 207.

STIGLER, GEORGE, 'The Theory of Economic Regulation' (1971) 2 (1) The Bell Journal of Economics and Management Science 3.

STIGLITZ, JOSEPH, 'Greece, the Sacrificial Lamb' (2015, July 25) The New York Times. <https://www.nytimes.com/2015/07/26/opinion/greece-the-sacrificial-lamb.html?mcubz=1>.

STRATHMAN, JAMES, 'Migration, Benefit Spillover and State Support of Higher Education' (1994) 31 (6) Urban Studies 913.

TAYLOR, JOHN, 'Sovereign Debt Restructuring: A U.S. Perspective' (2002) Remarks at the Conference "Sovereign Debt Workouts: Hopes and Hazards?" of the Institute for International Economics, Washington D.C. by the Under Secretary of Treasury for International Affairs <http://web.stanford.edu/~johntayl/taylorspeeches/Sovereign%20Debt%20Restructuring%20(2%20April%2002).doc>.

TIEBOUT, CHARLES, 'A Theory of Local Expenditures' (1956) 64 (5) Journal of Political Economy 416.

TREBESCH, CHRISTOPH, 'Inexcusable Sovereign Default' (2010) Working Paper. <https://sites.google.com/site/christophtrebesch/research/Trebesch-InexcusableSovereignDefault.pdf>.

TREMBLAY, JEAN-FRANCOIS, 'Fiscal Federalism and Public Service Provision in Canada' (2007) 3 (1) Public Policy Review 51.

TULLOCK, GORDON, 'Federalism of Scale' (1969) 6 Public Choice 19.

TULLOCK, GORDON, 'The Welfare Costs of Tariffs, Monopolies, and Theft' (1967) 5 (3) Western Economic Review 224.

TURNBULL, GEOFFREY, 'Fiscal Illusion, uncertainty, and the flypaper effect' (1992) 48 (2) Journal of Public Economics 207.

VAUBEL, ROLAND, 'Probleme der Bankenunion: Falsche Lehren aus der Krise' (2013) 46 (3) Credit and Capital Markets – Kredit und Kapital 281.

VON HAGEN, JÜRGEN, 'Fiscal Rules, Fiscal Institutions, and Fiscal Performance' (2002) 33 (3) The Economic and Social Review 263.

VON HAGEN, JÜRGEN and EICHENGREEN, BARRY, 'Federalism, Fiscal Restraints, and European Monetary Union' (1996) 86 (2) The American Economic Review 134.

VON HAYEK, FRIEDRICH AUGUST, 'The Use of Knowledge in Society (1945) 35 (4) American Economic Review 519.

VON HAYEK, FRIEDRICH AUGUST, 'Competition as Discovery Procedure' (2002, first 1969) 5 (3) The Quarterly Journal of Austrian Economics 9 (translated by Marcellus Snow).

VON MISES, LUDWIG, *The Theory of Money and Credit* (first published 1912, English version, Yale University Press 1953).

VON WEIZSÄCKER, CARL CHRISTIAN, 'Kapitalismus in der Krise?' (2015) 16 (2) Perspektiven der Wirtschaftspolitik 189.

WALRAS, LÉON, *Elements of Pure Economics* (original: *Éléments d'économie politique pure* 1874, tr William Jaffe Routledge 2010).

WALSH, MARRY WILLIAMS, 'How Puerto Rico is Grappling With a Debt Crisis' (2017, 16 May) The New York Times <https://www.nytimes.com/interactive/2017/business/dealbook/puerto-rico-debt-bankruptcy.html?rref=collection%2Ftimestopic%2FPuerto %20Rico&action=click&contentCollection=us&region=stream&module=stream_unit&version=latest&contentPlacement=20&pgtype=collection>.

WALSH, MARRY WILLIAMS, 'Puerto Rico: A Debt Problem That Kept Boiling Over' (2017, 5 May) The New York Times <https://www.nytimes.com/2017/05/05/business/dealbook/puerto-rico-debt.html>.

WALSH, MARRY WILLIAMS, 'Puerto Rico Declares a Form of Bankruptcy' (2017, 3 May) The New York Times <https://www.nytimes.com/2017/05/03/business/dealbook/puerto-rico-debt.html?rref=collection%2Ftimestopic%2FPuerto%20Rico> .

WALSH, MARRY WILLIAMS, 'Puerto Rico Defaults on Bond Payments' (2015, 3 August) The New York Times <https://www.nytimes.com/2015/08/04/business/dealbook/puerto-rico-decides-to-skip-bond-payment.html>.

WATERMAN, RICHARD and MEIER, KENNETH, 'Principal-Agent Models: An Expansion?' (1998) 8 (2) Journal of Public Administration Research and Theory 173.

WEIDEMEIER, MARK and GULATI, MITU, 'Market Practice and the Evolution of Foreign Sovereign Immunity' (forthcoming) Law & Social Inquiry.

WEINGAST, BARRY, 'The Economic Role of Political Institutions: Market-Preserving Federalism and Economic Development' (1995) 11 (1) The Journal of Law, Economics, & Organizations 1.

WILLIAMSON, OLIVER, *The Economic Institutions of Capitalism* (The Free Press 1985).

ZAX, JEFFREY, 'Is there a Leviathan in Your Neighbourhood?' (1989) 79 (3) The American Economic Review 560.

ZHANG, TAO and ZOU, HENG-FU, 'Fiscal decentralisation, public spending, and economic growth in China' (1998) 67 Journal of Public Economics 221.

ZODROW, GEORGE and MIESZKOWSKI, PETER, 'Pigou, Tiebout, Property Taxation, and the Underprovision of Public Goods' (1986) 19 Journal of Urban Economics 356.

Other resources

ASSÉNAGON ASSET MANAGEMENT SA v IRISH BANK RESOLUTION COOPERATION LIMITED [2012] EWHC 2090 (Ch).

BUNDESREGIERUNG, 'Neuregelung des bundesstaatlichen Finanzausgleichs 2020' (Pressemitteilung 369, 14 October 2016). <https://www.bundesregierung.de/Content/DE/Pressemitteilungen/BPA/2016/10/2016-10-14-beschluss-bund-laender.html>.

Decision of the German Federal Constitutional Court, BVerfGE 86, 148 (27 May 1992).

Decision of the German Federal Constitutional Court, BVerfGE 116, 327 (19 October 2006).

Decision of the German Federal Supreme Court, BVerfGE 125, 141 (27 January 2010).

EUROPEAN CENTRAL BANK, Agreement on emergency liquidity assistance (17 May 2017). <https://www.ecb.europa.eu/pub/pdf/other/Agreement_on_emergency_liquidity_assistance_20170517.en.pdf?23bb6a68e85e0715839088d0a23011db>

EUROPEAN CENTRAL BANK, Asset purchase programmes–information page (2018) <https://www.ecb.europa.eu/mopo/implement/omt/html/index.en.html≥.

EUROPEAN CENTRAL BANK, 'Details on securities holdings acquired under the Securities Market Programme' (2013, 21 February) Press Release <https://www.ecb.europa.eu/press/pr/date/2013/html/pr130221_1.en.html> .

EUROPEAN CENTRAL BANK, 'TARGET balances of participating NCBs: SDW Report Sheet' (2018) ECB Eurosystem – info page <http://sdw.ecb.europa.eu/reports.do?node=1000004859>.

EUROPEAN COMISSION, Budget info page (2018). <ec.europa.eu/budget/annual/index_en.cfm?year=2017.>

EUROPEAN COMISSION, Commission Decision of 30.08.2016 ON STATE AID SA. 38373 (2014/C) (ex2014/NN) (ex2014/CP) implemented by Ireland to Apple.

EUROPEAN COMMISSION, EFSM –information page (2017). <https://ec.europa.eu/info/business-economy-euro-0/economic-and-fiscal-policy-coordination/eu-financial-assistance/loan-programmes/european-financial-stabilisation-mechanism-efsm_en>.

EUROPEAN COMMISSION, Stability and Growth Pact – information page (2017) <https://ec.europa.eu/info/business-economy-euro/economic-and-fiscal-policy-coordination/eu-economic-governance-monitoring-prevention-correction/stability-and-growth-pact_en>.

EUROPEAN COMMISSION, 'The Second Economic Adjustment Programme for Greece' (2012, March) European Economy Occasional Papers No. 94 <http://ec.europa.eu/economy_finance/publications/occasional_paper/2012/pdf/ocp94_en.pdf>.

EUROPEAN COMMISSION, 'The Economic Adjustment Programme for Greece' (2010, 26 May) European Economy Occasional Papers No. 61 <https://publications.europa.eu/de/publication-detail/-/publication/64c89a77-ddc4-46f4-9bb0-18d7e80f6f0c/language-en>.

EUROPEAN COMMISSIAN and THE HELLENIC REPUBLIC et al., Memorandum of Understanding Between the European Commission Acting on Behalf of the European Stability Mechanism and The Hellenic Republic and The Bank of Greece (2015, August) <https://ec.europa.eu/info/sites/info/files/01_mou_20150811_en1.pdf>.

EM LTD. v REPUBLIC OF ARGENTINA, 695 F.3d 201 (Second Circuit, 20 August 2012).

ESM, Financial assistance–information page (2018). <https://www.esm.europa.eu/financial-assistance>.

ESM, Lending Rates–information page (2018) <https://www.esm.europa.eu/lending-rates>.

ESM, What is the Greek Loan Facility – information page (2017). <https://www.esm.europa.eu/content/what-greek-loan-facility-glf>.

FREIE HANSESTADT BREMEN, Bericht der Freien Hansestadt Bremen vom September 2016 zur Umsetzung des Sanierungsprogramms 2012/2016 (2016) <http://www.senatspressestelle.bremen.de/sixcms/media.php/13/20160912_Sanierungsbericht_September_2016_komplett.pdf>.

GOVERNMENT OF PUERTO RICO, *Fiscal Plan for Puerto Rico* (San Juan, Puerto Rico, 13 March 2017) <http://www.gaclaw.com/Puerto-Rico-Fiscal-Plan-March-13-2017.pdf>.

GERMAN FEDERAL MINISTRY OF FINANCE, European Financial Assistance (2017) <http://www.bundesfinanzministerium.de/Web/EN/Issues/Europe/European-Financial-Assistance/european-financial-assistance.html>.

HELLENIC REPUBLIC ASSET DEVELOPMENT FUND, 'Asset Development Plan' (2015, July) <https://ec.europa.eu/info/sites/info/files/ecfin_01_mou_annex1_20150730_en.pdf>.

IMF, 'Greece: Ex Post Evaluation of Exceptional Access Under the 2010 Stand-By Arrangement' (2913, June) IMF Country Report No. 13/156 prepared by J. Gordon, I. Karpowicz, S. Lanau, J. Manning, W. McGrew, M. Nozaki, and M. Shamloo.

IMF, 'Ireland: Ex Post Evaluation of Exceptional Access Under the 2010 Extended Arrangement' (2015, February) IMF Country Report No. 15/20 prepared by A. Chailloux, J. Gobat, H. Imamura, J. McHugh, H. Poirson Ward, and T. Krueger.

Leukerbad v Valais, 2C.4/2000 (3 July 2003, Federal Supreme Court).

NML CAPITAL, LTD. v REPUBLIC OF ARGENTINA, 699 F.3d 246 (Second Circuit, 26 October 2012).

REPUBLIC OF ARGENTINA v NML CAPITAL, LTD., 134 S.Ct. 2250 (U.S. Supreme Court, 16 June 2014).

SWISS NATIONAL BANK, 109th Annual Report 2016 <https://snb.ch/en/mmr/reference/annrep_2016_komplett/source/annrep_2016_komplett.en.pdf>

TRADING ECONOMIES, Greece: Credit Ratings (2018, 21 February). <https://tradingeconomics.com/greece/rating>.